ABOUT THE EDITOR

Richard Phillips teaches post-colonial criticism and cultural geography at the University of Liverpool, where he is reader in geography. His publications include *Mapping Men and Empire: A Geography of Adventure* (1997), *Sex, Politics and Empire: A Postcolonial Geography* (2006), and the co-edited *Decentring Sexualities: Politics and Representations Beyond the Metropolis* (2000). He is also the author of a series of articles for journals and magazines ranging from the *Annals of the Association of American Geographers* and *Antipode: A Radical Journal of Geography*, to *Race & Class* and *Red Pepper*.

D1354219

MUSLIM SPACES OF HOPE

geographies of possibility in Britain and the West

edited by Richard Phillips

Zed Books
LONDON | NEW YORK

Muslim spaces of hope: geographies of possibility in Britain and the West
was first published in 2009 by Zed Books Ltd, 7 Cynthia Street,
London N1 9JF, UK and Room 400, 175 Fifth Avenue, New York,
NY 10010, USA

www.zedbooks.co.uk

Editorial copyright © Richard Phillips 2009
Copyright in this collection © Zed Books 2009

The right of Richard Phillips to be identified as the editor of this
work has been asserted by him in accordance with the Copyright,
Designs and Patents Act, 1988

Set in Monotype Plantin and Gill Sans by Ewan Smith, London
Index: ed.emery@thefreeuniversity.net
Cover designed by www.alice-marwick.co.uk
Printed and bound in Great Britain by CPI Antony Rowe,
Chippenham and Eastbourne

Mixed Sources
Product group from well-managed
forests and other controlled sources
www.fsc.org Cert no. SGS-COC-2953
© 1996 Forest Stewardship Council
FSC

Distributed in the USA exclusively by Palgrave Macmillan, a
division of St Martin's Press, LLC, 175 Fifth Avenue, New York,
NY 10010, USA

A catalogue record for this book is available from the British Library
Library of Congress Cataloging in Publication Data available

ISBN 978 1 84813 300 6 hb
ISBN 978 1 84813 301 3 pb
ISBN 978 1 84813 302 0 eb

CONTENTS

ILLUSTRATIONS

ACKNOWLEDGEMENTS

Muslim Spaces of Hope was the theme of a public debate that took place at the Merseyside Maritime Museum in April 2008. I would like to thank the panellists – Ziauddin Sardar, Tahir Abbas and Arun Kundnani – who accepted my invitation to speak on this question. Others who participated, shaping the debate and the book that has come out of it, included members of Liverpool's Muslim communities, and students and researchers who had been attending a workshop entitled Muslim Geographies. These events were supported – practically, intellectually and morally – by Museums Liverpool and the University of Liverpool, and by individuals within these institutions, in particular Rachel Mulhearn at the museum, Drummond Bone and David Sadler, then vice-chancellor and head of geography at the university.

These events formed part of a research project, funded by the Economic and Social Research Council (ESRC Grant RES-000-22-1785). I am deeply grateful to the two research assistants who worked with me on this project – Naima Bouteldja and Jamil Iqbal – both for their formative contributions to the empirical research and also for their involvement in the conception and arrangement of the public debate and workshop behind this book.

Thanks are also due to those who have supported the production of this book. In addition to the authors, who have patiently responded to my editorial requests and suggestions, I would like to thank anonymous readers, who refereed earlier drafts of chapters, and also the three reviewers and the reader who reviewed this book proposal and manuscript for Zed. I have also appreciated the real interest in this book shown by Ellen Hallsworth and Ken Barlow, the commissioning editors at Zed.

And for their contributions and support, less easy to pigeonhole, I thank Lisa Shaw, Tinho da Cruz, Andy Davies, Dave Featherstone and Tom Greaves.

Introduction: Muslim geographies – spaces of hope?

RICHARD PHILLIPS

Debates about contemporary Islam and Muslims in the West have taken some understandably negative turns in the depressing atmosphere of the war on terror and its aftermath. This book argues that we have been too preoccupied with problems, not enough with solutions. It acknowledges but challenges what has come to be viewed as the 'Islamic problem' – the widespread perception or construction of Muslims as a troubled and troublesome minority – by asking what Muslims have to be hopeful about today, and how others might share this hope. It argues that there are grounds for hope in many areas of everyday life, and challenges assumptions and assertions that have been made about Muslims in the West. Segregation is set against integration, fear and hate against what cultural critic Paul Gilroy has termed convivial culture. Assertions of difference are put on hold, suggestions of compatibility entertained. Assumptions that Muslims are non-liberal and anti-modern are challenged with evidence about their negotiations of liberalism and modernity. And allegations about Islamic aloofness are set against nuanced evidence of their interaction with other social groups.

Muslims represent a growing and increasingly visible minority in many Western countries. In western Europe, they are the largest single minority religious group, estimated to number between 13 and 23 million people: nearly 5 per cent of the total population (Savage 2004: 26). Estimates of the numbers of Muslims in the United States vary widely, as Selcuk R. Sirin and Selen Imamoğlu explain in this volume, though it is widely accepted that there are between 2 and 8 million Muslim-Americans, and that this number is growing fast (Kosmin et al. 2001). Numbers are increasing fast in Canada too, where there are now upwards of 800,000 Muslims (Bakht 2008), and in Australia, where numbers are closer to the 400,000 mark (Kabir 2004). Not only through their numbers, but also through their increasing mobilization and politicization, members of this group have recently been treated as an exceptional – different and distinctly difficult – minority. And yet, debates about Islam and

Muslims can be located within broader hegemonic constructions of race and identity. These constructions vary in important ways between and within Western countries, but some general trends can be observed. Generally, the increased mobilization and scrutiny of Muslim identities have taken place in the context of a more general recasting of racism in terms of cultural and religious rather than biological or physiognomic difference, though visible differences continue to be crucially important in the construction of social categories (Modood et al. 1997; Modood 2005; Bonnett and Carrington 2000). More generally, the targeting of Muslims has been associated with new forms of an older phenomenon: imperialism. As Ziauddin Sardar writes in Chapter 1 of this book, 'My father's generation have vivid memories of British foreign policy in the 1950s and the 1960s in the Muslim world. And they are a generation shaped by the lived experience of colonialism.' These experiences were not all confined to 'the Muslim world', but were shared by others, particularly in the global South. Crude binaries of Muslims and non-Muslims echo colonial discourses, with their binaries of black and white, colonized and colonizer, within practices of divide and rule. So, though concerned primarily with Muslims, this book speaks to others who have been marginalized and colonized, and to wider debates about social difference, oppression and liberation.

Seeking a more positive tone within debates about Muslims in the West, this book advances a critical avenue that has been pioneered by a number of other writers and cultural critics. These include Jocelyn Cesari (2004), whose empirical research illuminates the progressive and politically engaged politics of many Muslims in the West, and Jytte Klausen (2005), who acknowledges and charts Muslims' participation in democratic processes and institutions. Meanwhile, Olivier Roy and Peter Mandaville have both argued that, neither anachronistic outsiders nor exceptional minorities, Muslims in Western countries negotiate many of the same forces and ideas that structure other peoples' lives, notably multiculturalism (Roy 2004), globalization (Mandaville 2001, 2007) and media (Poole 2002). This is an important point: it is widely presumed that Muslims are unique, and much of the discussion of this group is therefore divorced from wider debates about inequality, racism, multiculturalism and so on, when in fact Muslims face many of the same issues as other groups.

Framed as *Spaces of Hope*, this book advances debates about Muslims in the West not only from a cautiously optimistic angle, but also through a specifically geographical lens. This book was conceived and written around the time Barack Obama was campaigning for the United States presidency, and its language of hope may borrow something from that. Indeed, many of the things Obama invited Americans (and those of us who would have liked the chance to vote with them) to hope for – beginning with an end to racism and more immediately to the war on terror – are close to the heart of this project too. But to speak of hope, and specifically spaces of hope, is also to mobilize a particular political and rhetorical tradition, to borrow terms from David Harvey (2000), Doreen Massey (2005) and others who have framed social and political grievances and projects geographically.

Though framed in specifically geographical terms, this is not a narrowly geographical project. To adapt a phrase from the late map historian Brian Harley, who wrote that 'maps are too important to be left to cartographers alone' (Harley 1992: 231), I would argue, and I think this book demonstrates, that these spaces of hope, and more generally these Muslim geographies, are too important to be left to geographers alone. While contemporary human geography is sufficiently broad and lateral to encompass different understandings of space and geography, including material and metaphorical, tangible and textual, representational and non-representational spaces, it does not have a monopoly over conceptions of space, or more specifically over understandings of Muslim and Islamic spatialities. So this book brings a multidisciplinary approach to Muslims in the West and to 'spaces of hope', one that includes contributions from cultural criticism, post-colonial studies, fashion studies, politics, sociology and geography. The following paragraphs draw out a series of overlapping and interrelated Muslim geographies that run through this book, and then suggest ways in which these spaces, though by no means always or inevitably hopeful, may be regarded or mobilized as spaces of hope.

MUSLIM GEOGRAPHIES

The experiences and predicaments of Muslims in Western countries are shaped by and expressed through a series of geographies, which can be sites of oppression – including racism, deprivation and social exclusion – but also of liberation. Kevin M. Dunn and Alanna Kamp's ambivalent title – 'the hopeful and exclusionary politics of Islam in Australia' – illustrates the more general thread that runs through this book, in chapters that try not to oversimplify complex stories and spaces, in which problems and solutions, deep injustices and progressive politics intermingle.

The ambivalence of Muslim geographies reflects and speaks to a more general post-colonial condition. The engaging subtitle of Paul

Gilroy's polemical study of post-colonial Britain (2004) – 'Melancholia or convivial culture?' – presents too stark a choice. After empire, there is both melancholia and convivial culture: racism and anti-racism, tolerance and intolerance, deep injustice and genuinely progressive politics. Similar things were true during and within colonial empires, as the abolitionist and former slave Ottobah Cugoano once acknowledged, through the rhetorical question he quoted from the King James Version of the Holy Bible: 'Doth a fountain send forth at the same place sweet water and bitter?' (Cugoano 1787: 141). Cugoano's immediate point was that 'Black People' in England had been rightly cautious about accepting invitations to join the free and then private colony of Sierra Leone, while the British Empire was still embroiled in the slave trade and the institution of slavery: in search of sweet water, 'their doom would be to drink of the bitter' (ibid.: 142). Conversely, however, this makes the point that a place of enslavement can also be one of liberation. These words and sentiments have been echoed down the centuries, for instance by the Victorian feminist Josephine Butler, who suggested in the course of her campaigns on behalf of women forced into state-regulated prostitution in the British Empire that 'England has been sending forth to all these parts of the world two streams, one pure and the other foul' (Butler 1887: 4; Phillips 2006). Once again, places – including nations, cities, ships and other, less tangible sites – are capable of redemption, as sites not only of oppression but also of liberation.

Though ultimately concerned with spaces of hope, each of the chapters in this book is framed and underpinned by an acknowledgement of why this hope is needed: an acknowledgement of the negative experiences of many Muslims in the West. Beginning and ending this book, Ziauddin Sardar and Tahir Abbas set contemporary Muslim geographies in the context of major events, including the war on terror, but also of underlying, entrenched injustices. They both stress that deprivation – low incomes, poor housing, unemployment, poor health – is disproportionately high among Muslim minorities and their communities in Western countries such as Britain. This generalization must be qualified by recognizing the socio-economic mobility of some Muslim communities in Western countries, particularly in the United States, where many Muslims of Asian and Arab origin can be described as middle class and affluent; this notwithstanding the ongoing poverty and exclusion experienced by many of their co-religionists, particularly those who are African-American. It is not just that many Muslims in the West are deprived; the places in which they live are in many cases concentrations and, in themselves, sources of deprivation. Poverty and housing problems in the London borough of Tower Hamlets, where many Bangladeshi immigrants live, are examined in a number of chapters in this book. These include Ayona Datta's study of housing and Jane Pollard, Hilary Lim and Raj Brown's chapter on economic deprivation and investment strategies.

The lives and life chances of Muslims are also shaped by some less tangible spaces (Dwyer et al. 2008; Falah and Nagel 2005; Hopkins and Gale 2008). The most fundamental geographical construct, which shapes the lives of Muslims both within and without Western countries, is the idea of the West itself (Bonnett 2004). This, as Edward Said showed, is a fundamentally imperial construct (Said 1978, 1993). Western imperialism has been organized around a series of binaries, which pit Occident against Orient, West against East, Christian against Muslim or heathen, and assert the superiority of the former. Moreover, whereas other colonial and anti-colonial or post-colonial binaries – global North and South, developed and developing countries, First and Third World – are routinely deployed in other contexts, the binary most often applied to Muslims and Islam is that of East and West. So, while it makes sense to speak of Muslims in the West, it may be more controversial to speak of 'Western Muslims', though some contributors choose to do this (see also Ramadan 2004). Said (1978) elaborated the ambivalence of this and the other imaginative geographies introduced here. On the one hand, he acknowledged that they tend to be hegemonic constructs, projections of a will to power; on the other, they assume a reality of their own, and stand to be appropriated within counter-hegemonic projects. So, as Peter Hopkins explains in this book, the West and the other Muslim geographies illustrated here are problematic categories, which can nevertheless be productively employed.

Moving down one level from the grand scale of the Occident and the Orient, Muslim geographies are also shaped by nations (Hopkins and Gale 2008). A series of chapters in this book draw out ways in which Western nations structure the lives of Muslim minorities in specific ways: Kevin Dunn examines the experiences of Australian Muslims, Selcuk Sirin and Selen Imamoğlu those of their counterparts in the United States, while Sardar, Abbas and a number of other authors focus on the United Kingdom. Though concerned broadly with the West, this book pays particular attention to the United Kingdom and its constituent nations and provinces – Northern Ireland and Britain, which in turn is composed of Scotland, England and Wales, all of which combine in different ways to structure the lives of Muslims and other residents and citizens. The book explores how these and other nations function in different ways: as cultural and political units, as tiers of government, and as real and imagined geographies.

Of course, individual nation-states are not all-powerful. Tariq Ramadan (2004) has elaborated the importance of European institutions and culture in the lives of Muslims, arguing controversially that there are now not just Muslims in Europe but European Muslims. The lives of immigrant Muslims and their descendants and communities are also shaped in important ways by transnational geographies, which link nations such as Britain and Bangladesh. Or, more precisely, they link places within these nations, London or Scotland and Sylhet, for instance. Peter Hopkins speaks of Muslims in Scotland, arguing that this is an important space for many Muslims precisely because it is not a nation-state and is therefore free of some of the associations of the former imperial power of which it is a constituent. Hopkins argues that this stateless nation coheres around shared senses of belonging within a territorial unit, rather than the colonial heritage and shared ethnic identity that are mobilized in the definition of England and Englishness, and in other post-imperial nations and nationalisms.

Another important geographical construct – part idea, part reality – that structures Muslims' lives, and dominates debates about Muslims in the West, is that of segregation and its corollary, integration. It is often said that Muslims tend to form segregated communities, living separate lives. Sardar interrogates the causes and consequences of this phenomenon, contesting stereotypical images of Muslims as self-segregated and isolationist. The themes of segregation and integration preoccupy many of the contributors to this book, including M. A. Kevin Brice, who examines relationships between residential and broader social integration among British Muslims. A number of other chapters identify and map, if not segregation, then spaces that are predominantly occupied by Muslims. These range from homes, which as Datta shows may be adapted to a mixture of cultural and religious needs, to businesses, which may be organized along specifically Muslim lines, as Pollard, Lim and Brown show in their chapter on Muslim financial industries.

SPACES OF HOPE?

Having identified a series of Muslim geographies – ranging in scale from the global to the local, the abstract to the intimate; encompassing a mixture of material and imaginative, concrete and textual spaces (see also Netton 2008) – I now want to begin to suggest how these can be recast as potential spaces of hope.

First, geographies of oppression can be recast as what David Featherstone (2008) has termed 'maps of grievance' – points of departure for disruptive and progressive politics. Thus, Datta, Glynn, and Pollard, Lim and Brown all begin by acknowledging the depth of the problems faced by many Muslims, but in so doing they set the scene for engagements with the many ways in which it may be possible to address and contest deprivation, racism and exclusion. Similarly, Hopkins does not stop with an analysis of the pervasive orientalist rhetoric of East and West; he moves beyond this to analyse and illustrate how these spatial binaries and categories may be deconstructed. This resonates with wider efforts that have been made to challenge divisive constructions of Muslims – as aloof and resolutely other – by mapping Muslim geographies as geographies of connection and diversity (Aitchison et al. 2007).

To recast Muslim geographies as spaces of connection is, more generally, to interrogate and contest allegations that stereotype Muslims as self-segregated, metaphorical and literal ghetto-dwellers. A number of chapters in this book take a fresh look at allegations of this type. While Brice qualifies claims about segregation and finds some evidence of integration, other authors address the latter more directly, in chapters about mixed residential areas, city centres and shopping districts (Reina Lewis), and mixed cultural institutions (Sarah Mills). Sardar contests the charge that segregation is always bad, integration always good, and raises questions about where and when Muslims might integrate; where and when they might find some solace in places of their own; where and when they might be accommodated for who they are, and who they want to be. Thus, the groups that come together in certain cosmopolitan, multicultural and convivial public spaces – in streets and workplaces, for instance – may also spend some of their time in places that are more exclusively their own, which include mosques, of course, but also schools, businesses and homes. Datta shows how homes may be adapted to a mixture of cultural and religious needs, for people who are at once Bangladeshis and Muslims, for instance. Pollard, Lim and Brown show how Muslims empower themselves and their communities through the marketplace, and in businesses and workplaces. At a time of crisis in mainstream Western financial markets, we might speculate that Islamic finance has the potential not only to benefit Muslims, but also to inspire and inform others, who are desperately searching for ways in which to reform and replace their own financial systems.

Another way in which Muslim geographies can actively inspire others is illustrated by Magda Sibley and Fodil Fadli, in their chapter on the *hammām*. The *hammām*, or Islamic bathhouse, presents positive and tangible understandings of Islam – or, more accurately, a cultural world of which Islam is an integral part – to a wider European public. Also concerned with Islamic architecture, or rather with buildings that are designed to accommodate a mixture of religious and cultural needs, Datta shows how houses in London have been built and adapted for Bangladeshi Muslim families. Alongside these relatively exclusive spaces, it is possible to trace a series of spheres in which measured forms of segregation and integration coexist. Lewis and Mills both provide concrete examples of this, Lewis showing how young women bring their religious identities to the spaces of fashion retailing, Mills how children engage social and civic cultural practices, as Muslims and as active citizens.

A number of other chapters focus on the fruits of this convivial culture, tracing collaborative politics and projects and assessing their outcomes. Thus, Claire Dwyer and Varun Uberoi examine the role of British Muslims in 'community cohesion' debates, while Glynn also examines engagement between Western governments and Muslim minorities. While both these chapters are critical of governmental approaches to Muslims, some others find a somewhat more even playing field on which Muslims and others have come together. Writing with Jamil Iqbal, I show how Muslim-identified activists have engaged the British anti-war movements, in a chapter that resonates with broader claims that have been made about the (limited) empowerment of some Muslims who have engaged with democratic systems in Western countries (Klausen 2005).

Distilling into more general form these sorts of arguments about the ways in which Muslims negotiate hybrid identities by moving through spaces that are variously integrated and segregated, exclusive and in-clusive, Sirin and Imamoğlu show how Muslim-Americans follow what they call a 'positive path'. Their geographical metaphor, like much of this book, describes a space in which Muslims may not only live but move forward, forging pragmatic identities and progressive politics. This, the most general theme of the book, is revisited in the final chapter by Abbas. This chapter provides a polemical discussion of the problems of representation and participation in politics and the impact that they have for Muslims in Britain who are still vying for recognition and acceptance in the social world and political life in general.

This book is divided into four sections. The first – 'Spaces of hope?' – introduces the major themes that structure debates about Muslims in the West: integration and segregation; multiculturalism and cosmo-politanism; tolerance and inclusion. Second, a section entitled 'Convivial cities', shifts the emphasis to a series of more specific experiences, which illuminate Muslims' active participation in Western cultural life. These inventive, cosmopolitan cultural practices describe some creative adaptations to essentially Western cultural models; but they also demonstrate a two-way cultural traffic between the West and the Islamic world. The theme of Muslims making their own histories and geographies – if not in conditions of their own choosing – is developed further in the next section, which shifts the focus from cultural life to 'Economic and political empowerment'. A final section revisits the themes that are raised early on in the book, through detailed interrogation of material and metaphorical geographies of 'Integration and resistance', with an eye to the future, which this book seeks in some small way to shape.

REFERENCES

Aitchison, C., P. Hopkins and M.-P. Kwan (eds) (2007) *Geographies of Muslim Identities: Diaspora, Gender and Belonging*, Aldershot: Ashgate.

Bakht, N. (ed.) (2008) *Belonging and Banishment: Being Muslim in Canada*, Toronto: TSAR.

Bonnett, A. (2000) *Anti-Racism*, London: Routledge.

— (2004) *The Idea of the West: Culture, Politics and History*, Basingstoke: Palgrave Macmillan.

Bonnett, A. and B. Carrington (2000) 'Fitting into categories or falling between them? Rethinking ethnic classification', *British Journal of Sociology of Education*, 21.

Butler, J. E. (1887) *Revival and Extension of the Abolitionist Cause*, Winchester: John T. Doswell.

Cesari, J. (2004) *When Islam and Democracy Meet: Muslims in Europe and in the United States*, New York: Palgrave.

Cugoano, O. (1787) *Thoughts and Sentiments on the Evil and Wicked Traffic of the Slavery and Commerce of the Human Species*, London.

Dwyer, C., B. Shah and G. Sanghera (2008) '"From cricket lover to terror suspect" – challenging representations of young British Muslim men', *Gender, Place and Culture*, 15(2).

Falah, G.-W. and C. Nagel (eds) (2005) *Geographies of Muslim Women: Gender, Religion and Space*, New York: Guilford Press.

Featherstone, D. (2008) *Resistance, Space and Political Identities*, London: Wiley-Blackwell.

Gilroy, P. (2004) *After Empire: Melancholia or Convivial Culture?*, London: Routledge.

Harley, J. B. (1992) 'Deconstructing the map', in T. Barnes and J. Duncan (eds), *Writing Worlds*, London: Routledge.

Harvey, D. (2000) *Spaces of Hope*, Edinburgh: Edinburgh University Press.

Hopkins, P. and R. Gale (eds) (2008) *Muslims in Britain: Race, Place and Identities*, Edinburgh: Edinburgh University Press.

Kabir, N. (2004) *Muslims in Australia: Immigration, Race Relations and Cultural History*, London: Kegan Paul.

Klausen, J. (2005) *The Islamic Challenge: Politics and Religion in Western Europe*, Oxford: Oxford University Press.

Kosmin, B. A., E. Mayer and

A. Keysar (2001) *American Religious Identification Survey*, New York: City University of New York.

Mandaville, P. (2001) *Transnational Muslim Politics: Reimagining the Umma*, London: Routledge.

— (2007) *Global Political Islam*, London: Routledge.

Massey, D. (2005) *For Space*, London: Sage.

Modood, T. (2005) *Multicultural Politics: Racism, Ethnicity and Muslims in Britain*, Minneapolis and Edinburgh: University of Minnesota Press and Edinburgh University Press.

Modood, T., R. Berthoud, J. Lakey, J. Nazroo, P. Smith, S. Virdee and S. Beishon (eds) (1997) *Ethnic Minorities in Britain: Diversity and Disadvantage*, London: Policy Studies Institute.

Netton, I. R. (ed.) (2008) *Islamic and Middle Eastern Geographers and Travellers*, London: Routledge.

Peach, C. (2006) 'Islam, ethnicity and South Asian religions in the London 2001 census', *Transactions of the Institute of British Geographers*, NS 31.

Phillips, R. (2006) *Sex, Politics and Empire: A Postcolonial Geography*, Manchester: Manchester University Press.

Poole, E. (2002) *Reporting Islam: Media Representations of British Muslims*, London: I.B.Tauris.

Ramadan, T. (2004) *Western Muslims and the Future of Islam*, Oxford: Oxford University Press.

Roy, O. (2004) *Globalised Islam: The Search for the New Ummah*, London: Hurst.

Runnymede Trust (1997) *Islamophobia: A Challenge to Us All*, Report on the Runnymede Trust Commission on British Muslims and Islamophobia, London: Runnymede Trust.

Said, E. (1978) *Orientalism*, London: Routledge & Kegan Paul.

— (1993) *Culture and Imperialism*, London: Chatto & Windus.

Savage, T. (2004) 'Europe and Islam: crescent waxing, cultures clashing', *Washington Quarterly*, 27(3).

Travis, A. (2008) 'Officials think UK's Muslim population has risen to 2m', *Guardian*, 8 April.

ONE | **SPACES OF HOPE?**

1 | Spaces of hope: interventions

ZIAUDDIN SARDAR

In contemporary Britain being Muslim is a problem no matter what you do as a human being or as a British citizen. The problem begins with perception, the general perception that Muslims seek out and live in segregated communities. The perception is supported by a complex of stereotypical commonplace cultural ideas about the nature of Islam and Muslims. These ideas rationalize Muslims' supposed desire to remain different and distinct from British society, the better to sustain a separate identity. I argue that such assumptions are wrong, factually questionable and ultimately prevent us identifying the spaces of hope that exist to build more genuine, sustainable and mutually beneficial integration.

SEGREGATION

Muslim segregation is deemed a problem. Yet a realistic review of Britain today and in its history would suggest such spatial segregation is not peculiar to Muslims and not considered a problem, so long as those who segregate themselves are not Muslim. Take, for example, the growth of gated communities – nothing could be more segregated than the gated community. The rich and famous, the British billionaires and all those 'non-doms' we seem so pleased to attract to live in this country segregate and seclude themselves behind high walls, security cameras and need never interact with ordinary British people. They live penned-in lives as they make a utility of British residence – and that is not considered a problem.

There are minority communities long resident in Britain that lead segregated lives. Take the Chinese – a Chinese takeaway is likely to exist on every corner of every high street in Britain. Yet the Chinese community maintains its language and culture, through special classes for its children, for instance, without the attention of prying eyes. We are also quite happy to encourage the emergence of Chinatowns, with their distinctive remaking of the urban landscape, right in the heart of our major cities. So segregation and its visible markers are not necessarily a problem in this case. Nor is it a problem for Jews. I grew up near

Stoke Newington, which supported a large Jewish community. When I was growing up in the sixties they lived as an isolated, segregated community and lived perfectly wonderful lives without any problem. Now I live in North London on the fringes of the Finchley/Golders Green area that has been roped off, literally, in accordance with the Talmud to accommodate and ease the Sabbath requirements of the large Orthodox Jewish community. And until a few years ago one never saw Christmas lights on the main shopping thoroughfare of Golders Green; only the large installation at the bus and tube station of the Lubavitch Hanukkah candles, one lit with much fanfare for each day of the holiday. These days you will find both Christmas lights in the main street and the Hanukkah candles. But again this provides signs and symbols of a distinct community maintaining its identity which are not considered a problem.

We need to be clear about what these examples tell us. The rope around an area of North London is far more than notional. It is the tie that binds an entire community to the endurance of a discrete and distinct lived identity transmitted from generation to generation here in Britain. It is a line of demarcation; it claims real space that is not just physical but also cultural, spiritual, social, philosophical and ideological. It caused some argument in the local newspapers when first proposed, but passed and passes the attention of the majority of non-Jewish Britons entirely.

The case of Chinatowns is analogous yet slightly different. The demarcation of these spaces is distinctively visible. Think of Soho and its dragon arch, an outburst of bright red paint topped with its typically oriental curved tiled roof that serves as a gateway to an enclave of shops and restaurants that service the lifestyle of a community which determinedly transmits its heritage from generation to generation. These are spaces of hope which demonstrate the possibilities of acceptable diversity.

The first question I want to ask is this: why Muslims aspiring to domestication of their identity, creating the infrastructure that supports the lived identity they wish to pass from generation to generation, as other minorities clearly do, are considered segregated communities and inherently a 'problem'? The answer, I think, is simple. It is not 9/11; it extends beyond, back before and after that watershed. Muslims living in Britain have a record of campaigning, arguing and protesting to secure their right to the signs and symbols of their identity. For years, this spirit of insistence was summed up in demands for halal food and the hijab, the kernels around which community activism began. It progressed to include activism against racism and went on to object to specific instances of what has become known as Islamophobia in the protests against Salman Rushdie's novel *The Satanic Verses* and more recently the Danish cartoons of the Prophet Muhammad. And this is the nub of the problem. Securing Muslim identity impinges on the majority population in ways that are quite different in scale and scope than has been the case with other minorities. There are a number of points to be made here. Muslims do not present Britain with the prospect of a small exclusivist identity content to exist as an example of acceptable diversity on the margins within the undisturbed fabric of society as usual. Muslim identity is seen as part of a larger global identity which competes with loyalty to Britain. Both Chinese and Jewish identities are also part of larger, global identities; they come complete with ongoing attachments and loyalties to things beyond Britain. Muslims are similar, yet significantly different. Muslim identity is the product of a worldview that is universal and an alternative to British identity. It connotes not just ongoing attachments and loyalties to something beyond Britain but an enduring, competitive, proselytising identity capable of overtaking and displacing indigenous identity. Chinese and Jewish identity is not understood as capable of co-opting Britons. When Muslims complain and campaign to root their identity in Britain they are not seen as merely seeking justice, fairness and equitable provision, like other minorities, but rather as attempting to aggrandize themselves to secure a superior position that in and of itself undermines British identity.

The precise definition of Islamophobia is 'an irrational fear and hatred of Islam and Muslims', because it records the historic memory of Islam as a competitor and inimical civilization. When all activism is perceived through this mindset the reality of Muslim communal endeavours here in Britain is easily misconstrued, misunderstood and seen as potentially hostile to the host nation. The most legitimate and basic of rights – to freedom from racism, injustice and inequitable treatment in education, employment and health – become not reasonable and proper requests which are necessary elements of healthy integration but demands for special concessions that will both bolster segregation and act as incipient covert threats to British identity. The result is that we do not see the reality of how the Muslim communities of Britain regard themselves, nor take proper account of the conditions of Muslim life and adaptation to living in Britain. Most of all we fail to recognize the spaces of hope that already exist, which can and should become the basis for building a more inclusive integrated British future.

My argument is that what is perceived as segregation can be turned into hopeful space. The process begins by making a real appraisal of what is actually happening in communities around Britain. To recognize hopeful space we have to get beyond the stereotypes, unfounded assumptions and scaremongering. We have to defuse the fears of overheated imaginations with the more mundane realities of the ordinary, everyday lives and aspirations of Muslim communities.

Take Tower Hamlets, for instance, which is regarded as a classic example of a segregated community. The borough contains the largest concentration of Bangladeshis in Britain, clustered around two mosques. It is one of those boroughs where minorities, Bangladeshis prominent among them, are set to become the majority of residents. The prospect seems to fulfil all the worst fears of segregation displacing the host community and utterly changing the face of Britain. The fear obscures the rather different story of what has been and is happening in this one area of London.

There is nothing surprising, or indeed sinister, in the fact that a Muslim community should be found clustered around a mosque: it is the basic necessity for confessional communal survival. The problem is that in the case of Muslims this natural impulse is seen as both exclusive and a rejection of mainstream Britain. Further, the mosque is regarded as doubly subversive: acting as a base for both proselytizing and potential plots. Mosques are terra incognita for non-Muslims, who are largely unaware of what activities go on within, how they serve their congregation, and, not without some justification, regard them as hostile environments closed to non-Muslims. Mosques, for better but mostly for worse, are taken as symbolic of the segregation sought by an entire community, a segregation that is a characteristic of its way of life.

What we should understand is that the mosques came after the establishment of a community. We also need to acknowledge that Bangladeshis' residence in London is no new phenomenon. This is a community with a long British history, especially in London, the hub of Britain's long connection and interaction with the subcontinent. The arrival of purpose-built mosques is a logical progression of belonging, the long untold story of being at home in Britain.

The Bangladeshis, in their long history in Britain, have made a niche for themselves in the catering trade. The 'Indian' restaurant was the invention of those communities we now call Bangladeshi, Pakistani and Kashmiri, virtually exclusively a Muslim endeavour. These 'Indian' restaurants have their own history in Britain and, as in all histories, have changed and adapted over time. Not least of the transformations that took place in Tower Hamlets can be traced back to the one good deed of Mrs Thatcher. She introduced the legislation that allowed the people of Tower Hamlets to buy their council houses. And, clever chaps that they are, they bought their council houses for modest sums, rented them out to people working in the City and moved out to Walthamstow and Hackney themselves. The money generated was reinvested in the restaurants clustered in Tower Hamlets. The restaurants expanded in number, creating new jobs for members of the Bangladeshi community and new sources of prosperity. The restaurant industry around Brick Lane is specialized, yet in marketing and culinary terms has diversified, becoming more sophisticated and upmarket over the course of the last few decades. Everyone who works in the industry in this area knows everybody else. Far from being a classic case of segregation, what has been happening in Tower Hamlets is the generation of a thriving community with its own specialized economy, making the most of its opportunities and enhancing its contribution to British life. It is hardly surprising that the achievements of Brick Lane, centre of Bangladeshi culinary arts, are a source of pride for the community. And it was pride, the earned self-respect, which led them to refuse to be portrayed through what they regarded as standardized stereotypes. When a film company wanted to make the movie of Monica Ali's novel *Brick Lane* – the story of a second-generation British-Bangladeshi young woman's arranged marriage to an older and apparently ridiculous recent arrival from Bangladesh – the community said no, and the film-makers were forced to work elsewhere.

Another reason for the rejection of Ms Ali's vision of Brick Lane can be found by taking a more accurate appraisal of another development in Tower Hamlets: what has been happening among Bangladeshi women. They not only rented property to City people; they have actually taken to working in the City themselves! There is now a whole generation of young Bangladeshi women, highly educated, working in the City as accountants, insurance brokers, bankers and what have you. And they, in consequence, have changed the community.

Young women and young men born and educated in Tower Hamlets who are making careers for themselves are a new and unrecognized face of the Bangladeshi community. They have relinquished the fading dream of the older generation, the myth that one day they would all go back to Bangladesh. The dream of return created some of the dynamics taken as evidence of a segregated community intent on preserving a discrete identity and resistant to integration in the mainstream. It was the mindset of long-term residents who nevertheless regarded their place in Britain as temporary. The attitude reflected not just the motives behind migration to Britain, serial migration to earn enough to make a better life back in Bangladesh, but also a response to their disappointment at the cold reception they received in Britain. But again time and community history move on. The younger generations are committed to what their parents' generation have built despite all the obstacles they faced – a community that thrives but which is still far from ideal. The success of Bangladeshi restaurants is only one aspect of the reality of Tower Hamlets; others are entrenched poverty, crumbling housing stock and infrastructure, gaps in provision for education and leisure activities for the youth, difficulties with health provision and, most of all, the social effects of malaise and disaffection incubated by racism – Islamophobic attitudes that are the wider context of the lives of these young Britons.

League tables of social indicators place Bangladeshis at the bottom of the pyramid of British well-being. Indeed, when social statistics are broken down by ethnicity and correlated with religious affiliation it is apparent that Muslims generally have not fared as well as other minority groups. They lag behind in education, skills and employment, and when in employment often tend to be underemployed. Disadvantage has seemed to cohere around Muslim identity. Genuine integration requires unravelling the complex reasons behind this state of affairs. The social, economic and environmental disadvantages that afflict Muslim communities around the country are not primarily Muslim issues; they are the generic issues of blight, deprivation, neglect and decay. They afflict not just Muslims but also their non-Muslim neighbours. What matters is how these problems are now being addressed.

So I return to Tower Hamlets, where the new generation committed to their future in Britain have become engaged in tackling the endemic problems of the area with their own communal resources and approaches. You will find young people in the mosque running a drug centre, trying to do something about the scourge of addiction. Then there is the thriving local soccer league providing a constructive alternative outlet for the energy that too often gets channelled into gang membership. You will find people venturing out from the mosque and knocking on doors to persuade parents to become school governors and take a proactive role in their children's education. And their efforts have not been in vain. The schools, some of which were once marked for closure as failing institutions, have been brought back to life and transformed into some of the best schools in the area.

Thus, so-called segregation can be turned into a space of hope. It not only requires economic resources and opportunity; it depends upon the engagement of the hopes, aspirations and values of the community.

INTEGRATION

At the end of the day nobody wants to live in a ghetto. A ghetto is not merely a physical space, it is also a state of mind, a condition of being. The problem is: how do we empower people to get out? In the final analysis I am arguing that breaking down a ghetto is not something that can be done to a community; it requires the realization of hope that sets the community on course to transform itself. But is it possible that we can empower a ghetto to uplift its own condition and yet still remain a segregated community? Does economic uplift, improvement of the physical and social conditions, always mean the end of communal clustering, the desire to be with and among only people like oneself? So my second and most basic question is this: what shall I integrate with? Unless we can answer that fundamental question, there can never really be full integration.

Neither the question nor the answer is a one-way proposition – it's not just a matter of what shall I integrate with. It is always a question of who or what will permit me to integrate or, put another way, who will integrate with me. What I am trying to identify is whether integration is a one-way process or involves two sides: a mutual process of transformation. In Oldham, for instance, you have three communities: the Pakistani, the Bangladeshi and the white communities. If there is going to be integration, it's not just the Pakistanis and Bangladeshis who need to integrate; it must also include the white community. And in Britain, so far as I've seen, the people who refuse to integrate are not the Pakistanis or the Bangladeshis, but the whites.

I am suggesting that integration is a mutual process of being accepted and accepting. But to really appreciate what I mean we have to consider whether integration is and must be a process of renunciation by one or both parties, or is it a process of accommodation, of coming to terms with, of knowing and understanding more about each other? When integration becomes a two-way process, it becomes a source of hope, something that we all do together. It is a mutual process of breaking down the barriers of fear that prevent us identifying the reality of the other as something that is not too remote from ourselves and most definitely not threatening to our way of knowing, being and doing, to our way of life and being ourselves.

If we think about the process in this way we ought to be able to envisage the end product; so we also have to ask: how do we know when we have integrated? Living in an environment where there is a plethora of restaurants testifying to an immense diversity of peoples, styles and tastes – is that integration? Or is genuine integration something more profound? Is the end we seek a qualitative shift in how we conceive of and experience living as a nation? I think these are fundamental questions that need to be answered.

BRITISHNESS

This brings us to the fundamental question: how does Britain integrate with the rest of the world? In my opinion that is what the Britishness question comes down to at the end of the day.

British Muslim identity is very interesting and highly complex. I've recently finished writing a book called *Balti Britain: A Journey through the British Asian Experience* (2008). Researching the book took me on visits to various Muslim communities around the country, and in talking to Muslims, Pakistanis and Asians throughout Britain I discovered a very interesting thing. If you speak to an Asian in Scotland, whether Pakistani, Indian or Bangladeshi, it doesn't really matter, he or she will feel very strongly Scots. They will tell you: I'm a Pakistani Scot or I'm an Indian Scot. My response was to enquire: what is so Scottish about you? I would be told how people celebrate Hogmanay; some would say they occasionally wear a kilt, and all were proud of their accent, whether Glaswegian or something more dulcet. Probe further and you discover that in fact they perceive Scotland in a very specific light. First they see Scottish identity as open, something in which they can actively participate and become part of. Second, they see Scottish history in terms of their own history, as of a people persecuted and marginalized. I found this rather extraordinary, remembering as I do that Scotland provided innumerable soldiers and administrators to service the empire. To which my informants would reply, 'Oh no, the English forced them to do that. It wasn't them … they were OK.' In the common bonds of a strong sense of marginalization I found such a strong identification with Scotland had been forged that these Pakistani Scots and Indian Scots never ever described themselves as British.

If you go down to Wales you find something similar; in fact most Asians who live in Wales see Wales as England's first colony. Welsh history is a story of oppression, which enables Asians to identify with the Welsh, even though you find open racism in certain parts of Wales. There was a recent case in point. A Sikh schoolgirl was barred from attending Aberdare Girls School because she insisted on wearing her Sikh bracelet in defiance of the school's no-jewellery policy. The bracelet, the student insisted, was not jewellery but one of the five signs of Sikhism, a witness to her faith and identity. The case went to court and the student won. Exiting the courthouse, she read a statement to the waiting local media expressing her satisfaction with the outcome. What did she say? 'I remain a good Welsh Sikh girl'! I take particular note of this since my newly acquired son-in-law was born in Aberdare and he too, I find, is about as Welsh as you can get and proud of it. In all my travels and encounters, however, I never found one single individual, whether Indian, Pakistani or Bangladeshi, who said 'I am an English Pakistani' or 'I am Pakistani English' or 'I am Bangladeshi English'. When pressed they would say 'I'm a Brit' – I'm Pakistani British or I'm a British Pakistani or I'm a British Bangladeshi. Why? It seems to me that in the devolved condition of Britain today English identity is problematic. Scots and Welsh identity harks back to a different history; they conceive of identity in broad cultural terms as founded on the heritage of different language, poetry and music. And this sense of heritage is defined in opposition to England and ritually played out in sporting encounters and celebrated in the gladiatorial combat these permit whether they win, lose or draw. In contrast, however, English identity lays claim to all that Britain is, has and has done, with little, in fact virtually no, acknowledgement of regional participation, thus consequently offers little of the consolation of cultural signs and symbols that are open and inclusive. England's narrative is one of dominance, and as such it is made by and about that class which rules the roost and comprises the makers of history. England downplays its own diverse cultural heritages and in consequence seems to lack the passionate intensity of Wales or Scotland as well as the capacity to offer an open invitation of inclusion to migrants.

So Scots, Welsh and Irish identity is at base cultural, and culture encapsulates values, a way of looking at life and the world, a way of acting towards oneself and one's fellow countrymen and women that is distinctive. It is a cultural tradition that is all about a sense of belonging to a communal existence and a specific heritage. When we pose the question who are we talking about when we talk of British Muslims, the question then becomes: what is the British element in the identity of British Muslims? What values does one identify with Britishness? We are asked to invoke a litany about fairness, democracy, justice and decency. The trouble is that such values cannot be claimed exclusively by any one nationality. They are general human values; they belong to all humanity and occur in all traditions. They can be claimed by Muslims as Islamic values rather than British values. Identified at such a level of abstraction, British values do not bring people together with a sense of something unique, particular and special which they share; they do not provide the strong, affective bonds of emotional attachment. It may very well be that a certain reticence about strong emotion is a quintessential English characteristic. If we are to determine how we can recognize if and when we have really achieved integration, however, I think we need to debate what Britishness is – what is this identity to which we all inclusively can belong? As far as I am concerned there is no single answer – there are not even any answers; it's a form of becoming, something that needs to be negotiated continuously. Most certainly I think we urgently need to debate the subject in a broader context than that offered by the government. We need to create a debate that matches the hope we wish to invest in the process of integration as a mutual undertaking of mutual belonging.

There is absolutely nothing wrong with an individual having several loyalties, just as we all have several fluid identities. As members of a complex modern society it is natural that we should take identity from and express loyalty to various aspects of our lives. An accountant, for example, will tend to be supportive of the accounting community, will defend the high ideals and best practice of his or her profession and will certainly not let slip how effortlessly accountants can manipulate their knowledge to massage balance sheets and evade taxes and other such examples of sharp practice. Indeed, to protect their professional trade secrets they converse in Accountese, the technical term for their jargon-laden special language which serves to keep outsiders out. Apart from professional loyalty, we each of us have numerous other loyalties reflecting the organizations to which we belong, the associations we form in the course of our lives. What we believe is another source of identity and loyalty. Christianity, whether Roman Catholic, Anglican, Orthodox, Baptist or Wesleyan, Judaism and Buddhism are all transnational affiliations. So there is nothing inherently wrong in Muslims identifying with a global community.

The question of the moment, however, is whether this transnational identity inevitably leads to terrorism and is likely to undermine the safety of Britain. Muslims see the *umma*, the worldwide Muslim community, as their extended family. So if young British Muslims see fellow Muslims suffering, for example in Iraq, then they feel upset and angry. They feel involved, and the more stark the suffering, the more unjust the cause, the more upset they feel. And it is perfectly clear that British foreign policy shares responsibility for the appalling events in Iraq which we watched daily on television. It is not merely an affective disorder that afflicts only the young. The older generation, our first-generation immigrants in Britain, still remember the history of what the British did in Iran, what the British did in Iraq, the precursors of today's entanglements. My father's generation have vivid memories of British foreign policy in the 1950s and 1960s in the Muslim world. And they are a generation shaped by the lived experience of colonialism. The legacy of British foreign policy and its operation today have played a very important part in the rise of militancy among British Muslims. It is absurd to ignore this obvious fact.

MULTICULTURALISM

This brings me to multiculturalism. Here again Muslims are seen as a problem. Let me be very frank. Multiculturalism was not a problem before 2001; in fact I am not aware that anyone uttered a bad word about multiculturalism until 1999. It was widely accepted as a problem after 9/11; it became an even more acute problem after 7/7. Now it is commonplace for people to say that multiculturalism is dead or should die or should be killed outright. I would suggest they're not really making considered comments on multiculturalism. What the new consensus testifies to is that multiculturalism is a problem because of Muslims – the good things multiculturalism might bring have hit the insurmountable obstacle of Muslim sensibilities. The fear and concern created by the activities of certain Muslims have become the problem of multiculturalism in people's minds and overshadow all else.

For me multiculturalism in Britain is about two things that I regard as a source of hope. Primarily, multiculturalism is about empowerment; it is and always should be about empowering a minority. Recently I found myself on a platform with David Cameron, leader of the opposition, who said, 'Well, I'm not against multiculturalism, I'm against state multiculturalism.' When I enquired what state multiculturalism was, I was told it was the officious allocation of state funding to particular communities, an approximation of affirmative-action policies. I can see very little wrong with such policies. As I have already noted, Muslim communities experience high levels of deprivation. The problems will not vanish without the application of real resources. And without real resources being available, a cycle of deprivation will be transmitted from generation to generation, creating an underclass that can define itself by its Muslim identity. Such a situation invites disaffection and is not something we should wish to contemplate or countenance. Making resources available does not mean we cannot debate and scrutinize the policies and programmes selected, to determine whether they are the most effective or indeed even necessary. Most certainly, multiculturalism does not mean that only some deprived communities, defined by ethnicity or religious affiliation, should be helped. Deprivation is not in and of itself about one's cultural heritage and ancestry; it is about need, basic, common human need. The connection I make between multiculturalism and empowerment is that so long as deprivation exists it deforms hope, undermines self-respect and human dignity and defers the real business of achieving genuine integration. The empowerment I seek is about securing the necessary resources to enable members of deprived communities to become agents of transformation and betterment in their own lives and those of their community. What is essential is that this process of empowerment should encourage common cause across communal lines. Deprivation is no helpmate to integration. It is a prime culprit in creating antagonism between and among the disadvantaged. The empowerment we need must have access to real resources, real funding, but it must be smart money – used to help build bridges between similarly disadvantaged groups and communities. Empowerment has to be an essential element of multiculturalism. Empowerment is supporting the capacity to take responsibility for and lay claim to ownership of the circumstances and condition of one's life and lived environment.

The second essential element of multiculturalism is self-representation. Multiculturalism is seen as a problem in contemporary Britain because Muslims insist on self-representation. But what is to be self-represented is by no means self-evident. To be correct we should not speak of 'the Muslim community'; in Britain there are a diversity of Muslim communities. Unity in diversity is an authentic part of Islam, its civilization and history. Muslims speak many languages, have varied cultures, customs and practices, let alone differences of religious interpretation. Another characteristic of Muslim life is that we form innumerable organizations all of which lay claim to being the only right and proper face of Islam. We generate community leaders and have no system for democratically selecting them to give voice to the thoughts and feelings of particular groups, let alone the 'community' as a whole. Greater understanding of the fluidity, diversity and even disorganization of Muslim communal affairs might actually go a long way to soothing many of the fears and misconceptions held by the British public about Muslims. Such understanding is certainly a necessary part of achieving genuine integration. In Islamic history there has never been just one answer to any question. All questions are subject to context and circumstance, and that can be a source of hope.

The desire for self-representation is driven by the common currency of negative stereotypes, which structure what their non-Muslim neighbours think they know about Muslims and Islam. But we need to be not only self-representing but also self-aware. Muslims seek to represent their beliefs, tradition and heritage as the ideal. In countering the negative, Muslims offer only the positive, as if we all lived perfect lives. However understandable, it is not a convention that aids mutual understanding. And it raises problems for Muslims themselves. It has delayed the community becoming involved with issues that affect our young people, not just issues such as drug addiction, but also the increase in single-parent Muslim mothers. Issues of family breakdown, domestic abuse and child abuse do not pass us by. They are human problems, part of our flawed humanity as much as anyone else's. To properly represent ourselves we need to take ownership of all the predicaments of members of our communities and begin devising our own approaches to counselling, care and remedial assistance. This would be the most hopeful sign of real empowerment and the most honest form of self-representation, which would open up new discussions and opportunities for understanding with our non-Muslim fellow citizens. Self-representation is about reflecting how our communities and their members are maturing, adapting and transforming themselves in the context and circumstances of British life.

Self-representation is about articulating who we are, what we believe and what we think in terms appropriate and relevant to living in Britain today. Self-representation is about taking responsibility for making ourselves more comprehensible and better understood by our fellow citizens. Effective self-representation must be a proactive strategy that develops new channels and terms of communication, as well as new kinds of participation in the mainstream of British life.

So multiculturalism, the multiculturalist space I see as a space of hope, must be focused in two basic directions: empowerment and self-representation.

As I have tried to make clear, I understand both empowerment and self-representation as opportunities, the chance to take possession of our own fate as citizens of Britain, to become contributory participants in the life of this society. So long as we accept being seen as a problem, the problematique of being Muslim will obstruct and hinder genuine integration across all sectors of British society.

There are lots of spaces that Muslims occupy. We have a choice. We can see our circumstances as problems. Or they can be seen as spaces of hope. I would much rather look to spaces of hope. One way to make the switch to a new mindset is to step back and see things not in terms of Muslim this and Muslim that but in terms of race, in terms of inequality, in terms of marginalization, in terms of problems in inner cities, in terms of problems of unemployment, because ultimately that's what the debate should be about. To these debates and issues we will bring our own distinctive approach, but we should not wield our identity as a brand name. The greatest of the spaces of hope I look forward to is that in which we develop the capacity to explain ourselves better both to ourselves and to our fellow citizens as we share in the burdens and difficulties of making Britain a better society for everyone.

REFERENCE

Sardar, Z. (2008) *Balti Britain: A Journey through the British Asian Experience*, London: Granta.

2 | Muslims in the West: deconstructing geographical binaries

PETER HOPKINS

Public discourse, everyday discussion and commonsense understandings persistently reinforce the notion that 'Islam' and 'the West' are mutually exclusive. Whether it be through the rhetoric of politicians, the language of newspaper editors or the representation of different social groups on the television or in magazines, the prevailing sense is that 'the West' and 'Islam' are – in a number of different ways – incompatible, divergent, mismatched and often in conflict with each other. This sense of incompatibility is often bolstered by the employment of a complex series of binaries about the attitudes, values and behaviours of communities identified as 'Muslim' or as 'Western'. These binaries are constructed in such a way that a series of barriers, restrictions and limitations are often placed on there being constructive conversations, interactions or dialogue between different communities. Islam is set against the West, segregation against integration, liberalism and democracy against fanaticism and extremism. The central argument of this chapter is that, in order to create a more tolerant, understanding and equal society, there is an urgent need for academic researchers, policy-makers and others to break down, challenge and problematize these binaries.

Binary thinking is highly problematic. Post-colonial critics have unsettled the assumed superiority of Western society by problematizing the relationships between colonized/colonizer, core/periphery and self/other (Blunt and McEwan 2002). Furthermore, in recent years, ideas of 'hybridity and in-betweenness, flexibility and mutability have gained conceptual currency over fixity, stability and boundedness' (Smith 2005: 97) in the search for an understanding of social and spatial relations. This has provided a further set of concepts for exploring the complexities of social worlds that were once thought of as unique and distinct, yet are now acknowledged as being interconnected and related.

In this chapter, I focus upon three of the many binaries that are regularly reinforced in discussions about the place of Muslims in the West. First, I critique commonsense understandings of the oppositions between 'the West' and 'the Muslim Rest' by highlighting the diversities existing within each of these categories. Second, I interrogate contradictions and problematic assumptions inherent in mainstream debates about religious residential clustering, which revolve around claims about segregation and integration. Third, I concentrate on the representation of Muslims within Western societies – and in particular British society – highlighting the fact that Muslim individuals and communities tend to be ignored or demonized rather than represented in a positive light. Overall, the crux of the argument presented in this chapter is that a radical change in how Muslim communities and individuals are regarded within British society must take place if a fairer and more just society is to be created.

'THE WEST' VERSUS 'THE MUSLIM REST'

The idea that 'Islam' and 'the West' are mutually exclusive prevents dialogue and stifles positive social relations. As Halliday (1999: 892) observes:

No subject in contemporary public discussion has attracted more confused discussion than that of relations between 'Islam' and 'the West'. Whether it be discussion of relations between Muslim states and non-Muslim countries, or that of the relations between non-Muslims and Muslims within Western countries, the tendency has *on both sides* been, with some exceptions, towards alarmism and simplification.

The commonsense understanding, then, is that 'the West' is positive, advanced and democratic with 'Islam' being representative of intolerance, oppression and backwardness. Conversely, those outside of the West are constructed as subservient, inferior and at odds with 'the West'. As Halliday (ibid., 2003) notes, such stereotypes are problematic in that they both represent 'Islam' and 'the West' as monolithic categories with little or no internal diversity, variation or contradictions. One of the first steps in promoting positive social relations for Muslims in the West is therefore to open up debate about the meanings of the categories of 'Islam' and 'the West'.

The report of the Commission on British Muslims and Islamophobia entitled *Islamophobia: A Challenge for Us All* distinguishes between closed and open views of Islam (see Table 2.1). Closed views of Islam tend to see it as monolithic, separate, inferior, threatening and hostile, with any discrimination towards Islam being regarded as normal. Open views of Islam, however, recognize it as a diverse and genuine religion, connected with other faiths and of value. The sense here, then, is that

TABLE 2.1 Closed and open views of Islam

	Closed views of Islam	Open views of Islam
Monolithic/diverse	Islam seen as a single monolithic block, static and unresponsive to new realities	Islam seen as diverse and progressive, with internal differences, debates and development
Separate/interacting	Islam seen as separate and other – (a) not having aims or values in common with other cultures; (b) not affected by them; (c) not influencing them	Islam seen as interdependent with other faiths and cultures – (a) having certain shared values and aims; (b) affected by them; (c) enriching them
Inferior/different	Islam seen as inferior to the West – barbaric, irrational, primitive, sexist	Islam seen as distinctively different, but not deficient, and as equally worthy of respect
Enemy/partner	Islam seen as violent, aggressive, threatening, supportive of terrorism, engaged in a 'clash of civilizations'	Islam seen as an actual or potential partner in joint cooperative enterprises and in the solution of shared problems
Manipulative/sincere	Islam seen as a political ideology, used for political or military advantage	Islam seen as a genuine religious faith, practised sincerely by its adherents
Criticism of the West rejected/considered	Criticisms made by Islam of 'the West' rejected out of hand	Criticisms of 'the West' and other cultures are considered and debated
Discrimination defended/criticized	Hostility towards Islam used to justify discriminatory practices towards Muslims and exclusion of Muslims from mainstream society	Debates and disagreements with Islam do not diminish efforts to combat discrimination and exclusion
Islamophobia seen as natural/problematic	Anti-Muslim hostility accepted as natural and 'normal'	Critical views of Islam are themselves subjected to critique, lest they be inaccurate and unfair

Source: Runnymede Trust (1997: 5)

those who adopt this open position are willing to critique and analyse any criticisms made of Islam. Open views of Islam highlight the internal diversities of the Muslim faith, recognize that there are different ethnic groups, nationalities and regional practices, and emphasize that groups and individuals often follow the religion and engage with their 'Islamic' faith in a host of different ways. The result of these open views is the dissolution of perspectives which see Islam as one homogenous block. As Modood (2003: 100) points out:

> Muslims are not, however, a homogenous group. Some Muslims are devout but apolitical, some are political but do not see their politics as being 'Islamic' (indeed, may even be anti-Islamic). Some identify more with a nationality of origin, such as Turkish; others with the nationality of settlement and perhaps citizenship, such as French. Some prioritise fund-raising for mosques, others campaign against discrimination, unemployment or Zionism ... The category 'Muslim', then, is as internally diverse as 'Christian' or 'Belgian' or 'middle-class', or any other category helpful in ordering our understanding ...

So, it is crucial to recognize that '"Islam" tells us only one part of how these peoples live and see the world; and that "Islam" may vary greatly' (Halliday 1999: 897).

As well as deconstructing the ways in which Islam is presented as static and unresponsive, it is also crucial that the flatly positive idea of 'the West' is also critiqued and challenged (Bonnett 2004). It is crucial that – as well as being viewed in a series of positive ways – 'the West' is also recognized as diverse, contradictory and, at times, exploitative, unequal and intolerant.

It may be simple to recognize some of the diversity within 'Islam' and 'the West'; the mutual exclusivity of 'the West' and 'the Muslim Rest' is, however, often transposed on to other aspects of social relations that are viewed in stereotypical ways and then used as a justification for derogatory or discriminatory attitudes and practices. In particular, one of the most powerful set of social practices that are often entangled in these debates relate to gender relations and the practices of 'Islamic' and 'Western' men and women. Recently, too, the tensions associated with the gendering of the binary between Islam and the West have been bolstered by geopolitical events such as September 11th 2001: '"the West" once again lines up against "the Rest", displacing the niceties of recognition with the indignity of biometric profiling, tagging, tracking and targeting' (Hopkins and Smith 2007: 110).

The intersection of gender with discourses about 'the West' versus 'the

Muslim Rest' works to reinforce stereotypes about the embodiment, attitudes, values and spatial practices of Muslim men and women and often places them in opposition to or estranged from those of non-Muslim 'white' individuals. In my own work, I have explored how stereotypes about Asian masculinities have previously tended to represent Asian men as weak, effeminate and middle-class, especially in comparison to black (African or Caribbean) men, who are labelled as powerful and strong (Hopkins 2006). Recent geopolitical events have witnessed the reworking of stereotypes associated with Muslim men, however (Dwyer et al. 2008). Bolstered by discourses promoting the mutual exclusivity of Islam and the West, many Muslim men are now often stereotyped as aggressive, fundamentalist, angry and as potential terrorists. They are seen as out of place in the West, a threat to the gendered order of Western society and a disturbance to the moral order of Western society.

Similarly, assumptions about Muslim women's behaviours, attitudes and practices are also often represented as being at odds with norms associated with Western femininities. Dwyer (1998: 53) observes that a complex set of discourses work to reinforce dominant perceptions of what it means to be a Muslim woman. These discourses mobilize 'a set of widely held shared beliefs, or "commonsense" understandings, which are repeatedly reproduced through different media and institutional practices'. Overall, these discourses operate to construct Muslim women as the 'embodiment of a repressive and "fundamentalist" religion' and as 'passive victims of oppressive cultures'. As such, there is a strong set of stereotypes that represent Muslim women as passive, oppressed victims of patriarchy, who are not allowed to work and are forced to veil (ibid.; Mohammad 1999; Puar 2007). More recently – in a radical refocusing of stereotypes – Muslim women have often been regarded with suspicion and possibly even associated with terrorism, as a result of the simplistic assumptions made about their gendered, racialized and religious identities. The binaries of 'modern' and 'fundamentalist' are therefore mapped directly on to 'Western' and 'Islamic', resulting in the reinforcing of polarized discourses about Muslims in the West. Furthermore, stereotypes associated with these binaries are regularly reworked in a variety of ways as a result of different geopolitical events, yet the strength of them is such that they remain as binaries, albeit reshaped in different ways.

SEGREGATION VERSUS INTEGRATION

A second aspect of the Muslim/West binary that operates at a variety of geographical scales revolves around the tendency of Muslims to be residentially concentrated in particular urban locations. As Peach (1996: 379) clarifies, the sense is that segregation is negative:

> Segregation has a bad name. References, when it refers to people, are almost always pejorative. It seems that it is acceptable to segregate land uses, but that social segregation carries a whiff of apartheid and is generally dismissed as a totally negative and abhorrent phenomenon ... Ethnic segregation is seen as divisive, as preventing understanding, as reducing social interaction between groups and individuals and as leading to mistrust.

The racialization of religion has now resulted in ethnic segregation being viewed through a religious lens and so policy concerns now often focus on the residential clustering of Muslim populations rather than particular ethnic groupings (Phillips 2006). In the UK in particular, such discourses have been reinforced by official reports about the disturbances in Bradford, Oldham and Burnley in 2001 which argue that a key issue is that white and ethnic minority communities are living 'parallel lives'. 'Central to this assertion is the claim that people of South Asian origin, particularly British Muslims, are failing to be active citizens by withdrawing from social and spatial interactions with wider British society' (ibid.: 25). The issue here focuses upon 'Muslim self-segregation,' and so the commonsense approach to this social phenomenon is to 'see Muslim individuals and communities as isolationist and separatist.' As Sardar argues in this volume, Muslim segregation is often regarded as particularly problematic, despite the fact that many other forms of segregation – from gated communities to the clustering of Chinese or Jewish populations – pass without comment.

Despite the strength of dominant discourses about Muslim residential clustering and the suspicion and lack of trust that such discourses engender, the binary 'segregation versus integration' is highly problematic for a number of reasons. Much like the assumption that 'Islam' is the problem while 'the West' is regarded as overwhelmingly positive, there is also a strong sense that Muslim segregation is simply down to the residential practices of Muslims with the white population being regarded in an overwhelmingly innocent and positive light. Yet, in analysing census data about religion and ethnicity in the London 2001 census, Peach (2006: 367) found that 'there 'is considerable residential separation between Muslims of different ethnic origins', and so the dominant determinants of location are 'family, ethnicity and region of origin' (ibid.: 368) rather than religion per se. As Peach (ibid.: 368) concludes, 'political Islam and everyday Islam are different. At the residential and marital level, Islam is not a monolithic religion. Ethnicity, region of origin and language play a part in differentiating traditions within the Ummah.' Dominant discourses about Muslim self-segregation have also been challenged by Deborah Phillips (2006), who has highlighted a diverse range of social and spatial factors that influence the residential location of different groups:

> Although it emerged that British Muslim families value residential clustering, for reasons of culture and tradition, familiarity, identity and security, the desire for separation from others is not self-evident. Their spatial segregation in poorer neighbourhoods largely reflects bounded choices, constrained by structural disadvantage, inequalities in the housing market (past and present), worries about racism ... (ibid.: 34)

' As such, the idea that Muslims are choosing to withdraw, segregate and isolate themselves is overly simplistic.'While some Muslim families might choose to live near other Muslim households, other Muslims are forced to locate in residentially segregated neighbourhoods as a result of structural issues connected with the housing market (such as estate agents showing Asian clients houses in Asian areas) as well as concerns about racial harassment. As Peach (1996: 379) observes, segregation is not all bad. Segregation is, in fact, one of the key methods of accommodating difference. There are positive as well as negative reasons for segregation (ibid.: 379):

> The positive side is that concentration allows the group to maintain its social cohesion. It maintains cultural values, it strengthens social networks, it allows the passing of critical thresholds for the support of institutions and shops. Within the urban sphere, it is possible to maintain group cohesion through spatial concentration. Urban concentration allows the groups to pass the threshold size at which ethnic shops and religious institutions can be maintained and the proximity to members of the groups that allows the language and norms of the groups to be maintained. (ibid.: 386)

Furthermore, the residential choices and institutional control of white communities clearly also shape patterns of residential clustering (Phillips 1998).'This influences patterns of religious residential clustering in a number of ways, such as – for example – the decisions of white households to move out of ethnic minority neighbourhoods (white flight). / Furthermore, although residential segregation is often viewed as a problem created by minority communities, the vast majority of white communities tend to residentially cluster in particular locations, with research finding that white people tend to live in communities where they form over 80 per cent of the local population (Johnston et al. 2002). So, 'whereas most of the members of the various ethnic groups live in areas where they are exposed to white majorities, most of the members of the host society live in relatively homogenous areas and experience little local exposure to other ethnic communities' (ibid.: 608–9).

There is therefore a need to challenge the commonsense understanding that Muslim communities choose to self-segregate when, instead, a series of complex processes are at work in shaping the social and spatial patterning of religious residential segregation. Binary thinking that sets segregation against integration and Muslims against the West needs to be challenged and refocused. Furthermore, one of the main factors identified in causing segregation is racism: racist practices within the housing market, other forms of institutional racism, racist residential decisions of white households, as well as fears among Muslim families about experiencing racial harassment in particular residential locations – all work to influence decisions and practices connected with deciding where to – and where not to – live. So, alongside the need to challenge dominant discourses about Islam versus the West, as they are expressed through discourses of segregation versus integration, there is an urgent need to stand up against the racist attitudes, practices and values of the different agents involved in shaping the residential patterning of neighbourhoods.

ABSENT OR DEMONIZED IMAGES VERSUS POSITIVE REPRESENTATIONS

A third set of binaries – and a medium through which other binaries are produced and reproduced – relate to the various representations of Muslims in television programmes, news coverage, online media and daily newspapers. Appadurai (1996: 35–6) discusses globalized issues relating to 'mediascapes' and 'ideoscapes'. The former refers to the 'electronic capabilities to produce and disseminate information (newspapers, magazines, television stations)', with the latter being 'concatenations of images [that are] often directly and have frequently to do with the ideologies of states'. There is much evidence to suggest that – with respect to the representation of Muslims – mediascapes and ideoscapes work to present Islam and Muslims in an overwhelmingly negative light (e.g. Dwyer 1998; Poole 2002). 'Dominant representations of Muslims present them in a negative manner, demonize their behaviours and practices, and associate them with suspicious and alien attitudes and values.'

There is much evidence from research that coverage of Islam and Muslims in the media is overwhelmingly negative. Poole (2002) found that there is a strong tendency for newspaper coverage to move towards the sensational when reporting Islam, and Samad (1998: 428–9) has noted that '... there was a strong perception that whether as Asians, Muslims or as Pakistanis, they were represented in the media in a negative manner and that as viewers their interests were not taken into consideration'. Similarly, in my own work, 'the media was persistently critiqued for portraying a negative or slanted view of Islam and Muslims and thereby influencing the views and attitudes of the general public' (Hopkins 2004: 268); and Dunn et al. (2007) have found similarly negative coverage of Muslims in their work in Australia. Furthermore, in the current geopolitical context, Kundnani (2002: 74) observes that

> Since September 11, media attention has focused on Muslim funda-mentalists in the UK, such as Abu Hamza al-Masri, of Finsbury Park mosque, and Sheikh Omar Bakri, leader of the Al-Muhajiroun group, who have become household names ... [however] little effort has been made to point out how small their respective followings are.

The tendency in terms of media coverage, then, is to focus on the sensational, the extreme and the exotic, all of which operates to re-inforce simplistic understandings and crude representations of Muslims in the West. As such, the overwhelming tendency is for Muslims to be represented through a series of demonized images or ignored completely rather than to be viewed through positive representations. For example, many of the young Muslim men I worked with (Hopkins 2008) were very critical of the ways in which the media constantly sensationalized and misrepresented their religious faith and everyday behaviour while also choosing to ignore the positive contributions their families and communities made to wider society. There is therefore a need to chal-lenge the misrepresentation of Muslims in various everyday media, or their absence therefrom, in order to encourage more engagement with positive representations of the ways in which Muslims live their everyday lives. Sarah Mills's work with the Muslim Scout movement in the UK (published in this volume) is an ideal example to highlight the positive and creative ways in which Muslim communities are engaging with organizational structures within British society, yet coverage of such an example is very rarely found within various forms of everyday media.

The persistence of these demonized images operates to associate all Muslims with the practices, attitudes and values of a very small minority of Muslims who are classified as having extreme views or practices. This process of normalization works to associate 'the Muslim community' with the perspectives and values of a minority of Muslims, thereby stigmatizing all Muslims. Muslim communities therefore become imagined through discourses such as the 'Asian gang' (Alexander 2004), fundamentalist religious leaders, controversial veiling practices and hierarchical and controlling family relations. We rarely read accounts or see images associated with the standard everyday practices of Muslim families and communities, such as those associated with the compassion and warmth experienced by Muslims attending the local mosque, Muslim young men who train hard every week as part of their football team, or Muslim families who work long hours to make sure their parents and children can live decent lives. Academic research has a role to play here too, as work here also tends to focus on the margins. Alexander (ibid.: 544) observes that there are '... parallels between media and academic analyses, which raises pertinent, and disquieting, questions about the ways in which selected academic discourses have fed into, and upon, populist soundbite understandings of race and ethnicity'.

When Muslims are not being represented through negative images and discourses, they tend to be absent. As Dunn (2004: 334) observes: 'there are two central ways in which a minority cultural group can be constructed as Other: deviance and absence'. As such, the focus on the negative side of the binary of absent or demonized images versus positive representations works to construct Muslims as either unworthy, illegal and out of place (owing to their being absent) or as a threat to the moral order of society (owing to their being stereotyped as deviant). There is an urgent need therefore to move beyond the absence or demonization of Muslims, in order to recognize the diversity of practices, values and attitudes that constitute such an important part of their everyday lives (see also Kevin M. Dunn's chapter in this volume). In order to open up spaces of hope, then, it is crucial that there is media coverage that includes positive representations of Muslim communities and individuals, yet it will take considerable time to reach a point where the negative stereotypes associated with Muslims in the West are eventually put to rest.

OPENING UP SPACES OF HOPE

Working towards a more positive conclusion, I would like to emphasize three further points. First, moving fully beyond and outside of the binaries identified in the chapter results in a radical rethinking of the status of Muslims in Western societies. Rather than being regarded as contradictory to Western values, segregated from mainstream society and associated with a range of negative representations, Muslim individuals and communities are respected for their contributions to Western nations and recognized as valued members of society. Rather than being seen as intolerant, fundamentalist and threatening, Muslims are regarded as progressive citizens open to dialogue and discussion on a range of social issues. This requires a radical rethinking of the place of Muslims in the West, alongside transforming assumptions about segregation and radically reshaping the nature of media coverage and engagement. Overall, however, this is very challenging to achieve as a result of the ways in which the overlapping and interlocking binaries discussed in this chapter dominate public discussion, forcefully govern media coverage and engagement and ultimately influence the shape of social life.

Related to the re-evaluation of the place of Muslims in the West and the re-evaluation of simplistic binaries about 'the West' versus 'the Muslim Rest', it is crucial that the diversity of Islam is recognized fully, alongside understanding that what it means to identify as Muslim varies considerably from individual to individual. Some Muslims pray five times a day, others only on a Friday, others when they can, and others not at all. Some have completed the pilgrimage to Mecca more than once, others never have and possibly never will (Modood 2003). This will undoubtedly require a refocusing of media coverage of Muslim individuals and communities. Alongside this, it is crucial that public understanding of the religion of Islam and what it means to be a Muslim is improved in order that everyday interactions between different communities take place in a culture of understanding and mutual respect, rather than in the context of suspicion and lack of understanding (Dunn et al. 2007; Hopkins 2004).

Third, and finally, opening up conversations with Muslims in the West creates space for acknowledging Muslim communities and individuals as genuine partners for joint working, whether this is in community partnerships, through interfaith dialogue or as partners in collaborative research (Spalek and Imtoual 2007; Spalek et al. 2008). This might involve working with local Muslim organizations in exploring issues of shared interest, partnering Muslim agencies in research applications or providing training or other forums for discussions with Muslims, perhaps through community forums or policy discussions. By giving voice to Muslim communities through participatory and collaborative research, researchers have the potential to work alongside Muslim communities in order to engage with communities, reshape public understandings of Islam and work towards creating a more just and ultimately hopeful society.

CONCLUSION

In conclusion, I have tried to use this chapter to disturb, unsettle and dislodge some of the commonsense stereotypes and dominant discourses that work to marginalize Muslims in the West. In doing so, I have critiqued an interweaving and overlapping set of binaries that seek to support the apparent contradiction between 'Islam' and 'the West'. In particular, I have focused upon the reification of three binaries – Islam versus the West, segregation versus integration and absent or demonized images versus positive representations – that are regularly reinforced through commonsense understandings and everyday discourse, all of which work to set Muslims and Islam against the West. The presence of Muslims in the West tends to be viewed through this interweaving set of binaries, which work to 'stereotype' them in negative and unhelpful ways and 'stigmatize' their communities. Furthermore, these binaries are often viewed in the context of particular geopolitical events (e.g. Northern riots, 9/11, London bombings), whereby heightened attention is given to Muslim families and communities in terms that work to exclude them from mainstream society. As such, Muslims tend to be viewed simultaneously through a complex set of stereotyping and stigmatizing binaries and in the context of particular events that operate to shape the character and nature of social relations and interactions. It is therefore necessary to move beyond these problematic binaries if the possibility of creating a more just society is to be fulfilled.

Clearly, the deconstruction of these binaries is very challenging given their dominance within popular culture, everyday representation and public life, and a number of important changes are required in order to create a more hopeful society. First, the nature of government policy and public discussion needs to be refocused in a way that highlights the positive contributions of Muslim communities, rather than focusing on the negative. Again, the tendency here is to focus upon issues of radicalization, extremism or immigration, on the exotic. More attention could usefully be focused on the array of positive contributions made by Muslim communities in the West and the ordinary aspects of their everyday routines and practices. Second, Muslim communities tend to be viewed through particular identities – such as religion, race and gender – while others are overlooked. Approaching Muslim communities through acknowledging other identities – such as age, disability and locality – may assist in the reimaging of Muslim individuals and families along more diverse lines. Perhaps these challenges could be combined with the three highlighted by Dunn (in this volume) – offering alternative portrayals of Islam in the West; defusing the political efficacy of

Islamophobia; and normalizing Islam as a Western religion – in order for spaces of hope to be opened up within Western societies.

REFERENCES

Alexander, C. (2004) 'Imagining the Asian gang: ethnicity, masculinity and youth after "the riots"', *Critical Social Policy*, 24(4).

Appadurai, A. (1996) *Modernity at Large: Cultural Dimensions of Globalization*, Minneapolis: University of Minnesota Press.

Blunt, A. and C. McEwan (2002) *Postcolonial Geographies*, London: Continuum.

Bonnett, A. (2004) *The Idea of the West: Culture, Politics and History*, New York: Palgrave Macmillan.

Dunn, K. (2004) 'Islam in Sydney: contesting the discourse of absence', *Australian Geographer*, 35(3).

Dunn, K., N. Klocker and T. Salabay (2007) 'Contemporary racism and Islamophobia in Australia', *Ethnicities*, 7(4).

Dwyer, C. (1998) 'Challenging dominant representations of Muslim women', in T. Skelton and G. Valentine (eds), *Cool Places: Geographies of Youth Culture*, London: Routledge, pp. 50–65.

Dwyer, C., B. Shah and G. Sanghera (2008) '"From cricket lover to terror suspect" – challenging representations of young British Muslim men', *Gender, Place and Culture*, 15(2).

Halliday, F. (1999) '"Islamophobia" reconsidered', *Ethnic and Racial Studies*, 22(5).

— (2003) *Islam and the Myth of Confrontation*, London: I.B.Tauris.

Hopkins, P. (2004) 'Young Muslim men in Scotland: inclusions and exclusions', *Children's Geographies*, 2(2).

— (2006) 'Youthful Muslim masculinities: gender and generational relations', *Transactions of the Institute of British Geographers*, 37.

— (2008) *The Issue of Masculine Identities for British Muslims after 9/11*, Lampeter: Edwin Mellen Press.

Hopkins, P. and S. J. Smith (2007) 'Scaling segregation; racialising fear', in R. Pain and S. J. Smith (eds), *Fear: Critical Geopolitics and Everyday Life*, Aldershot: Ashgate.

Johnston, R., J. Forrest and M. Poulsen (2002) 'Are there ethnic enclaves/ghettos in English cities?', *Urban Studies*, 39(4).

Kundnani, A. (2002) 'An unholy alliance? Racism, religion and communalism', *Race and Class*, 44(2).

— (2007) *The End of Tolerance: Racism in 21st Century Britain*, London: Pluto Press.

Modood, T. (2003) 'Muslims and the politics of difference', *Political Quarterly*, 74(1).

Mohammad, R. (1999) 'Marginalisation, Islamism and the production of "Other's" "Other"', *Gender, Place and Culture*, 6(3).

Peach, C. (1996) 'Good segregation, bad segregation', *Planning Perspectives*, 11.

— (2006) 'Islam, ethnicity and South Asian religions in the London 2001 census', *Transactions of the Institute of British Geographers*, 31.

Phillips, D. (1998) 'Black minority ethnic concentration, segregation and dispersal in Britain', *Urban Studies*, 35(10).

— (2006) 'Parallel lives? Challenging

40 | TWO

disdiscourses of British Muslim self-segregation', *Environment and Planning D: Society and Space*, 24(1).

Poole, E. (2002) *Reporting Islam: Media Representations of British Muslims*, London: I.B.Tauris.

Puar, J. (2007) *Terrorist Assemblages: Homonationalism in Queer Times*, Durham, NC: Duke University Press.

Runnymede Trust (1997) *Islamophobia: A Challenge for Us All*.

Samad, Y. (1998) 'Media and Muslim identity: intersections of generation and gender', *Innovation*, 11(4).

Smith, S. J. (1989) *The Politics of Race and Residence*, Cambridge: Polity Press.

— (2005) 'Black: white', in P. Cloke and R. Johnston (eds), *Spaces of Geographical Thought: Deconstructing Human Geography's Binaries*, London: Sage.

Spalek, B. and A. Imtoual (2007) 'Muslim communities and counter-terror responses: "hard" approaches to community engagement in the UK and Australia', *Journal of Muslim Minority Affairs*, 27(2).

Spalek, B., S. El-Awa and L. McDonald (2008) *Police–Muslim Engagement and Partnerships for the Purposes of Counter-Terrorism*, Birmingham: University of Birmingham.

3 | The hopeful and exclusionary politics of Islam in Australia: looking for alternative geographies of 'Western Islam'

KEVIN M. DUNN AND ALANNA KAMP

This chapter gives voice to the everyday experiences of Australian Muslims. The voices evocatively report on the 'everyday experiences of racism' of these citizens (after Essed 1991). The experiences are endured in the street, on public transport, and in dealings with institutions and shopkeepers. The aforementioned spaces can be seen as 'contact zones' across which Muslims and non-Muslims interact (Wise 2005). While these are everyday spaces of intolerance and prejudice, they are also places of indifference and neutrality. Most often, people get along with each other and they tolerate difference, or better still, they accommodate and embrace cultural differences. Noble (2009) and Wise (2005) have reported on how most everyday cross-cultural interactions are 'unpanicked' in the sense that cultural difference is negotiated in other ways besides conflict or anxiety. That is not to suggest that racist incidents are unimportant. We outline in this chapter the socially and personally debilitating impacts of racist incidents against Muslim Australians and highlight that they are too frequent (Noble 2005; Poynting et al. 2004). We also outline, however, the desires and recommendations of Australian Muslims, and review some of the actions taken to improve relations between Muslims and non-Muslims. These voices provide everyday geographies of hope.

The problematic perceptions of Islam and the West are also outlined in this chapter, and each is matched with some hopeful findings, initiatives and suggestions that come from both Muslims and non-Muslims in Australia. A handful of scholars have attempted to map such recommendations. For example, in reflecting on the British circumstance, Hopkins (2004: 268–9) suggested three sets of remedy: changing the racialization of Islam that occurs through the media, improving public understandings of Islam, and expanding public recognition of Islamic heterogeneity. Specific Australian examples of each of these forms of remedy are reviewed in this chapter, although we also look at suggestions regarding experiences of racism and civic leadership. The recommendations for improving perceptions, certainly in the Australian circumstance, are more likely to have flowed from community organizations, advocacy groups and anti-racism agencies. Given our own research history and community links, this chapter carries an emphasis on the lessons that flow from the experiences and hopes of Australian Muslims.

The data for this chapter are the voices of Australian Muslims, as detailed in the reports of Islamic organizations and anti-racism agencies. The most used data source in this chapter is the *Race, Faith and Gender* report of the Islamic Women's Welfare Council of Victoria (IWWCV). As with other Islamic organizations, we have provided advice to the IWWCV on the data-gathering instruments that were originally used for their study. The IWWCV and others, such as the Islamic Council of New South Wales (ICNSW), have produced reports that we have edited, and Dunn has presented keynotes and other addresses at the workshops and report launches of these groups. Dunn has similarly served in an advisory capacity for the inquiries and reports undertaken by anti-racism agencies such as the Human Rights and Equal Opportunity Commission's Ismaؙ Project (2004). We have a strong familiarity with the data collected in those projects, and this partly explains our use of them in this chapter. The studies have been comprehensive empirical exercises, collecting vast amounts of both qualitative and quantitative data. The quotations used in the reports, some of which are reproduced in this chapter, are deeply evocative of the experiences, desires and recommendations of Muslims. Well-crafted reports with strong evidentiary bases and evocative material can have considerable public policy impacts.

In writing this chapter we have asked some of our community contacts to critically review our arguments and to vet our characterizations of the experiences, desires and recommendations of Australian Muslims. We have asked them to 'return some of the favours' described above. The feedback received made us reconsider the citing of some Muslim scholars, for example those who were seen as only notionally Islamic, and so we expanded the set of references to include other Muslim commentators. Our community contacts challenged the overly rosy ways in which we had initially characterized some of the initiatives undertaken to address Islamophobia in Australia. As a consequence, the chapter paints a more rounded picture of the experiences, desires and recommendations of Muslims in the West.

MUSLIMS IN AUSTRALIA: SETTLEMENT, ISSUES AND INTERNATIONAL TRENDS IN ATTITUDES

The largest birthplace group among Australian Muslims is Australia (36.4 per cent) (Dunn 2004a). The two major overseas birthplace sources between 1970 and 1990 were Lebanon and Turkey, but there have also been flows of Muslim immigrants from the Pacific and South-East Asia – Fiji, Indonesia, Malaysia and Singapore, for example. More recent migration sources have included the Indian subcontinent, Iran, Iraq, Bosnia and Afghanistan. Australian Islam is very ethnically diverse. Muslims have come to Australia as refugees, family migrants and skilled immigrants across different and overlapping eras of immigration – during the White Australia Policy era (late 1800s to 1970s), in the Anglo assimilation times (post-Second World War to 1990s) and in the era of multiculturalism (1980s onwards). As with Muslims in other Western nations such as the United Kingdom (see Peach 2006), settlement experiences in Australia have varied with diverse socio-economic outcomes both within and across birthplace groups. The way that Islam is practised in the West also varies dramatically within each country (Dunn 2004a; Hopkins 2004: 268–9; Yasmeen 2008: 31–41). This variation is sustained by the local bases of mosque and centre organization, as well as the specific socio-economic and cultural contexts of the cities and suburbs where Western Muslims reside.

Within these spaces – nations, cities and suburbs – Western Muslims have faced the traditional pessimistic and disparaging accusations that many transnational communities have endured in modern history: they are accused and suspected of being the 'threat or enemy within' (Waldinger and Fitzgerald 2004: 1192). Such problematic views towards Muslims are manifest in simplistic proclamations about the emergence of a clash of civilizations between Islam and the West in Western societies (Maddox 2005: 173–4, 345). For example, Cardinal Pell, the leader of the Catholic Church in Australia, has suggested that the difference between Islam and Christianity is like a cold war divide (ICNSW 2005; Zwartz 2004: 3). Accusations of this kind fundamentally locate Muslims as non-Western.

Views that Muslims are incompatible with Australian society have also been found among the general Australian population. A survey undertaken in Australia in 2003 revealed that 41 per cent of respondents thought that Islam posed a minor threat of some sort to the nation, and a further 15 per cent thought that a major threat was posed (Dunn 2004b). In another large survey of Australian attitudes on diversity, racism and out-groups, Dunn et al. (2004) found that Muslims and people from the Middle East were consistently the most mentioned groups thought not to belong within Australian society. In NSW (sample [n]: 5,056) Muslims constituted 28 per cent of all the mentions of groups that did not belong, and the same proportion were people from Middle Eastern backgrounds (ibid.: 414–16).

Similarly, recent opinion polling from the Pew Global Attitudes Project (Pew Research Centre 2008) found that although a majority of people in Western nations have favourable views towards Islam and its followers, there remains a good deal of unfavourable sentiment towards Muslims. In the United Kingdom, 63 per cent of respondents claimed to have favourable views on Muslims. In the USA it was 57 per cent, and in Australia it was 60 per cent (ibid.: 15–17). These figures were generally better than for mainland European countries; for example, Germany (40 per cent), Spain (33 per cent) and Poland (35 per cent). The proportions holding negative views of Muslims were the same for the UK and USA (23 per cent), slightly worse in Australia (29 per cent) and then worse again elsewhere in the West (France 32 per cent; Germany 50 per cent; Spain 52 per cent; Poland 46 per cent). The proportion of Australian respondents holding negative views of Muslims (29 per cent) found by Pew (ibid.) is lower than the level of perceived threat from Muslims (56 per cent) found by Dunn (2004b). Notwithstanding these inconsistencies between surveys, there is a substantial minority in all the participating Western countries who hold views on Muslims that could be problematic for productive inter-communal relations.

Understandings of Muslims' perspectives on the West as well as Westerners' perspectives on Muslims may be crucial in working towards positive cross-cultural interactions. In a global questionnaire survey, Pew Research Centre (2006) examined both viewpoints. The sample included Muslims residing in majority Muslim countries as well as those residing within Western nations. Pew surveyed 14,030 people in thirteen countries between March and May 2006 to gather attitudinal data. Muslims in Islamic countries associated the West with geopolitical instability and saw Westerners as immoral, greedy and selfish (ibid.: 13–17). Non-Muslims in the West perceived Muslims as generally threatening and as specifically disrespectful of women. In this 2006 survey, Muslims in Western countries were those least likely to hold stereotypical views on both 'the West' and the 'Muslim world'. These Muslims are in a sense in between Islam and the West; they are 'Western Muslims'. Their presence, actions and connections may be an essential key to contesting the Western stereotypes of Islam (Dunn et al. 2007). In fact, the everyday lives of most Muslims are robust resistances of the simplistic binary between

Islam and the West (Manji 2004; Ramadan 2004). This mundane resistance through everyday life and presence is itself a geography of hope. Of course, Muslims vary in their views on the compatibility and consistency of Western and Islamic ways (see Yasmeen 2008: 42–5). None the less, the presence of 'Western Islam' and 'Western Muslims' is a political resource in so far as it confounds the assumption of a binary or clash between civilizations.

THE POLITICS OF ANTI-ISLAMIC SENTIMENT

In November 2007, the long-standing Australian Liberal Party government (a Conservative party by British analogy), led by John Howard, was voted out of office. In the lead-up to the federal election, it was becoming clear that the Howard government was in a good deal of trouble. In previous federal elections it had capitalized by taking tough policy and policing stances on issues to do with asylum seekers, many of whom were Muslim (Lygo 2004; Maddox 2005: 166–92; Marr and Wilkinson 2003). The Howard government was also implicated in the creation of moral panics about 'race', and about the poor integration of Islamic youth and their radicalization (Poynting et al. 2004). The Howard leadership was mostly careful in its use of what has been called subtle racism – that is, criticizing cultural traits rather than 'racial' or religious groups and vigorously denying any use of racism (ibid.: 153–5). Government commentaries on asylum seekers never overtly suggested that the tough stance on refugees was an anti-Muslim activity. It has been argued, however, that code-words were used to construct the asylum seekers as Other, and the deployment of Islamic stereotypes (militants, etc.) with reference to the unnamed asylum seekers made it clear to voters who it was (ethnically) that the government was attempting to exclude (Klocker and Dunn 2003; Dunn et al. 2007).

In the week before the 2007 Australian federal election it was revealed that the Liberal Party was, again, implicated in an attempt to capitalize on anti-Muslim sentiment. Some Liberal Party members in the Western Sydney seat of Lindsay had manufactured leaflets which they distributed to suburbs in electorally marginal areas. The leaflets were constructed so as to pretend they had been made and distributed by an Islamic group, with the fabricated name of the Islamic Australia Federation. The leaflet stated that a mosque was to be built locally and that the Labour Party was supportive: 'Labour supports our new Mosque construction and we hope, with the support and funding by Local and State governments, to open our new Mosque in St Mary's soon.' Furthermore, the leaflet stated that the Labour Party had supported arguments for the forgiveness of the

Bali bombers. The intention was to suggest that the Labour Party were sympathetic to Muslims: 'In the upcoming Federal Election we strongly support the ALP as our preferred party to govern this country and urge all other Muslims to do the same.' The areas where these leaflets were distributed were not places where a large number of Muslims live, nor was there any actual or over-the-horizon proposal to establish a mosque in that area. They were places, however, where Liberal Party members thought Islamophobic people lived. The leaflet was a stark demonstration of how Islamophobia was seen by political parties as a political instrument. It overtly revealed the political interest in stereotyping Islam.

A well-established set of stereotypes of Islam have evolved in Western countries (Said 1981). They include perceptions of Muslims as fanatical, intolerant, fundamentalist, militant and misogynist (Dunn 2001). Another strong stereotype refers to the general otherness or alien-ness of Islam within a Western context (Dunn 2005; Klocker and Dunn 2003). In regard to male Muslims in particular, scholars in the United Kingdom have commented on how the constructions of this group have evoked strong senses of animality (Hubbard 2005). Some of the perceptions of threat referred to earlier in this chapter are associated with these stereotypes. The relative importance of the stereotypes varies according to the subject matter under discussion. For example, in the context of international relations and overseas civil strife the constructions of militancy have been more prominent (Dunn 2001), whereas the stereotype of misogyny has been more prominent in public opinion on the status of Muslim women (IWWCV 2008), and the perceptions of animality, intolerance and fundamentalism have been stronger among non-Muslims' comments on whether Muslims fit into Western societies and on whether they represent a cultural threat (Dunn 2004b; 2005). These stereotypes have been shown to have a detrimental effect on municipal planning determinations for mosques and on tolerance of refugees, and are generally linked to racism against Muslims in Europe and elsewhere in the West (IHF 2005; HREOC 2004).

Many Muslims see the media as being largely responsible for the reproduction of Western stereotypes about Islam, as the following interviews illustrate:

> The [name of a newspaper] is really bad. I can't read it anymore. How come when a non-Muslim commits a crime, then there is no reference to their religion. I mean … how often do you see spread across the front page, 'Christian commits rape'? (Lebanese-Australian female, quoted in IWWCV 2008: 49)

Immediately post 9/11, women were looked at or spat at ... all sorts of vilification. And in part I would seriously say that the blame lies with the media in terms of how they portray, that is why I have never seen any programme with a positive portrayal of Muslim contributions to the country. (African-Indian-Australian female, quoted in Yasmeen 2008: 51)

ʌ Drawing attention to the cultural and religious heterogeneity of Islam could help to confound the static generalizations that are core to stereotypes. /

> The media has a lot to answer for. We are only ever represented in negative ways, or they really like to make use of images of women wearing the niqab or burqa. How about representing the full diversity of Muslim women? (Turkish-Australian female, quoted in IWWCV 2008: 49)

Muslim Australians have complained that the Australian media convey very narrow representations of Muslims and Islam, that the representations are unfair compared to the treatment of Christians, and they have demanded a more rounded portrayal of Islam and Muslims. Encouragingly, Klocker and Dunn (2003) found that some sections of the media maintain a critical perspective on government statements and actions regarding Islam, and (some) public opinion retains a healthy cynicism regarding both media and government.

The reproduction of Western stereotypes of Islam and Muslims has meant that what passes for knowledge of Islam in Australian society is a concern. The 2003 survey on attitudes towards Islam in Australia asked a random selection of Australians to summarize their knowledge of Islamic beliefs. Forty per cent of respondents could give no answer at all. Half those surveyed knew only a little about Islam. Only one in six Australians had a good understanding of Islam and its followers (Dunn 2005). Other data collected in Australia reveal that non-Muslims are aware of this ignorance. When asked whether non-Muslims in Victoria have a good understanding of the Muslim way of life, 69 per cent disagreed. Only 19 per cent agreed with that proposition (IWWCV 2008: 79–80). Ignorance is fertile soil in which virtually any idea can take root, and thus such a lack of knowledge of Islam in combination with the reproduction of stereotypes may be detrimental to positive inter-communal relations. What respondents in the 2003 survey did perceive as knowledge about Islam was a mix of critical comments as well as odd perceptions of core beliefs and key religious practices. Survey responses were sprinkled with self-deprecation and honesty: 'Are they the people who can't eat cows? No. They have a God.' Among the more ludicrous answers: 'They [Muslims] make peace rings and place them on the streets – not too sure if it's true'.

Contemporary sentiment towards Muslims in Western countries is typified by ignorance and stereotypes. Most ordinary Australians acknowledge this problem, with the majority also agreeing (71 per cent) that Australians need to be more tolerant of Muslims.

AUSTRALIAN MUSLIMS' EVERYDAY EXPERIENCES OF RACISM

Human rights agencies and Islamic organizations have found that anti-Islamic sentiment has become too common in the West. This is confirmed through consultations with Muslims:

> But I didn't speak to anyone about it [the racist experience], just people in my community. Didn't know who to go to. Besides, it's not as if it happens once in a blue moon, it happens all the time, and they spit at us, and pull our hijabs and call us black. (Somali-Australian female, quoted in IWWCV 2008: 37)

The IHF (2005) made reference to a deterioration in the social climate for European Muslims since the September 11th 2001 terrorism attacks and the subsequent War on Terror:

> *i* In the aftermath of 9/11, the social climate facing Muslims has deteriorated in the countries covered by this report [...] pre-existing prejudice and discriminations against Muslims have been reinforced. The xenophobic prejudice against Muslims has resulted in attacks on Muslims in the streets and other public spaces. (IHF 2005) *{*

Anti-terror laws, media representations and the experience of racist comments had all made European Muslims feel under suspicion and as foreigners within their own societies (Choudhury et al. 2006). Muslims in Victoria referred to the federal government's anti-terrorism campaigns as making them feel under suspicion (HREOC 2004: 66–8; IWWCV 2008: 49):

> The message seemed to be look out for suspicious looking Muslims, so I walk down the street thinking how many people are trying to work out if I am the person they should be suspicious of. (Young Palestinian-Australian female, quoted in IWWCV 2008: 49)

Muslim women in Victoria reported on the degradation of their

assessment is not to improve policing responses to the everyday racism that Muslim youth experience; rather, it aims to improve the policing of Muslim youth. The Australian Human Rights Commission have also initiated an inquiry into the Protection of Freedom of Religion, and are considering the extent to which there is 'adequate protection against discrimination based on religion' and how well 'incitement to religious hatred' is being managed (Australian Human Rights Commission 2008: 8). The short answer, after hearing the voices of Muslims in Australia, is that anti-racism legislation is not currently providing Muslims with protection against racism:

> I know about the Equal Opportunity Commission, but people don't go there ... mostly because of the hassle, and you need to prove it and it takes so long, so we have heard stories of people getting nowhere when they complain, so we don't bother. (Female, quoted in IWWCV 2008: 106)

> I know people who have called the police when they have been very seriously verbally abused in the street and from the front of their houses but the police don't come so they don't bother ringing them anymore. ... many of us are scared and where do we go for protection? (Female, quoted in ibid.: 106)

Interview informants told the IWWCV (ibid.: 6) that 'Our community needs to be educated about who to report problems to, and about our rights'. Australian Muslims have asked for complaints mechanisms that they would be able to use effectively. They also made it clear that they were prepared to take action in circumstances where they felt safe to do so:

> I don't want to just let it [the racist incident] go, because they think then that they can just get away with it. So as long as I don't think that I will get physically attacked or raped, I will tell them that they are wrong. (Female, quoted in ibid.: 60)

Muslim women expressed a desire to be seen as 'normal' everyday people, this raising questions about what normalization might entail:

> There are many people who are making an effort to get to know us personally and I think that is the answer. They need to see us as women, mothers, daughters, who feel all the same things they do ... we love our children and value our lives here just like everyone else. (Female, quoted in ibid.: 111)

Figure 3.1 These posters, developed by Australians Against Racism Inc., were placed on billboards in Sydney in 2004. The subheading reads 'Religion is not the only label they wear'. *Source*: Australians Against Racism Inc., photography by Cassandra Mathie, copy by Steve Sorec, and graphic design by blackant@iinet.net.au.

Normalization should not equate with assimilation or dissipation. One of the criticisms of campaigns aimed at humanizing Australian Muslims is that they tend to present a very assimilative representation of Islam. Figure 3.1 is a photograph of billboards that were established in 2004 to counteract Islamophobia. The group behind the campaign was Australians Against Racism Inc. They had worked for two years to design two posters and then raised the required funds (A$120,000 plus) to put the posters on to billboards in Sydney. Critics have pointed to the whiteness of the young women represented in the billboards and the unitary representation (hijab-wearing and young). Some of that criticism has come from organizations like the IWWCV. Later posters developed by the Council challenge this aspect of uniformity and focus on presenting a more diverse picture of Islam in Australia (Figure 3.2).

⁄ Just as there are stereotypes of Islam as the Other, there are important constructions of the Self that affect the treatment of Muslims in Western countries.⁄Narrow constructions of national identity will curtail attempts to normalize Islam within Western countries. In Australia, for example, there is a need to expand popular understandings of Australian-ness beyond Anglo-Celtic/Christian, such that non-Christians can symbolically feel part of a multi-faith citizenry. Yasmeen (2008: 75) has argued for a new language of communal harmony that better acknowledges the religious diversity in Australia and which asserts the citizenship of

Figure 3.2 Anti-Islamophobia poster developed by the Islamic Women's Welfare Council of Victoria. The subheading statements reinforce the diversity of the background and religious practices of Muslim women in Australia. *Source*: Islamic Women's Welfare Council of Victoria, 2005.

non-Christians as well as an expectation that they should feel safe and secure.

Muslim women in Victoria affirmed that non-Muslims needed to meet and hear from more Muslims: 'Schools and community centres should invite people from our communities to talk about our culture and inform people that we are not like you see on TV' (female, quoted in IWWCV 2008: 59). Muslim women in Victoria acknowledged the need for Muslims themselves to reach out to, and contact and mix with, non-Muslims. This was deemed important to the normalizing of Islam in a Western country like Australia:

> We [Muslims] need to also take some action. We need to be more visible and get out into many groups in the community so that people get to know us and realise we are just like them except we wear a scarf because of our religion. (Female, quoted in ibid.: 111)

They also suggested some of the ways in which Muslims could take action to expand everyday contact with non-Muslims:

> It is also up to us as Muslims to do something, not just stand around waiting for someone to do something for us. Last year my kids were involved in the sausage sizzle [barbecue] at their school ... So I went and bought halal sausages and cooked them there and told the school where to buy them for the future. So they agreed and I was happy I had made the effort. (Female, quoted in ibid.: 112)

> Well if your kids are at school, for example go and do all the things that other mothers do. Volunteer for the tuck shop, go on excursions with the kids and teachers, be part of the school community. Not many Muslim mothers do that. (Female, quoted in ibid.: 112)

We outlined earlier the negative impacts of experiences of racism. Positive encounters that Muslims have with non-Muslims in public spaces also have strong effects (HREOC 2004: 53, 86–7; IWWCV 2008: 110). Muslim women described how much they valued positive interactions:

> I feel lots of people go out of their way to help us to show that not all Australians are racist and against Muslims. They help in the schools, in community centres we are made to feel very welcome. (Female, quoted in IWWCV 2008: 110)

These insightful suggestions from Muslims are the actual and grounded geographies of hope.

SOURCES AND SPACES OF HOPE

⌐ We suggested earlier that while there is a good deal of stereotyping of Muslims in the West, there is none the less some ambivalence and ambiguity of public opinion! The mediation of antipathy and spread of stereotypes are not complete. There is a degree of flexibility in people's opinions that offers some hope for relations between Muslims and non-Muslims (Klocker and Dunn 2003). The IWWCV commissioned a telephone survey of non-Muslims (n: 600) which found that 60 per cent of respondents thought that the portrayal of Muslims in the mass media was unfair and biased, and 85 per cent agreed that media portrayals influenced how Muslims were treated and viewed by non-Muslims. Yasmeen's (2008: 65) interviews with 108 non-Muslims in Western Australia also uncovered a strong degree of scepticism regarding the media treatment of Islam, pointing to sensationalism, the linking of Islam to terrorism, and the cumulative effect of those upon stereotyping. This scepticism regarding media treatment, and the cognizance of harmful media effects, is a healthy basis from which to offer more rounded portrayals and hence to advance this form of remedy.

The diversity and varied experience of Muslims should be better acknowledged in the popular discourses about Islam in the West. For example, if Australian Islam is seen as diverse, this makes it more difficult for the aforementioned generalizations to make sense. These ruptures against stereotyping are sources of hope. Events of the last few years have generated a stronger public interest in Islam. A member of the Indonesian Muslim community in Victoria stated to the HREOC researchers that: 'Since 11 September and the Bali bombings, people at work are starting to learn about what is Islam. ... I am the only Muslim. Because of this I have been asked a lot about Islam' (statement to the Isma₤ Project 2003; HREOC 2003: 9). Public information campaigns to broaden and improve community attitudes towards Islam should capitalize upon this period in which non-Muslim interest in Islam is high in Western countries. In Australia, there is considerable scope for widening community knowledge of Islam as a faith, and of Islam as it is practised throughout the Asia-Pacific region. The main representations of Islam in that region are narrow caricatures⌐– of bearded traditionalists who are a threat to Western tourists. More collaborative research between government agencies, academics and leading Islamic associations would generate more rounded impressions of the nature and diversity of Islamic practice in the region (for example, Indonesia and Malaysia, but also countries where Muslims are a minority, such as Singapore and Thailand), and should lend itself to dissemination through popular media products.

A key means of normalizing Islam would be to give more prominence to the history and presence of Islam, or the historical links between Islam and other major faith traditions (Naylor and Ryan 2002: 45). From the early history of 'European Australia' (after the British invasion), there was a very important Islamic presence. Afghan cameleers were asked to come to Australia to assist with some of the foundational work of colonialism, such as building large-scale transport and communication infrastructures, and generally assisting with the transport of materials across Australia's pioneering frontier (Cigler 1986: 11; Rajkowski 1987; Stevens 1989). The Islamic Council of NSW has published a documentary and pamphlets on the early presence and contributions of Muslims to the development of European Australia.

Discourse and content analyses of media products have consistently reported on the negative representations of Islam. The extent and nature of this negativity, as described in this chapter, can be efficiently assessed in stocktakes of media and other cultural products. Research on media can provide an evidentiary base for interventions. At the federal level the Department of Immigration and Citizenship (2008: 18) has recognized the need for 'monitoring media coverage to identify key community relations issues by broad location'. Cultural groups that suffer systematic negative media representation should be formally assisted to monitor the way in which they are portrayed in news media and other cultural products. Such formal assistance of media watchers could extend to supporting the advocacy and insertion of alternative representations. This would involve having well-briefed and erudite spokespeople. Islamic organizations could be assisted with the development of a panel of quote-makers available to provide media workers with statements/quotations/grabs when needed and on specific topics, and able to communicate in the domestic vernacular (accent). The policy thrust would be to specifically empower a group that endures oppressive representation. As part of the National Action Plan (against Islamic radicalization) in Australia, grants will be allocated to some community groups for media training, including:

- Assisting community leaders to become competent and assertive communicators, using English and non-English media, including newer information technology such as the Internet, to deliver accurate and positive messages about their communities.
- When appropriate, actively countering biased and inaccurate information, including through newer technologies such as the internet. (Ministerial Council on Immigration and Multicultural Affairs 2007: 14)

operationalize the Australian discourse of the 'fair go' could be used in campaigns to undermine generalizations about Muslims. These catch-phrases could operate as put-downs and reprimands to be deployed when vilifying comments are made.

CONCLUSIONS

This chapter has given voice to the complex experiences of everyday anti-Islamic racism while also providing insight into the more positive everyday experiences of tolerance and acceptance. These experiences take place in everyday places and spaces – in the street, on public transport, in dealings with institutions and shopkeepers. Understanding the everyday experiences of Muslim Australians allows us to develop ways in which 'everyday racism' can be countered by 'everyday anti-racism' and thus provide sources of hope for the positive interaction of Muslims and non-Muslims in Australia. The three sources of hope outlined in this chapter are: the offering of alternative portrayals; defusing the political efficacy of Islamophobia; and means by which to normalize Islam as a Western religion. First, drawing out the cultural and religious heterogeneity of Australian Islam confounds the static generalizations that are core to racialization. Public ignorance of Islam, and the political prominence of 'the Muslim issue', means that Western interest in such information is high. Second, negative constructions of Islam are a political device within some Western nations. Muslims abroad and within have been used by Western politicians and opinion leaders to fortify political constituencies. Critical analysis of the political misuse of Islam is essential, as is the lauding of productive references to Islam by political leaders. Hope depends upon public support for Muslims and good leadership and commitment from anti-racism agencies and other public authorities. This must include a productive consensus in which hostility and racism against Muslims are constructed as deviant and treated as a threat to good public order. Third, the intention of, and mechanisms for, the normalization of Islam were outlined. Normalization will require certain representations, but it also benefits from good cross-cultural contacts. The conditions that help determine productive interactions were reviewed. Normalization and alternative representations together generate a public resilience to political racialization. The constructing of alternative geographies of Islam in the West needs to be both a political and an academic project. It will require strong links between researchers, Islamic organizations and government institutions.

REFERENCES

Allport, G. W. (1954) *The Nature of Prejudice*, New York: Doubleday.

Australian Human Rights Commission (2008) *Freedom of Religion and Belief in the 21st Century*, Discussion Paper, Sydney: Human Rights and Equal Opportunity Commission.

Bedar, A. and J. El Matrah (2005) *Media Guide: Islam and Muslims in Australia*, Fitzroy, Melbourne: Islamic Women's Welfare Council of Victoria (IWWCV).

Choudhury, T., M. Aziz, D. Izzidien, I. Khreeji and D. Hussain (2006) *Perceptions of Discrimination and Islamophobia: Voices from Members of Muslim Communities in the European Union*, Austria: European Monitoring Centre on Racism and Xenophobia.

Cigler, M. (1986) *The Afghans in Australia*, Blackburn: Australasian Educa Press.

Council of Australian Governments (2005) Council of Australian Governments' Communiqué: Special Meeting on Counter-Terrorism, 27 September, www.immi.gov.au/media/publications/multicultural/pdf_doc/coag270905.pdf, accessed 10 December 2008.

Department of Immigration and Citizenship (2008) *Living in Harmony: Program Review*, Canberra: Australian Government.

Dunn, K. M. (2001) 'Representations of Islam in the politics of mosque development in Sydney', *Tijdschrift voor Economische en Sociale Geografie*, 92(3).

— (2004a) 'Islam in Australia: contesting the discourse of absence', *Australian Geographer*, 35(3).

— (2004b) 'Attitudes to Islam in Australia: measuring Islamophobia', Geography Teachers Association of NSW Conference: Population Issues, Parliament House, Sydney, 13/14 August.

— (2005) 'Australian public knowledge of Islam', *Studia Islamika*, 12(1).

Dunn, K. M., J. Forrest, I. Burnley and A. McDonald (2004) 'Constructing racism in Australia', *Australian Journal of Social Issues*, 39(4).

Dunn, K. M., N. Klocker and T. Salabay (2007) 'Contemporary racism and Islamophobia in Australia: racialising religion', *Ethnicities*, 7(4).

Dunn, K. M., J. Forrest, R. Pe-Pua, M. Hynes and K. Maeder-Han (2009) 'Cities of race hatred? The spheres of race and anti-racism in contemporary Australian cities', *Cosmopolitan Civil Societies: An Interdisciplinary Journal*, 1, in press, epress.lib.uts.edu.au/ojs/index.php/mcs.

Essed, P. (1991) *Understanding Everyday Racism: An Interdisciplinary Theory*, Newbury Park: Sage Publications.

Hopkins, P. (2004) 'Young Muslim men in Scotland: inclusions and exclusions', *Children's Geographies*, 2(2).

HREOC (Human Rights and Equal Opportunity Commission) (2003) *Interim Report of Ismaع Project: The situation of Muslim and Arab peoples in Australia after 11 September 2001*, Sydney: HREOC.

— (2004) *Ismaع Listen: National Consultations on Eliminating Prejudice against Arab and Muslim Australians*, Sydney: HREOC.

Hubbard, P. (2005) 'Accommodating Otherness: anti-asylum centre protest and the maintenance of white privilege', *Transactions of the Institute of British Geographers*, 30.

ICNSW (Islamic Council of New South Wales) (1989) Submission to the Human Rights and Equal Opportunity Commission Inquiry into Racist Violence, Submission no. 4.28, Zetland: Islamic Council of New South Wales.

— (2004) *Challenges for Australian Muslims: Discrimination, Anti-Terrorism, and the Media*, Chullora: Islamic Council of New South Wales.

— (2005) *A Response to Cardinal Pell's Crusade against Islam*, Chullora: Islamic Council of New South Wales.

IHF (International Federation for Human Rights) (2005) *Intolerance and Discrimination against Muslims in the EU – developments since September 11*, IHF.

IWWCV (Islamic Women's Welfare Council of Victoria) (2008) *Race, Faith and Gender: Converging Discriminations against Muslim Women in Victoria: The Ongoing Impact of September 11, 2001*, Northcote: Islamic Women's Welfare Council of Victoria.

Klocker, N. and K. M. Dunn (2003) 'Who's driving the asylum debate? Newspaper and government representations of asylum seekers', *Media International Australia*.

Kobayashi, A. and L. Peake (2000) 'Racism out of place: thoughts on Whiteness and an antiracist geography in the new millennium', *Annals of the Association of American Geographers*, 90(2).

Levett, C. (2008) 'Curiosity call to a house of prayer', *Sydney Morning Herald*, 13 December.

Lygo, I. (2004) *News Overboard: The Tabloid Media, Race Politics and Islam*, Sydney: Southerly Change Media.

Maddox, M. (2005) *God under Howard: The Rise of the Religious Right in Australian Politics*, Crows Nest: Allen & Unwin.

Manji, I. (2004) *The Trouble with Islam: A Muslim's Call for Reform in Her Faith*, Sydney: Random House.

Marr, D. and M. Wilkinson (2003) *Dark Victory*, Crows Nest: Allen & Unwin.

Ministerial Council on Immigration and Multicultural Affairs (2007) *A National Action Plan to Build on Social Cohesion, Harmony and Security*, Ministerial Council on Immigration and Multicultural Affairs, www.immi.gov.au/living-in-australia/a-diverse-australia/national-action-plan/_attach/National-Action-Plan-2007.pdf, accessed 10 December 2008.

Naylor, S. and J. R. Ryan (2002) 'The mosque in the suburbs: negotiating religion and ethnicity in South London', *Social and Cultural Geography*, 3.

Noble, G. (2005) 'The discomfort of strangers: racism, incivility and ontological security in a relaxed and comfortable nation', *Journal of Intercultural Studies*, 26(1/2): 107–20.

— (2009) 'Everyday cosmopolitanism and the labour of intercultural community', in A. Wise and R. Velayutham (eds), *Everyday Multiculturalism*, in press, London: Palgrave.

Peach, C. (2006) 'Muslims in the 2001 Census of England and Wales: gender and economic disadvantage', *Ethnic and Racial Studies*, 29(4).

Pedersen, A., N. Contos, B. Griffiths, B. Bishop and I. Walker (2000) 'Attitudes toward Aboriginal-Australians in city and country settings', *Australian Psychologist*, 35(2).

Pedersen, A., I. Walker and M. Wise (2005) '"Talk does not cook the rice": beyond anti-racism rhetoric to strategies for social action', *Australian Psychologist*, 40(1).

Pettigrew, T. F. and L. R. Tropp (2005) 'Allport's intergroup contact hypothesis: its history and influence', in J. F. Dovidio, P. Glick and L. A. Budiman (eds), *On the Nature of Prejudice: Fifty Years after Allport*, Victoria: Blackwell.

Pew Research Centre (2006) *Europe's Muslims More Moderate. The Great Divide: How Westerners and Muslims View Each Other*, Washington, DC: Pew Global Attitudes Project.

— (2008) *Unfavorable Views of Jews and Muslims on the Increase in Europe*, Washington, DC: Pew Global Attitudes Project.

Poynting, S., G. Noble, P. Tabar and J. Collins (2004) *Bin Laden in the Suburbs; Criminalising the Arab Other*, Sydney: Sydney Institute of Criminology.

Putnam, R. D. (2007) 'E pluribus unum: diversity and community in the twenty-first century – the 2006 Johan Skytte prize lecture', *Scandinavian Political Studies*, 30.

Rajkowski, P. (1987) *In the Tracks of the Camelmen*, North Ryde: Angus and Robertson.

Ramadan, T. (2004) *Western Muslims and the Future of Islam*, Oxford: Oxford University Press.

Rifi, J. (2008) 'Open letter', *El-Telegraph*, 3 October.

Said, E. W. (1981) *Covering Islam*, New York: Pantheon Books.

Stevens, C. (1989) *Tin Mosques and Ghantowns: A History of Afghan Cameldrivers in Australia*, Melbourne: Oxford University Press.

Victorian Health Promotion Foundation (2007) *More than Tolerance: Embracing Diversity for Health*, Melbourne: Victorian Health Promotion Foundation.

Vrij, A. and B. J. Smith (1999) 'Reducing ethnic prejudice by public campaigns: an evaluation of a present and a new campaign', *Journal of Community and Applied Social Psychology*, 9.

Waldinger, R. and D. Fitzgerald (2004) 'Transnationalism in question', *American Journal of Sociology*, 109(5).

Walker, I. and M. Crogan (1998) 'Academic performance, prejudice, and the jigsaw classroom: new pieces to the puzzle', *Journal of Community and Applied Social Psychology*, 8.

Wise, A. (2005) 'Hope and belonging in a multicultural suburb', *Journal of Intercultural Studies*, 26(1/2): 171–86.

Yasmeen, S. (2008) *Understanding Muslim Identities: From Perceived Relative Exclusion to Inclusion*, National Action Plan to Build on Social Cohesion, Harmony and Security.

Zwartz, B. (2004) 'Islam could be new communism, Pell tells US audience', *Sydney Morning Herald*, 12 November.

TWO | **CONVIVIAL CITIES**

4 | Veils and sales: Muslims and the spaces of post-colonial fashion retail[1]

REINA LEWIS

This book's theme of spaces of hope might not necessarily bring fashion retail immediately to mind, but I want to suggest in this chapter that fashion plays an important part in how we understand the different spaces we inhabit. As other chapters demonstrate, spatial relations are made up of human interactions with natural and built environments – producing a set of embodied experiences that variously create, inform, enforce, reinstate or challenge our senses of our social selves. In a book about Muslims in Britain and the West, I am especially interested in how *dress* features in the processes by which bodies come to be read as Muslim – and how these processes are spatialized. I have taken as my case study the human relations of fashion retail in order to explore how dress informs the ways in which Muslims see and are seen in specific spaces at specific times.

In the UK, post-9/11 and post-7/7, dress and body management have taken on a renewed centrality in the anxious marking of bodies in relation to faith and ethnicity – think, for example, of how majoritarian commentators increasingly interpret the persistence of so-called 'ethnic' dress as a failure of integration. In oft-repeated episodes of the moral panic about Islam in Britain, women's Islamic dress is positioned as antithetical to the positive qualities associated with hip cosmopolitanism. While middle England prides itself that the nation's favourite meal is the Indo-Anglian hybrid of chicken tikka masala, and trendies demonstrate their cultural capital through the consumption of diverse cultural foods, forms and fashion styles, the British Muslim woman wearing the hijab is not presumed to be engaging in cool postmodern fashion bricolage. Instead she is likely to be essentialized as a victim of Muslim patriarchal control or as evidence of the security risk posed by Muslims' presumed lack of social/national integration.

In 2006, the issue of the niqab hit the British press when former Foreign Secretary Jack Straw revealed that he asked women wearing a face veil to remove it during consultations in his constituency office.[2]

Briefing the national press about an article he had written for the local paper of his Lancashire constituency, Straw characterized the niqab as 'a visible statement of separation and difference', arguing that it was an obstacle to communication in that 'the value of a meeting, as opposed to a letter or phone call, is that you can – almost literally – see what the other person means, not just hear what they say'.[3]

In a horribly familiar pattern the media furore prompted by Straw saw the figure of the veiled woman positioned by all sides as the key signifier in a set of debates about nation, culture, identity, modernity and belonging. As in previous instances the veiled woman is spoken for more often than she speaks herself, standing yet again as an object of obsessive attention in a majoritarian discourse, functioning in a classically orientalist way simultaneously as a cipher for the mysteries and threats of Islam and as an object of pity in need of rescue. Significantly, in this instance, the voices (if not the faces) of veiled women have sometimes been more apparent. But the revivalist positions they most often enunciate present piety as form of individuating self-expression achieved through the willing abnegation to transcendant will, and so provide little comfort to many Western feminists whose Enlightenment framework equating autonomy with freedom and independence is directly posed against a model of obedience and subjugation.

But, like the confidently spoken young teaching assistant Aisha Azmi, who eventually lost her tribunal against the school that sacked her for wearing a niqab in class, revivalist women in head covering or face veil utilize a discourse of choice to explain and defend their decision to veil.[4] This persuasive rhetoric combines the secular-Enlightenment-derived notion of conscious choice with an allegiance to a universalizing revivalist politics that decrees veiling to be a divine requirement (Mahmood 2005). The exponent of veiling is presented as a self-directed sovereign subject – a riposte to the presumption of many in the Straw debate that veiling is always and only a sign of female subordination and lack of individuation. Rather than allowing the discussion to be overtaken by debate about respect for ahistorical religious differences premised on a view of minority cultures as homogenous and unchanging, I want to resituate the 'veil' (by which here I mean any form of Islamic modest outerwear) as an item of *clothing*, not just as a sign of religious allegiance. In doing this I resist attempts by both religious revivalists and hostile majoritarian commentators to close down definitions of the veil, in favour of an emphasis on its multiple potential meanings for the women who wear it and those who observe them so that we can see veiling as a dress act that, like all clothed performances, is historically and geographically located.

So, allow me to take you back to Saturday, 6 August 2005 ...
One month after the 7/7 bombs in London, and Oxford Street is
buzzing with shoppers. Retail figures are down and travel on the tube
has diminished by a third, but the sales are in full swing and bargain
hunters are not to be deterred. Walking from Oxford Circus to Marble
Arch reveals a significant number of visibly 'Muslim' women: hip twenty-
somethings in black boot-cut trousers and skimpy T-shirts wear their
black head wraps tight with a fashionable ghetto-fabulous tail cascading
down their backs from their high topknots as they check out bargains
in Top Shop; older women in embroidered shalwar kameez with filmy
dupatta thrown loosely over their heads mooch about Marks and Spencer;
in Selfridges, mothers in black abayas with niqabs over their faces select
children's clothes. And in their activities as consumers the women in
hijab, and those not in hijab, are likely to be served by shop assistants
who also veil. A trawl down the street reveals women in British Home
Stores in cream jilbab; in Marks and Spencer, young women wear the
uniform-issue long-sleeved shirt with a store-issued (non-branded) black
scarf; in New Look, young women keep the changing rooms under control
in coloured headscarves worn over the items from this season's selection
that constitute the store's 'feelgood fashion' uniform choices. All this in
a month when assaults on Muslims, or those perceived as Muslim, have
increased dramatically from the police figures of this time the previous
year, and in a week when some Muslim 'leaders' have been quoted in
the press advising women that they should relinquish their veils if their
public prominence makes them likely targets for abuse or attack.

In this context writing about shopping, fashion and veils seems ever
more appropriate as a way of decoding some of the bewildering issues
experienced in contemporary post-colonial spaces. Simply to pitch those
three terms together generates immediate interest because veils are seen
by those outside veiling communities, and sometimes by those inside,
as inimical to fashion and largely as outside of the commercial circuits
of the fashion industry. With shops, or fashion shopping, operating as
an indicator of modernity, and with Islam often presented as resistant
to modernity, the presence of veiled shop girls becomes a potent mix
of two contrasting spatial and social codes, often still interpreted as a
temporal clash.

But the temporal nature of perceived religious differences also structures many varieties of Islamic revivalist discourse, reversing the values
ascribed to the opposition between Islam and commerce, 'tradition' and
modernity, modesty and fashion. Yet, while revivalist identities are often
positioned as self-consciously oppositional to Western consumption,

the commercial development and distribution of new forms of Islamic dress (such as the Turkish *tesettür*) demonstrate that religious identities are increasingly experienced and expressed through the self-conscious consumption of goods marked (and marketed) as the opposite of secular/ Westernized commodities and lifestyles (Navaro-Yashin 2002; Secor 2002; on lifestyle, Miller et al. 1998).

DRESS AS A SPATIALIZED PRACTICE

The creation of women as consumers has long been seen as a central element of Western modernity (Benson 1986; Lancaster 2000; Wilson 2003). Since the development in the second half of the nineteenth century of the department store as a space for respectable female luxury expenditure, shopping has gained a significance for the constitution and performance of modern femininities that is recognized around the world. The spatial relations in the shop, between staff and between staff and customers, are inevitably related to the spatial relations outside the shop, as bodies move from one space to another, performing different elements of their identities as they go (from daughter at home, to worker in the shop, to consumer in the lunch-hour perusal of other retail outlets, to passenger on public transport), only some elements of which are legible to the external observer and all of which require different cultural competencies to be decoded.

But through all this the veil, in all its forms, suffers from an almost generic illegibility in that the dress acts of most veiling women in the UK are observed by a majority non-veiling and non-Islamic audience who cannot adequately deduce the significance of their veiling choices. Women who veil are almost inevitably read as Muslim by a majority audience that rarely imagines they might be Hindu or Sikh. In a situation where ethnicity and religion are often united in their expression through dress in the minds of their practitioners (Dwyer 1999), the likelihood of veiled women being presumed Muslim by those outside their communities is high.[5] As such, Islamophobic prejudice or well-intentioned protectionism will rain on any woman who veils, regardless of her actual ethnic or religious identity. Although 'the' veil is often fetishized as a thing in itself, this garment (in all its varieties) can, like all dress, best be understood as what Joanne Entwistle calls a 'situated bodily practice' (2000: 3). Clothes and fashions acquire social meaning through being worn on dressed bodies whose ability to present in socially appropriate ways relies on the internalization of learned 'techniques of the body' – literally how to hold oneself, to walk, to dress (Mauss 1973 in ibid.: 14). Nobody is born knowing how to walk in high heels, but many women in Western cultures learn the body management necessary to enact this particular gender-specific and socially sanctioned embodied practice. Wearing any form of veil similarly requires the development of particular techniques of body management, such as the processes by which Hindu girls in an Indian village 'learn' to wear the veil, progressing from the lighter half-sari adopted in late childhood to the complex techniques demanded by stricter forms of face and head covering as they grow towards marriageable age (Tarlo 1996).

Not only is dress an embodied practice, it is also spatialized and temporal – dressed bodies are given meaning though their location in specific times and places which have their own rules of dress and comportment. The different places that dressed bodies inhabit are relational, acquiring distinction and meaning from their relationship to what lies 'beyond' (Massey 1994). Individuals, therefore, never belong to only one spatial community: they engage with overlapping sets of spatial relations whose socializing effects produce differences of gender, sexuality, class, race and ethnicity.

But for veiled bodies, the diverse audiences that witness their spatialized dress practices provide additional complications. The veiled body in the contemporary post-colonial city travels across what Anna Secor usefully names as different 'veiling regimes': 'spatially realized sets of hegemonic rules and norms regarding women's veiling, which are themselves produced by specific constellations of power' and which vary in terms of 'formality, enforcement, stability, and contestation' (Secor 2002: 8). These regimes of veiling, which also include the normatization of non-veiling, inhere in different spaces and are enforced and challenged to varying extents (officially by state police in Saudi Arabia, or unofficially by the regulatory role of gossip and elders in close-knit minority ethnic communities in London). Combine the socializing dynamism of space with the concept of spatialized veiling regimes, and the veiled woman – sometimes presented as the passive victim of patriarchal cultures – emerges as an agent actively negotiating the spaces she encounters.

Women, with varying degrees of 'choice' in different contexts, can be understood to exercise a series of cultural and subcultural competencies in their adherences to and destabilizations of veiling regimes, often moving between different regimes in the space of a single day and over the course of their lives. But the performative elements that make up these veiled manifestations are not universally comprehensible. This is where the travelling of bodies in the post-colonial city becomes so significant: the veiling and non-veiling inhabitants of a district like Southall in West

London (which has a long-established and substantial South Asian community) may well be sufficiently familiar with their South Asian neighbours to distinguish between the dress (and regional affiliations) of Hindu, Sikh or Muslim women, but when the veiled woman moves beyond the district she is likely to be incorporated within a discourse that – operating without the spatialized cultural competencies that might render her 'legible' in Southall – frames her as Muslim.

VEILING AS A SPATIAL SYSTEM

The veil is not just a garment that is worn in particular locations: it is itself a spatializing device that facilitates the gender segregation of society for those communities that adhere to codes of gender seclusion. There are several misconceptions about the veil that need to be addressed: first, although the veil is today predominantly associated with Islam, it is a garment that is pre-Islamic in origin and one that has been adopted by diverse religious and ethnic communities, especially in the Middle East. Second, in the Middle East, the veil often signified status rather than piety or ethnic allegiance. Third, there is no single garment that equates to the veil: different versions of clothing that are held suitably to preserve modesty in gender-mixed environments have been adopted by different communities (often with different names for the same garment). Furthermore, the form of these garments or combinations of garments changes over time, quite often within the lifespan of a single woman. Thus, attempts to legislate which type of body covering is properly Islamic can only be seen as partial and located. Fourth, the veil is intended primarily as outerwear, as a garment that preserves modesty between the sexes when outside the gender-secluded space of the Islamically structured home (or when non-familial men are present in the domestic space, as may be the case more often these days). It is this last element which brings us most closely to questions of spatiality. As Fatima Mernissi (1985) has argued, the veil can be understood as a sartorial mechanism by which the gender seclusion of the harem system – the Islamic organization of domestic space that keeps a distance between women and those men to whom they are not closely related – is extended beyond the harem walls. Based on the presumption of an active female sexuality, harem seclusion and the veil serve to keep men and women separated to protect the community from the chaos of *fitna*, or uncontrolled sexual energy that would be released by inappropriate sexual contact.

For the Islamic world, harem and veiling, properly understood, require codes of modesty from both genders: men as well as women should dress modestly, and should deport their bodies in ways that will not prompt inappropriate cross-sex contact. Thus for women in territories largely governed by Muslim habits of body management, the wearing of a veil constitutes a legible display that prompts similarly respectful performances from male bodies in her vicinity, such as not staring at her face. In a Western post-colonial environment of mixed religions, genders and ethnicities, there is no such social contract. (Ironically, one of the behaviours that was held retrospectively to mark out the 'extremist' tendencies of one of the London bombers was his habit in his recent ultra-orthodox incarnation of refusing to meet the eyes of any woman in public. This practice, when repositioned to post-colonial, post-industrial northern England, read as misplaced zealotry to others in his community, rather than as good modest manners.)

DRESS AS A TEMPORAL PRACTICE: VEILING, SHOPPING AND NON-WESTERN MODERNITIES

In the development and representation of modernities in what might broadly be called the Muslim world, the veil in particular and female dress in general were a source of continual tension in debates about modernity and its compatibility with Islam from the early nineteenth century. As in subsequent and contemporary discussions, the figure of woman stood for both defence of tradition and the march of modernity. For modernizing rulers like Mohamad Ali in Egypt (reigned 1805–49) and successive Ottoman sultans who sought to harness the advantages of modern Western technologies (from railways to cameras), the social behaviours that accompanied Western commodities were not necessarily to be emulated. The indigenization of Western technologies and goods was therefore a process of selective adaptation rather than straightforward adoption (Frierson 2000), as Ottoman-style leaders adapted Western imports to suit local social mores. It was through clothing that Western designs were most pressingly brought to bear on non-Western bodies, with women style innovators from the progressive elites ordering couture from Paris and commissioning local seamstresses to adapt conventional garments (Frierson 2000; Graham-Brown 1988; Davis 1986). Whether individuals' use of Western commodities signalled a conscious or only a vague sense of modernity or progressiveness (Duben and Behar 1991), by the turn of the twentieth century most sectors of the urban population were regularly engaging with Western goods. Women, in all their variety of veils, were going out to shop – an activity seen by themselves and their male peers as both potentially liberating and potentially dangerous.

Local modernization processes contributed to and relied on the development of new (gendered) spatialities. Women from segregated households in Istanbul and Cairo and other major cities started to go out to shop, in the bazaars of the old city quarters and, in Istanbul, to the shops of Pera, the international quarter. These excursions were made possible by a combination of two potentially conflicting spatial relations: the modernizations of the Tanzimat reforms that aimed in part to open up mixed gender spaces outside the home, and the Islamic conventions of the veil. Though this meant that veiled women were increasingly more visible on public streets, the nuanced social stratification of who was seen where and engaged in which consumer activities was often only perceptible to inside observers. Lelya Sazhanımeffendi, writing about her youth in the household of Sultan Abdulmecit in the 1850s and 1860s, recalls that when the imperial princesses visited the Grand Bazaar their shopping was managed through a partial seclusion in the bazaar's mosque, a space understood as socially restricted by the other elite (but not royal) ladies, who took care 'never to stop in any of the dependencies of the Mosque in order not to give the impression of imitating the Imperial Harem' (Lelya Sazhanımeffendi 1920 in Lewis and Micklewright 2006: 181). In Alexandria by the 1890s, the young Hoda Shaarawi, later a prominent nationalist and feminist leader, was thrilled to visit the new department store – a spatial incursion achieved only after substantial negotiations with her parents' household. '[A]shamed' of the scene caused by her overzealous eunuch and the retinue that accompanied her, Shaarawi eventually persuaded her mother to visit the store, at which point permission to shop alone was granted (Shaarawi 1987 in ibid.: 192).

In travelling through the city visiting shops, and creating taste communities for transnational commodities and associated behaviours, Ottoman women, of the elite especially, were developing a cosmopolitan sensibility that incorporated engagement with Western cultural forms into an already existing regional internationalism. Local wardrobe decisions were understood to have international ramifications. Ottomans and Egyptians were well aware that the image of the veiled harem lady was seen by the West as an indicator of the state of civilization of their entire society and took pains to counter orientalist stereotypes, often through attention to the dressed visibility of Muslim women. By the twentieth century unveiled Muslim women were working in shops: in the 1920s, the new Turkish republic used the public presence of unveiled female bodies to advertise its modernity to itself and to the West in a version of modernity that was to become increasingly and aggressively secular under Mustapha Kemal (Atatürk) (Durakbaşa 1993; Göle 1996). When

Demetra Vaka Brown, a Greek Ottoman-American, returned to a wartorn and occupied Istanbul in 1922 to interview the first generation of unveiled shop girls, it is clear that they were motivated by a sense of participating in a project of nation-building – and that this imbued with honour their public unveiled retail labour. But to what extent are contemporary British shop girls in veils heirs to these insurrectionary activities?

REGULATING BODIES IN SPACE: SHOP DRESS CODES

All the fashion retail outlets mentioned earlier in this chapter can be found in most UK high streets and shopping malls. Unlike the independent boutique, these companies require their staff to dress according to a uniform code, be it branded in-house uniforms, selections from the current range, or the mix of store uniform and franchise merchandise worn in the department store.

Associated with the rise of women as shopworkers in the last quarter of the nineteenth century, shop dress codes (and later uniforms) were designed to establish the respectability of their largely female staff. Often accompanied by strict rules about behaviour, dress codes created an identity for the establishment through the regulation of employees' bodies inside and outside the store. Within an often paternalistic management style (especially in the large department stores), the respectability of shop work as a form of employment was one of the attractions for working-class women who saw it as a step up, and for middle-class women who were reassured that the propriety of social relations in the store would help make shop work a respectable career (Lancaster 2000; on the contemporary context see Leslie 2002). Women's dress at work was a key factor in the manufacture of these decorous social relations, while association with the glamour and modernity of fashion retail was itself a lure (which continued into the twentieth century; Winship 2000).

Today, in relation to the veil, employers are bound by the new British regulations concerning discrimination at work. The previous legislation outlawing racial discrimination could not cover Muslims as such, extending only to those faith communities established in law as an ethnic group, such as Jews or Sikhs. For the multi-ethnic Muslim population, it needed the 2003 Employment Equality (Religion or Belief) Regulations to extend protection against discrimination at work, or in vocational training. Significantly, the law covers discrimination 'on the grounds of perceived as well as actual religion or belief (i.e. assuming – correctly or incorrectly – that someone has a particular religion or belief)' (www.dti.gov.uk/er/equality). The emphasis on perceived religion attests to a state recognition of the instability and potential illegibility of performances of religious identity.

For shopworkers this means that the employer now has an obligation to permit and to facilitate the expression of religious identity as defined by employees and therefore must not discriminate against or in any way treat differently an employee who wishes to wear a veil. An employee's right to expression is limited by the provision for unspecified exceptions, and, when I started on this project in 2004, my discussion with the British arbitration service ACAS revealed that there were as yet no cases concerning the veil at work in the public domain. At that time it was generally anticipated that exceptions to the new regulation would be in terms of health and safety: for example, a Sikh man might not be permitted on safety grounds to wear a *kirpan* (ritual sword) when working in an airport. In the early stages of this work, but after the London bombs, my straw poll of human resources departments at high-street employers found a widespread acknowledgement that women could wear a veil 'if their religion demanded it'. This is a situation specific to Britain: for employees of international retailers who work in branches elsewhere in the world, clothing rights at work (beyond those permitted by individual companies, some of which have an equal opportunities code of practice) are subject to local state law. While recent changes to British law have been designed to bring British regulation in line with the European Employment Equality Directive (2000), for employees in other EU states who find themselves denied the right to wear a veil the European Court of Human Rights will provide the point of last appeal. Since my initial enquiries, however, the situation in Britain has changed and veiling has featured so prominently in debates about social inclusion and belonging that I cannot imagine employers being willing or able casually to answer questions about veiling at work. Recent court cases have made Muslim veiling a prominent employment issue, and have shifted the focus from covering the head to covering the face.

Since the 1980s, policies of multiculturalism in Britain have permitted the 'tolerance' of visible signs of ethnic and religious diversity – in stark contrast to the aggressive secularism of the (Muslim) republic of Turkey and the (Catholic) republic of France. But in the early years of the twenty-first century, challenges to accepted British veiling regimes by young women revivalists have tested the sartorial limits of multiculturalism. In 2002, teenager Shabina Begum took her Luton school to court after being refused permission to wear a jilbab rather than the uniform option of shalwar kameez and headscarf (which had been negotiated with the area's large South Asian community). Contested up to the House of

Lords, where she eventually lost (www.publications.parliament.uk/pa/ld/
ldjudgmt.htm), Begum's actions in seeking to distinguish herself through
the assertive performance of a revivalist identity had obvious implications for other Muslim girls in the UK. Where some have 'upveiled' in
solidarity, others have been compelled to wear an unwanted jilbab, once
the alibi of school uniform was eroded (Hari 2005).

In 2006, at the same time as the British press was full of the Jack
Straw story, two court cases that questioned the ability of women in
niqabs to carry out professional duties hit the news within weeks of
each other, feeding the ferment of commentary and demonstration. In
one, the young teaching assistant Aisha Azmi lost her case at industrial
tribunal (appeal pending) against the school that sacked her for wearing
a niqab in the classroom. The school, which had hired her to help non-
native speakers improve their English, claimed that the children needed
to see as well as hear her forming the words. In the other, legal advocate
Shabnam Mughal won a partial victory over the judge in an immigration
tribunal who suspended proceedings when she refused to remove her
niqab. In an interim decision Mr Justice Hodge, president of the Asylum
and Immigration Tribunal, advised that the niqab be permitted in court
unless a judge's inability to hear meant that 'the interests of justice are
not served' (*Independent*, 10 November 2006: 23).

Couched not in terms of health and safety, but on the assertion that
the niqab impedes verbal and visual communication, these challenges
to veiling habits normatize Western modes of body management and, in
the case of Straw especially, naturalize the culturally specific presumption that visual expression is an accurate guide to inner feeling. At the
time of going to press, these challenges to expressions of faith-based
identities are provoking widespread cultural crises for minority and
majority communities. While face covering of any form is a minority
practice among the UK veiling population, this intense focus on the
niqab has effectively shifted the commonsense definition of the 'veil'
from head covering to face covering – with an attendant ratcheting up
of political activity. Revivalist young women take up the niqab as a badge
of anti-establishment honour, while the government issues consultation
documents specifically offering schools the opportunity to ban niqabs
from their premises.

CONCLUSION: SELLING SPACES

Just as Claire Dwyer has demonstrated with school students who know
that they are judged in relation to the veiling practices of other students
and teachers (Dwyer 1999), the appearance behind the shop counter of a

veiled body immediately repositions the other bodies around it. Staff can find themselves having to explain to non-Muslim colleagues why they do not veil, or veil in a different way, and potentially having to justify their choices to other co-religionists on the workforce. In the private sector context of fashion retail, the veiled shopworker foregrounds new questions about staff selection, training and retention. On one hand employers may find that the presence of visibly Muslim staff, especially in the climate of the 'war on terror', brings on an increase in discriminatory behaviour from customers or from staff, and will need to provide staff training to deal with this. On the other hand, the dress acts of shop staff may facilitate comfortable retail geographies for Muslim consumers, as shoppers and workers circulate cultural knowledges about which stores are likely to have veiled staff or be Muslim-friendly employers.

Given that in the UK as elsewhere most Muslim women wear the veil in conjunction with 'non-Islamic' fashion items, these local retail geographies (Crewe 2003) are also connected to the supranational entity of the *umma* in ways that are spiritual, material and stylistic. Within the expanding and increasingly diversified Islamic lifestyle media (and I am thinking of international titles and websites like the American/ Canadian *Muslim Girl*, as well as UK publications like *Emel*), Muslim lifestyle journalists emphatically represent veils *as fashion*, with changing trends in colours and style securing veil-wearing as a form of individuating self-expression explicitly tied to modern lifestyle consumer culture (Kılıçbay and Binark 2002; Balasescu 2003; Jones and Leshkowich 2003; Durakbaşa and Cindoğlu 2002; El Guindi 1999).

The sartorially distinct forms of veiling adopted by young hijabis not only distinguish them from previous generations (teen rebellion writ large), they also create a religiously authoritative persona whose dress – signalling a personal knowledge of holy texts – distinguishes her (in the Turkish context, for example) from rural, peasant or generational cultures of habitual rather than doctrinal veiling. These new and constantly evolving forms of Islamic chic create so many carefully delineated taste communities that, with 'up-veiling' adopted sometimes as much out of social aspiration as out of piety, it is not only majoritarian observers who may 'fail' to decipher individual women's veiling intentions (Boubekeur 2005; see also Jones and Leshkowich 2003). If we accept that ethnic identities are not essential and pre-existent but are achieved socially and relationally, then the design, retail and consumption habits of Muslim women can be recognized, as Claire Dwyer and Philip Crang suggest, as a 'matrix for the fashioning of ethnicities' (Dwyer and Crang 2002: 411; see also Mani 2003; Puwar and Raghuran 2003).

With the political and discursive creation post-7/7 of new categories for British Muslims of 'moderate' and 'extremist', recent attempts by the courts to arbitrate between acceptable and unreasonable forms of veiling play out across the bodies of Muslim women the wider debate about nationality and belonging – again premised on essentialized categories of gender and identity. Given the alarming hypervisibility accorded to the veiled woman, reminding ourselves that women who veil (in any way for any reason) operate within overlapping spatialities and competing but mutually constituting dress systems may be a way to think through some of the bewildering challenges of dress politics in post-colonial Britain.

NOTES

The ideas for this chapter were developed through a series of conference presentations, and I wish to thank particularly the conveners of and respondents at: 'Faith and Identity in Contemporary Visual Culture', University of Manchester; 'Beyond "Feminism and Multiculturalism"', LSE Gender Institute; 'Muslim Women in Europe: Bodily Performances, Multiple Belongings and the Public Sphere', the European University Institute Mediterranean Programme 2007. I have also benefited from discussions with Richard Phillips and Daniel Monk.

1 This chapter is an edited and abbreviated version of an article that first appeared in *Fashion Theory*, 11(4), 2007, pp. 423–42.

2 I use the word 'veil' to refer generically to the variety of garments and ways of wearing them used to achieve the modest public dress felt by some to be required by cultures informed by Islam. This includes various methods of covering (all or some of) the hair, ears, neck, shoulders (often referred to as the hijab), and, less commonly in the UK, a face covering (often referred to as the niqab). The covering of parts of the head and upper body is achieved through many different methods, and may be combined with the wearing of an overgarment that obscures the contours of the entire body (variously, abaya, jilbab). The design, feel and production processes of these garments change over time, and the terms used can reflect regional, national, religious and political affiliations.

3 www.telegraph.co.uk/news/main. jhtml?xml=/news/10/06/nveils106.xml.

4 Aisha Azmi was suspended and subsequently sacked by Kirklees Council in 2006 because she refused to remove her niqab in a classroom where she was assisting a male teacher. Ms Azmi claimed that she was prepared to remove her veil in front of children or women teachers, but not male teaching colleagues. In October 2006 her claims of discrimination and harassment against Headfield Church of England junior school were dismissed, but she was awarded damages of £1,000 for 'injury to feelings'. The case prompted public comment from government ministers while it was still sub judice; www.guardian.co.uk/education/2006/nov/24/schools.uk.

5 This chapter concerns itself specifically with Muslim forms of veiling, and generically with the

ways in which veiled bodies are incorporated as Muslim within a dominant discourse. For reasons of space, I have restricted my compara-

tive geographical and temporal focus to the modernizing centres of the late Ottoman Empire and the modern Turkish republic.

REFERENCES

Balasescu, A. (2003) 'Tehran chic: Islamic headscarves, fashion designers, and new geographies of modernity', *Fashion Theory*, 7(1): 39–56.

Benson, S. P. (1986) *Counter Cultures: Saleswomen, Managers, and Customers in American Department Stores 1890–1940*, Urbana and Chicago: University of Illinois Press.

Boubekeur, A. (2005) 'Cool and competitive: Muslim culture in the West', *ISIM* [International Institute for the Study of Islam in the Modern World] *Review*, 16: 12–13.

Crang, P. (1994) 'It's showtime: on the workplace geographies of display in a restaurant in southeast England', *Environment and Planning D: Society and Space*, 12: 675–704.

Crewe, L. (2003) 'Geographies of retailing and consumption: markets in motion', *Progress in Human Geography*, 27(3): 352–62.

Davis, F. (1986) *The Ottoman Lady: A Social History from 1718–1918*, New York: Greenwood Press.

Duben, A. and C. Behar (1991) *Istanbul Households: Marriage, Family and Fertility, 1880–1940*, Cambridge: Cambridge University Press.

Durakbaşa, A. (1993) 'Reappraisal of Halide Edib for a critique of Turkish modernization', Unpublished PhD thesis, Department of Sociology, University of Essex.

Durakbaşa, A. and D. Cindoğlu

(2002) 'Encounters at the counter: gender and the shopping experience', in D. Kandiyoti and A. Saktanber (eds), *Fragments of Culture: The Everyday of Modern Turkey*, London: I.B.Tauris, pp. 73–89.

Dwyer, C. (1999) 'Veiled meanings: young British Muslim women and the negotiation of differences', *Gender, Place and Culture*, 6(1): 5–26.

Dwyer, C. and Crang, P. (2002) 'Fashioning ethnicities: the commercial spaces of multiculture', *Ethnicities*, 2(3): 410–30.

Edib, H. A. (2005 [1926]) *Memoirs of Halidé Edib*, Piscataway, NJ: Gorgias Press.

El Guindi, F. (1999) 'Veiling resistance', *Fashion Theory*, 3(1): 51–80.

Entwistle, J. (2000) *The Fashioned Body: Fashion, Dress and Modern Social Theory*, Cambridge: Polity.

Frierson, E. B. (1999) 'Cheap and easy: the creation of consumer culture in late Ottoman society', in D. Quataert (ed.), *Consumption Studies and the History of the Ottoman Empire 1550–1922*, New York: State University of New York Press, pp. 243–60.

— (2000) 'Mirrors out, mirrors in: domestication and rejection of the foreign in late-Ottoman women's magazines', in D. F. Ruggles (ed.), *Women, Patronage, and Self-Representation in Islamic Societies*, New York: State University of New York Press, pp. 177–204.

Gilbert, D. (2000) 'Urban outfitting:

the city and the spaces of fashion culture', in S. Bruzzi and P. Church Gibson (eds), *Fashion Cultures: Theories, Explorations and Analysis*, London: Routledge, pp. 7–24.

Göçek, F. M. (1996) *Rise of the Bourgeoisie, Demise of Empire: Ottoman Westernization and Social Change*, New York: Oxford University Press.

Göle, N. (1996) *The Forbidden Modern: Civilization and Veiling*, Ann Arbor: University of Michigan Press.

Graham-Brown, S. (1988) *Images of Women: The Portrayal of Women in Photography of the Middle East 1860–1950*, London: Quartet.

Hari, J. (2005) 'Multiculturalism is not the best way to welcome people to our country', *Independent*, 5 August 2005, p. 35.

Jones, C. and A. M. Leshkowich (2003) 'Introduction: the globalization of Asian dress: re-orienting fashion or re-orientalizing Asia', in S. Neissen, A. M. Leshkowich and C. Jones (eds), *Re-Orienting Fashion: The Globalization of Asian Dress*, Oxford: Berg, pp. 1–48.

Kılıçbay, B. and M. Binark (2002) 'Consumer culture, Islam and the politics of lifestyle', *European Journal of Communication*, 17(4): 495–511.

Lancaster, B. (2000) *The Department Store: A Social History*, Leicester: Leicester University Press.

Leshkowich, A. M. and C. Jones (2003) 'What happens when Asian chic becomes chic in Asia?', *Fashion Theory*, 7(3/4): 281–300.

Leslie, D. (2002) 'Gender, retail employment and the clothing commodity chain', *Gender, Place and Culture*, 9(1): 61–76.

Lewis, R. (1996) *Gendering Orientalism: Race, Femininity and Representation*, London: Routledge.

— (2004) *Rethinking Orientalism: Women, Travel and the Ottoman Harem*, London: I.B.Tauris.

Lewis, R. and N. Micklewright (eds) (2006) *Gender, Modernity, Liberty: Middle Eastern and Western Women's Writings, a Critical Sourcebook*, London: I.B.Tauris.

McDowell, L. and G. Court (1994) 'Performing work: bodily representations in merchant banks', *Environment and Planning D: Society and Space*, 12: 727–50.

Mahmood, S. (2005) *Politics of Piety: The Islamic Revival and the Feminist Subject*, Princeton, NJ: Princeton University Press.

Mani, B. (2003) 'Undressing the diaspora', in N. Puwar and P. Raghuram (eds), *South Asian Women in the Diaspora*, Oxford: Berg, pp. 117–36.

Massey, D. (1994) *Space, Place and Gender*, Cambridge: Polity Press.

Mernissi, F. (1985) *Beyond the Veil: Male–Female Dynamics in Muslim Society*, 2nd edn, London: al Saqi Books.

Micklewright, N. (2000) 'Public and private for Ottoman women of the nineteenth century', in D. F. Ruggles (ed.), *Women, Patronage, and Self-Representation in Islamic Societies*, New York: State University of New York Press, pp. 155–76.

Miller, D., P. Jackson, N. Thrift, B. Holbrook and M. Rowlands (1998) *Shopping, Place and Identity*, London: Routledge.

Navaro-Yashin, Y. (2002) 'The market for identities: secularism, Islamism, communities', in D. Kandiyoti and A. Saktanber (eds), *Fragments of Culture: The Everyday of Modern*

Turkey, London: I.B.Tauris, pp. 221–53.

Puwar, N. and P. Raghuram (eds) (2003) *South Asian Dress in the Diaspora*, Oxford: Berg.

Rosaldo, R. (1993) *Culture and Truth: The Remaking of Social Analysis*, London: Routledge.

Secor, A. J. (2002) 'The veil and urban space in Istanbul: women's dress, mobility and Islamic knowledge', *Gender, Place and Culture*, 9(1): 5–22.

Tarlo, E. (1996) *Clothing Matters: Dress and Identity in India*, London: C. Hurst.

Vaka, D. (Mr Kenneth Brown) (2005 [1923]) *The Unveiled Ladies of Stamboul*, Piscataway, NJ: Gorgias Press.

White, J. (2002) 'The Islamist paradox', in D. Kandiyoti and A. Saktanber (eds), *Fragments of Culture: The Everyday of Modern Turkey*, London: I.B.Tauris, pp. 191–220.

Wilson, E. (2003) *Adorned in Dreams: Fashion and Modernity*, revised and updated edn, London: I.B.Tauris.

Winship, J. (2000) 'Culture of restraint: the British chain store 1920–39', in P. Jackson, M. Lowe, D. Miller and F. Mort (eds), *Commercial Cultures: Economies, Practices, Spaces*, Oxford: Berg, pp. 15–34.

5 | Citizenship and faith: Muslim scout groups

SARAH MILLS

One of the accusations levelled at Muslims in the West is a lack of engagement with established institutions and organizations in civil society. As this book seeks to ask what Muslims have to be hopeful about today, and how others may share this hope, we need to uncover the hidden and marginalized stories of where Muslims are not only participating in these spaces, but can also act as the driving force for new growth within organizations. This chapter seeks to draw attention to one such story from the UK Scout Association, through which Muslims have created new spaces for their youth in cities across Britain.

It is common for organizations to become essentialized with a particular set of ideas or membership, despite the often multiple internal differences and diversity within such structures. The Scout movement is notoriously stereotyped as being white, androcentric, middle-class and Christian, yet it is a multi-faith, multi-ethnic movement, and is open to male and female members in most of the 218 national territories where Scouting exists. Scouting in the United Kingdom is still largely white, with only 4 per cent of the Association's total membership from minority ethnic communities compared to 8.8 per cent of the national population (Scout Association 2006: 1); it may surprise many, however, that it is far more diverse than its publicly perceived image. Indeed, Scouting in the UK is home to a variety of ethnic and religious minority communities and has created local and national spaces of inter-faith dialogues and events for adults and young people over the last century. Through this chapter, I will develop this argument to show how one such community, Muslims in the UK, has in recent years negotiated its own concrete space within an organization that has always had a theoretical space for Muslims built into its flexible religious policy. This space has been realized through the Muslim Scout Fellowship (MSF), a body of Muslim Scout leaders who support and open Muslim Scout groups. This chapter will examine how since the late 1990s they have become one of the fastest areas of growth within the UK Scout Association. It will go on to argue that Muslim Scout groups, as separate but not exclusive spaces for young Muslims, can be used to overturn many of the assumptions that are made about Muslims and to rebuke claims often made by certain sections of the media about their supposed aloofness. The chapter will then focus on one such Muslim Scout Group, the 1st Cathays (Al-Huda) Scout Group based in Cardiff, Wales. It will discuss how a small number of individuals created an appropriate space for local Muslims through negotiating an alternative way of being a Scout. This example will also be used to present a number of arguments about how the group, both in the mosque and on camp, reflects its members' multiple identities and reaffirms faith-based beliefs. The central argument, though, is that Muslim Scout groups are one example of where an institution can provide support and space for British Muslims to mobilize communities, and in doing so begin to change and redefine the institution itself.

GEOGRAPHIES OF MUSLIM YOUTH

There have been important engagements in academic literature focusing on Muslim youth in Western countries, both in how young Muslims experience inclusion and exclusion within shifting national and international contexts (Hopkins 2004) and how they have defined their own identities through cultural representations (Dwyer 1998, 1999). Peter Mandaville (2001) has argued that Islam as lived experience can be seen 'in the things that Muslims – particularly those of the younger generation – are reading, writing, thinking and doing: in youth groups, on the Internet and in "transnational space"' (ibid.: xii). While there has been work on how young Muslims access youth groups (Parmar 1995), sports programmes (Kay 2007) and spaces of leisure (Green and Singleton 2007), attention has predominantly focused on ideas of risk, fear and social exclusion – important themes that have taken on new and different meanings post-9/11 with young Muslims experiencing racism both in the USA (Peek 2003) and Britain (Hörschelmann 2008). This chapter, while in essence still exploring a space designed for young Muslims, will instead be used to make a number of other arguments about Muslim youth and communities in Britain.

Contemporary debates about multicultural politics, ethnicity and religion and the broader socio-political context post-9/11 and -7/7 have given rise to a number of undesirable assumptions and accusations directed at Muslims in the West (see Abbas 2005; Modood 2005; Modood et al. 2006; Aitchison et al. 2007). One of these has been a perceived lack of engagement by Muslims with mainstream social groups and, significantly, institutions. The example in this chapter of the Scouts, an institutional space within civil society with its own nostalgic and romanticized place in British society, can illustrate how an organization designed for young people can be negotiated through religious difference and used to challenge such accusations.

THE SPACE OF YOUTH (CITIZENSHIP) MOVEMENTS

In broader studies on youth, the spaces of voluntary youth organizations have been marginalized, despite a recent 'institutional turn' within the social sciences (Jessop 2001; Philo and Parr 2000). Indeed, most studies on institutional spaces for young people have focused on schools (Fielding 2000; Kraftl 2006; although see Kyle 2007 on the Boys' Brigade). A number of youth organizations were founded in Britain at the end of the nineteenth and beginning of the twentieth century as organized attempts by volunteers to provide a programme of activities for young people (Wilkinson 1969; Springhall 1977). Although differentiated from one another (and youth clubs) by their uniforms and other pseudo-militaristic elements, the ultimate aim of *all* such youth organizations was, and to a large extent still is, to foster 'good citizenship'. This continued focus on informal citizenship training can be positioned against the changing attitudes to citizenship education within formal state education in British schools (Heater 2001; Bullen and Whitehead 2005; Weller 2007). Indeed, while governmental interest in citizenship initiatives in schools has waxed and waned with changing attitudes to youth, political engagement and democracy, conversely, informal voluntary youth organizations in civil society have consistently focused on youth citizenship. As adventurous spaces tied up with ideas of empire (Phillips 1997), youth organizations presented their members with an 'ideal' young citizen to try to emulate; usually one competent in outdoor skills and who adhered to the moral codes taught by adult leaders. Individual youth organizations, however, while holding citizenship as their common aim, could decide and negotiate the *type* of young citizen they wanted to encourage. This was often articulated through exclusions in their membership criteria along lines of gender, language, territory and religion.

Many youth organizations were constructed exclusively for a particular religious community, such as the Christian-based Boys' Brigade (Springhall et al. 1983; Kyle 2007) and the Jewish Lads' and Girls' Brigade (Kadish 1995). In contrast, by far the most popular youth organization founded in Britain, the Scout movement, has been much more flexible in its religious policy. Founded in Britain in 1908 by Robert Baden-Powell, Scouting has had an estimated total membership of 350 million over the last century, aided by global expansion (see Rosenthal 1986; Warren 1986a; Jeal 1989; Proctor 2002; Boehmer 2004). While Baden-Powell maintained that belief in a higher power was central to the development of a young person (and citizen), he stressed that Scouting was independent of any single religion and that boys of all faiths were welcome.[1] This led to a number of alternative Scouting spaces for religious communities in the UK, including Scout groups sponsored by religious bodies which actively ran troops and donated premises in exchange for attendance at religious services.[2] This sponsorship structure still exists in Scouting today; it is, however, becoming less and less popular. Instead, new Scouting groups have emerged that may meet in places of worship, but are specifically targeted at recruiting a particular religious community and tailored more exclusively for their religious requirements. These groups have been used as part of development projects run by the Scout Association as well as initiated by interested individuals within a number of faith-based communities. Muslim Scouting is one such example where a mixture of these approaches, with varying degrees of success, has been used to make spaces for Muslim youth in cities across the UK. This domestic growth can also be positioned in a global context as the Scout movement recently celebrated its centenary with over twenty-eight million members, a third of whom are Muslim.

It is these new spaces within UK Scouting which I now turn to as the focus of this chapter. It is important to first note the distinction here between definitions of an 'institution' and an 'organization'; this, however, goes beyond the scope of this chapter (see Del Casino et al. 2000; Valins 2000). As useful as it would be in terms of explanation to distinguish between 'Scouting' as an *institution* (a nostalgic, romanticized set of meanings about what it means to be a Scout that has shifted over time and space) and the 'Scout Association' as a national *organization* (a fixed and bounded entity with personnel and a headquarters), the two feed into one another and are mutually constitutive (see Kyle 2007: 37). It is worth highlighting that in this chapter I am considering the UK Scout Association as an organization, and specifically the growth of Muslim Scouting within it, but with an understanding that this feeds into a broader institutional geography about the meanings and representations of Scouting.

CREATING MUSLIM SCOUTING SPACES: THE MUSLIM SCOUT FELLOWSHIP

Scouting has a long history of working with Islamic communities in the UK. While there were small numbers of Muslim adults and young people in early Scouting in Britain, it was not until the post-Second World War immigration from Commonwealth countries that Muslims became more visible in the organization. A number of interviewees from the Muslim Scout Fellowship (MSF) commented how there had been a natural growth in Muslim Scouting as families from Scouting backgrounds in their country of origin came to the UK and joined existing groups. Indeed, growth across all ethnic and religious minorities in Scouting has largely followed immigration patterns, and I would argue that the changes in membership demographics of the Scout Association can be used as a lens through which to view the shifting religious landscape of Britain over the last century. Gerholm and Lithman (1990) suggest that, over time, the Muslim population has lost its transient character and become stable, settled and seeking spaces of its own. They argue that this process is ultimately about making a place for Islam and entails a long series of measures, both concrete (such as legalities of building mosques) and diffuse (such as the right to expect a neutral image in the media). In Britain, these legal struggles have mainly focused on schools – for example, the right to withdraw children from religious education and holidays for principal Muslim celebrations (Nielsen 1990; Joly 1990). One could argue that with these educational struggles now relatively secure, there are other arenas in which communities are seeking to create a place for Islam and 'make inroads into British institutions so that a space can be gradually opened for Muslims' (Gerholm and Lithman 1990: 48). I would argue that one of these, in recent years, has been the Scout Association.

The natural growth of Muslim Scouting through largely family-based links did not have the scope or resources to address the lack of provision for young people in Muslim communities across Britain. In light of this, and in the context of broader debates in British society about inclusion and diversity, there was a push by the Scout Association in the late 1980s to extend Muslim Scouting to new areas and target cities in a nationwide project as part of their wider Ethnic Communities Development Programme.[3] This was the Islamic Scout Development Project, which ran from 1987 to 1990 and focused on bringing Scouting to Muslims, for example through camps at the Scout Association headquarters in Essex and opening Muslim Scout groups in areas such as Tower Hamlets and Derby.[4] Although this project expressed a desire by the Association to make Scouting more available to Muslim communities, it was ultimately unsuccessful and naive, undermining its long-term sustainability. An independent evaluation report commissioned by the Scout Association suggested that community contacts were poorly supported by local Scouting personnel owing to a number of prejudices and a lack of cultural awareness.[5] The projects' principal flaws, identified by a number of interviewees, were not bringing the Muslim community to the forefront of the schemes and failing to train Muslim leaders; instead, existing (white) non-Muslim leaders were appointed from nearby groups. It was this decision which meant the handful of Muslim Scout groups that had been established did not have sufficient support from their local community and soon closed.

Nevertheless, in the early 1990s a core group of around ten Muslim Scout leaders based in London and Bristol, along with interested community contacts, decided that a new approach was needed to get Muslim communities involved in Scouting. They saw they could harness the enthusiasm of second- and third-generation Muslims who wanted to provide organized activities for young Muslims and therefore set up training courses and taster days for interested individuals. This informal network of leaders then began to develop Muslim Scouting in three ways; first, by targeting and increasing Muslim participation within existing groups through provision of leaders and planning activities; second, starting Muslim sections that worked as part of an existing Scout group; and finally, supporting the opening of brand-new Muslim Scout groups. This network was officially formalized as the MSF in 2005, and today they are one of the most active Scout fellowships in the UK.[6] Although increasingly involved in the broader work of the Scout Association, such as supporting nationwide events and international camps, the main work of the MSF remains opening and supporting Muslim Scout groups.

Muslim Scout groups are defined as 'open' Scout groups: they are not exclusively for Muslim children and, similarly, Muslim children can attend any other open Scout group in the UK. They are, however, specifically designed to provide a more Islamic environment in which Scouting can take place. There is not one archetypal Muslim Scout group; although they have common features, each is unique in its set-up to accommodate the needs of the local community. There has been a rapid growth in Muslim Scout groups over the last few years and there are currently twenty-two Muslim Scout groups in major cities across the UK, including London, Birmingham, Leeds, Manchester, Edinburgh and the focus of this empirical research, Cardiff.

'DUTY TO ALLAH': 1ST CATHAYS (AL-HUDA) SCOUT GROUP

The 1st Cathays (Al-Huda) Scout Group (hereafter 1st CAH) based in Cardiff is similar in its style and structure to that of any Muslim Scout group currently active in the UK. The story of its creation can also be found in the narratives of many other Muslim Scout groups across Britain. They began meeting informally in 2002, led by a teenager named Salah. He moved to the area from London, where he was involved in the MSF and recognized the need for 'something' in Cathays owing to the lack of activities for young people outside of school and madrasa[7] at the local Darul' Isra Mosque. A Muslim Scout group was well suited to this task, Salah felt, owing to the existing framework of support Scouting offered and its flexibility. Unlike the experimental Muslim Scout groups in the 1980s, the 1st CAH is not sponsored by the Darul' Isra Mosque, although it remains closely affiliated with it and utilizes its premises. After recruiting leaders and gaining the trust of local parents, Salah, the MSF and Scout Association began the long process of establishing the group and training leaders. The group was officially registered and opened in 2006 with around one hundred members, becoming the first, and only, Muslim Scout group in Wales.

It is worth reflecting on this national context before examining the case study in more depth, as the Welsh identity of the group is significant. Paul Chambers and Andrew Thompson argue that 'among sections of Wales's ethnic minority populations, religious faith is both an integral element of their ethnic identity and something through which their Welsh identity is mediated and constructed' (2005: 349). This additional layer of identity is important and yet it is often neglected within multiculturalism literature, which instead privileges the British experience. In reality, the multiple identities of religious minorities living in Wales complicate now popular terms such as 'British Muslim'. Ziauddin Sardar reflects on this 'multi-layering of identity', which he argues is tied up in the complexity of Britishness itself (2008: 48–9). He suggests that minority nations and internally colonized regions within the UK – notably Scotland and Wales – distance themselves from jingoistic constructions of British national identity, which are embroiled with imperial histories and identities (ibid.: 72). In other words, Muslims find it easier to identify with these minority nations than they do with Britain or England. This has been enhanced by their distance from the established church – the Church of England – and by religious change. A decline in Nonconformism and increased religious pluralism from post-war immigration has led to an emerging multi-faith Wales and multiple ways of 'being Welsh' (see Williams et al. 2003). Islam has become progressively stronger in South Wales, and Cardiff in particular has a long history of Islamic immigration through the in-migration of Somali and Yemeni seamen towards the end of the nineteenth century. Chambers and Thompson (2005) argue Muslim that communities in

Wales have benefited from the historic relationship between religion and nationhood (see Bogdanor 1999: 144) but have also gained from the new system of post-devolution governance in Wales, for example through the establishment of the Interfaith Council for Wales in 2002 and the Muslim Council of Wales in 2004. While Cardiff, and in particular Tiger Bay, has been revitalized as a result of the National Assembly, however, its redevelopment has further marginalized Muslim areas of the city in nearby Butetown and, significantly, Cathays (Threadgold et al. 2008). The role of place in the narrative of this Muslim Scout group becomes important, then, as it is located right in the heart of the Cathays area of the city. As I will highlight later in the chapter, this inner-city urban setting and the Welsh context both feed into the activities and identity of the group in multiple ways.

The 1st CAH comprises three age-graded sections: Beavers (6–8), Cub Scouts (8–10) and Scouts (10–14). Respecting Islamic approaches to gender, there are two separate meetings of each section for boys and girls, who meet at different times once a week. This is just one example where the rules of the organization have been renegotiated through religious difference, as for most other Scout groups in the UK it is now compulsory for all of its sections to be open to both sexes. This contrasts the original separate Scouting structures in Britain for boys and girls, which have shifted over time, as well as how other national Scouting bodies approach gender (Proctor 2002). A number of other negotiations have led to important differences between Muslim and other Scout groups in the UK, and these can be illustrated through the example of the 1st CAH. These differences were crucial to the group's initial popularity and its continued success. While its members were attracted to and have embraced traditional features of being Scouts, through this process of negotiating a space for Muslim Scouts and these differences, they are redefining the very same practices and performances that characterize the institution. This relationship will be explored in the next two subsections; first, looking at the more banal and subtle features of 'being a Scout'; and second, through camping and citizenship training in the landscape.

CEREMONIAL AND SARTORIAL SCOUTS

There are a number of features of Scouting that are common to all members, such as making the Scout Promise, taking part in opening ceremonies, and wearing the Scout uniform. Through adapting these routine performances and material items, Muslim Scouts have negotiated alternatives and, in turn, provoke us to rethink and challenge how we view such institutions. These features of 'being a Scout' are, to draw upon the ideas of Michael Billig (1995), relatively banal, and yet they are extremely important when considering how a space has been opened up for Muslim Scouts.

In order to join the 1st CAH, like any other Scout group, a young person or adult must make the Scout Promise. This declaration of membership, in its original form, pledges duty to God and the Queen:

> On my Honour,
> I Promise to Do My Best
> To Do My Duty to God and to the Queen
> To Help Other People,
> And to keep the Scout Law.

The Scout Promise has evolved over the last century, however, to include optional alternatives for various religious communities.[8] Muslim Scout groups such as 1st CAH, and indeed Muslim children who belong to other Scout groups, can choose to make the following alternative Scout Promise:

> In the name of Allah, the Most Beneficent, the Most Merciful,
> I Promise to Do My Best
> To Do My Duty to Allah and to [the Country in which I am now living/the Queen]
> To Help Other People,
> And to keep the Scout Law.

It was noted by a number of interviewees that this alternative Promise was a more appropriate way for them to 'become' Scouts, and they felt more comfortable declaring this version of the oath. The Scout Promise, in whichever form, is repeated whenever a new member joins the group and is also declared simultaneously at special Scouting events on important dates across the world. So while Muslim Scouts perform this part of the Scout identity under their own terms and in an appropriate way, crucially it is their participation in the very act of declaring the Promise which means they retain and strengthen the common bond that unites Scouts worldwide.

Scouting ceremonies, such as the opening of regular weekly Scout meetings, are another common feature of Scout groups that have been negotiated at the 1st CAH. Most Scout group meetings in the UK would begin with the children standing 'at ease' in horseshoe shape and then being called 'to alert' by the leaders. This is followed by 'flagbreak', where one child steps forward and pulls ropes releasing a Union flag from a pulley; the flag is first saluted by that child, and then by the rest of the group. Conversely, Scout meetings are opened at the 1st CAH by the children lining up in Patrols of five or six which are then called to attention in Arabic. The leader calls: '*Bismillahhirahmanirahim*'[9] and then a child recites a small piece from the Koran. While routine and discipline are common features in both cases, the opening ceremony of 1st CAH is more clearly mediated through religious belief than the former example. It also highlights the complex relationship between ideas of nationhood, citizenship and religion through the absence of the Union flag in the 1st CAH meeting place, and by extension its presence in most other Scout groups. Interestingly, while their British context remains hidden, the Welsh identity of 1st CAH is still visible through the Welsh Dragon badge embroidered on to each shoulder of its members' uniforms. There are links here with Billig's (1995) concept of banal nationalism. He argues that the metonymic image of banal nationalism is 'not a flag which is being consciously waved with fervent passion; it is the flag hanging unnoticed in the public building' (ibid.: 8). To extend Billig's metaphor, the non-verbal and non-ceremonial presence of the Welsh flag sewn on to the children's uniforms is a barely conscious reminder, or flagging, of the Welsh nation. This further emphasizes the importance of that additional layer of Welsh identity mentioned earlier in the chapter.

Uniform is the most visible marker of being a Scout (Proctor 1998). There is provision in the Scout Association's rules for religious dress, such as the hijab, to be incorporated into Scout uniform, and this demonstrates an institutional flexibility regarding religious requirements and visible symbols of faith when compared to recent incidents in British schools and workplaces (see Reina Lewis's chapter in this book). Scout uniform has another function at 1st CAH of demonstrating their religious identity in Scouting. Its various components provide a way for Muslims to display their multiple identities and in this sense clothing can be seen as a site of cultural representation and marker of difference (see Dwyer 1998: 54–8). For instance, their chosen neckerchief design (scarves that are worn around the neck) includes an embroidered logo on the back, seen here in Figure 5.1. This combination of the Islamic sign of the crescent moon where the star has been replaced by the Scout sign of a fleur-de-lis visually encapsulates their dual identities as both Scouts and Muslims.

These examples of the Scout Promise, opening ceremonies and uniform demonstrate how the 1st CAH has been constructed and differs from other Scout groups in the UK. While these more banal aspects

Figure 5.1 Sartorial scouting (*source*: Lisa Sandercock)

could easily be overlooked, they contribute to the overall feel of the group and what it stands for. This is further reflected in the group's chosen name, 'Al-Huda', which translates from Arabic as 'the guided ones' or 'guided path'. As well as echoing Baden-Powell's philosophy of guiding youth through outdoor knowledge and a code of living, for example in his naming of the separate but linked Girl Guide movement, the name 'Al-Huda' also has spiritual and moral connotations of guiding youth through Islamic observance. The 1st CAH's name thus combines these literal and metaphorical meanings and reflects their faith-based identity. To summarize, these three features reflect their Islamic faith in subtle but significant ways. The more spectacular demonstrations of the group's religious identity, however, occur outside of the mosque and away from the city – on camp.

LANDSCAPE AND CAMPING

Scouting is often associated with camping, the outdoors, adventure and rural landscapes. These themes will be used in this second subsection to demonstrate another way Muslim Scout groups have embraced traditional aspects of Scouting, appropriated them and, in doing so, have to some extent reshaped the wider organization they themselves are part of, or at the very least have thrown into question who can be a Scout by contesting dominant stereotypes of who belongs to the Scout movement.

The idea of 'being in the landscape' to develop senses of self and citizenship is as important to the Scout movement today as it was a century ago (on landscape and citizenship, see Matless 1995). One of the motivations for weekly meetings of all Scout groups is to learn Scouting skills that can be put into practice on camp, to learn techniques in mainly urban settings that can then be actualized in rural landscapes. For example, these exercises include 'tracking', where signs and arrows are used to direct others, usually through the woods using sticks and stones, but in this case around the mosque and with pieces of paper.

These Scouting skills, rewarded through the badge system of the Scout Association, are then performed on the regular camps run by the 1st CAH. While retaining several key features of a Scout camp such as pitching tents, campfire songs, open-fire cooking and so forth, there are important differences to a Muslim Scout camp. These include the provision of halal food in camp cooking as well as set times in the programme for prayers throughout the day. These distinctions are crucial for parents to know that the adventurous activities Scouting provides are done within the context of Islamic boundaries and that their children will be catered for in accordance with their faith. Furthermore, the visual performance of Islamic observance on camp, through praying on mats and tarpaulins in these rural landscapes, further strengthens the social and religious character of Muslim Scout groups. This has been taken one step farther by some Muslim Scout groups, which have embarked on the haj as part of a Scout trip abroad (see BBC 2006). These more spectacular performances of religious identity can be positioned in contrast to the more banal aspects of being a Muslim Scout discussed in the previous subsection.

Camping is seen by leaders at the group as the core traditional Scouting activity and a beneficial rural experience for its young members, who live in an inner-city urban area. These ideas about nature, youth and citizenship can be seen in the context of broader research on the relationship of young people to both rural and urban landscapes (Philo 1992; Matthews et al. 2000; Ward 1990a, 1990b) as well as recent work on campsites (Dunkley 2008; Paris 2008). A common stereotype interviewed Muslim Scout leaders felt they as Muslims had been labelled with was 'unadventurous', and this gave them a desire to contest that image. The 1st CAH, as well as other Muslim Scout groups, are actively rebuking those claims through participating in Scout camps and adventurous outdoor activities. Figure 5.2 illustrates the performance of setting up a campsite, which challenges those dominant misconceptions of Muslims as 'out of place' in rural landscapes (on these themes, see Kinsman 1995; Neal and Agyeman 2006).

As well as rural landscapes being associated with whiteness, David Matless (1998) has argued that over time they have become associated with senses of Englishness through various histories and spatialities. The

Figure 5.2 Pitching a tent (*source*: Mohamad Fez Miah)

1st CAH, as a Welsh Muslim Scout Group, complicate that relationship through camping in two ways: first, through their own domestic camps in Wales, which contest the dominant anglicized stereotype of the Scout movement, and second, through visiting campsites in England and making Muslims from Wales more visible in these landscapes of Englishness.

The presence of Muslim women in these landscapes (see Figure 5.2) also breaks down established gender stereotypes (see Dwyer 1998 on resisting dominant representations of young Muslim women). This quote from a female leader at the first ever MSF camp demonstrates her enthusiasm about camping: 'It's amazing ... I'm really happy to be here. There is a misconception that Muslim women stay at home all day doing nothing – but being Muslim doesn't stop us doing the assault course and the shooting – and beating the boys!' (quoted in James 2005: 33).

There is, though, a more serious element to these camps of taking children 'out of their comfort zone', as a leader from 1st CAH explains: 'We as Muslims and Scouts have the opportunity in camping ... to show them [young people] that it's not all about an easy life, you've got a challenge to be stronger, to appreciate the environment, the world, other people, everybody. That's why I like it' (Cub Scout leader, female section; interview with author).

So while the group has developed a unique experience of a Muslim

Scout camp in an appropriate format for its members and their parents, it is clear that traditional ideas and meanings associated with camping and nature influence the rationale behind their Scout camps. This example thus illustrates the chapter's much broader aim of showing how Muslims are using, transforming and negotiating Scouting spaces in the UK.

CONCLUSION

In this chapter I aimed to bring into the spotlight one example where Muslims are engaging in an institutional space in civil society: in this case a space designed for young people and, significantly, one with a historical relationship to the wider British sphere – the Scout movement. In drawing attention to the example of Muslim Scout groups and MSF, I wanted to show the inaccuracy of a number of unfavourable claims levelled at the Muslim community in recent years regarding their supposed detachment in the context of national institutions. I also explored the lengthy process of finding and negotiating appropriate ways of being a Scout and a Muslim through the case study of the 1st Cathays (Al-Huda) Scout Group in Cardiff. I argued that while initially attracted to the fundamental features of Scouting, the group's differences (both in the more banal aspects of Scouting and camping) have not only defined the 1st CAH and made their faith more visible, but have begun to redefine and reshape the traditional meanings and understandings of Scouting and its broader institutional geography. In this conclusion, I want to reflect on two broader points of participation and integration.

There is a wider debate here about participation by British Muslims in existing national institutions. Indeed, participation in established institutions can be viewed as a conservative strategy by British Muslims and there is, one could argue, a certain ambivalence regarding participation in such institutional spaces and whether in fact it is always desirable. The growth of Muslim Scouting in the UK demonstrates a real desire for participation and one that is motivated by providing fun, engaging and challenging opportunities for the young people within their communities. Indeed, the process of creating the 1st CAH as a new space in Cardiff was empowering for those Muslims involved and reaffirmed their place within the local community and the capital. I would argue, though, that Muslim Scout groups go *beyond* participation in that they are grassroots developments displaying creativity and purpose as well as opportunities for public engagement through volunteering and community events. They can also be seen as spaces where important negotiations are taking place, for example about the ways in which Muslims in Scouting and the wider organization engage and interact with each other. These Scout groups can be seen as dialogues that are beginning to remake Scouting in its own image; in that sense, they are desirable and can be powerful spaces of change rather than neutral participatory spaces.

This example also raises important questions of integration and fears of segregation. Tied into these ideas is the much broader issue of multiculturalism as a set of state-directed discourses and practices that are negotiated with minority groups, and while these debates are highly relevant, I want to focus more explicitly here on integration. One could view Muslim Scout groups as merely sidestepping various elements of the Scouting ethos and that meeting in separate spaces, rather than truly integrating into existing Scout groups, is regressive. On the other hand, I would contend that it is the very format of Muslim Scout groups and these negotiated ways of being a Muslim Scout which have ultimately led to the success of Muslim Scouting. Without these new spaces, there would not be the regular participation of thousands of Muslim adults and young people in Scouting across the UK. This level of growth would not have occurred through trying to integrate Muslim communities into rigid existing structures, and this was clearly demonstrated by the failed evangelical attempts in the 1980s to take Scouting to Muslim communities. While I would agree that there are limits to the divergence from Scouting until one is no longer recognizable as a 'Scout', I would argue that Muslim Scouts are still very much within those boundaries and are part of the broader institution of Scouting in the UK. There are wider debates here about integration, what it means and how it can be achieved, and these are themes that Tahir Abbas and Ziauddin Sardar both examine in this book. They ask whether integration is a one-way process or does it involve two sides. Indeed, this question is crucial in such debates and, in the context of this chapter, raises important points about how an institution can, or should, 'integrate' with various communities while still retaining its fundamental beliefs, rather than framing integration as a one-way process demanding acquiescence from minority groups. In their respective chapters, Abbas and Sardar also ask *where* integration is taking place, and the frustrations of knowing *how* to integrate for British Muslims. It is worth highlighting here that in Muslim Scouting, integration with other young people is taking place, but at a different spatial scale through joint meetings on a regional and national level; perhaps this example of rescaling can offer one possible answer regarding these questions.

As this book searches for sources of optimism in an often uniformly bleak landscape, the continued development of the MSF and the growing number of Muslim Scout groups in cities across the UK provide much hope for Muslims. I would argue that in order to move towards more important political goals regarding integration and addressing the injustices minority communities face, this has to begin with allowing ethnic and religious minorities to negotiate space, or, better still, to make their own spaces and flourish in them.

NOTES

I would like to thank the Economic and Social Research Council for funding assistance (Grant number: ES/F00737X/1). Thanks also to the Scout Association archival staff and all my research participants for their help and enthusiasm, as well as readers of this chapter and their helpful comments.

1 See Scout Association Archive (hereafter SAA): TC33, TC399, PWE 2 44. See also Warren (1986b); Proctor (2002: 142–3).

2 SAA: TC36, TC431.

3 SAA: TC423.

4 SAA: TC342.

5 SAA: TC342.

6 A fellowship in Scouting is a body of like-minded Scout leaders with a particular interest or area of development – for example, the Catholic Scouting Fellowship.

7 Madrasa, or Madrasah, is Arabic for any type of school (religious or non-religious) and classes usually take place at mosques.

8 See SAA: TC119.

9 This translates as 'In the name of Allah the Most Beneficient the Most Merciful'.

REFERENCES

Abbas, T. (ed.) (2005) *Muslim Britain: Communities under Pressure*, London: Zed Books.

Aitchison, C., P. E. Hopkins and M.-P. Kwan (eds) (2007) *Geographies of Muslim Identities: Diaspora, Gender and Belonging*, Aldershot and Burlington, VT: Ashgate.

BBC (2006) 'Scouts hajj experience', BBC Online, available at: www.bbc.co.uk/birmingham/content/articles/2006/01/27/faith_scouts_hajj_feature.shtml.

Billig, M. (1995) *Banal Nationalism*, London: Sage.

Boehmer, E. (2004) 'Introduction', in R. Baden-Powell (1908), *Scouting for Boys: A Handbook for Instruction in Good Citizenship*, Oxford: Oxford University Press.

Bogdanor, V. (1999) *Devolution in the United Kingdom*, Oxford: Oxford University Press.

Bullen, A. and M. Whitehead (2005) 'Negotiating the networks of space, time and substance: a geographical perspective on the sustainable citizen', *Citizenship Studies*, 9(5).

Chambers, P. and A. Thompson (2005) 'Coming to terms with the past: religion and identity in Wales', *Social Compass*, 52(3).

Del Casino, V. J., A. J. Grimes, S. P. Hanna and J. P. Jones, III (2000) 'Methodological frameworks for the geography of organizations', *Geoforum*, 31.

Dunkley, C. M. (2008) 'A therapeutic taskscape: theorizing place-making, discipline and care at a camp for troubled youth', *Health and Place*, doi: 10.1016/j.health-place.2008.02.006.

Dwyer, C. (1998) 'Contested identities: challenging dominant representations of young British Muslim women', in T. Skelton and G. Valentine (eds), *Cool Places: Geographies of Youth Cultures*, London: Routledge.

— (1999) 'Contradictions of community: questions of identity for young British Muslim women', *Environment and Planning A*, 31(3).

Fielding, S. (2000) 'Walk on the left! Children's geographies and the primary school', in S. L. Holloway and G. Valentine (eds), *Children's Geographies: Playing, Living, Learning*, London: Routledge.

Gerholm, T. and Y. G. Lithman (eds) (1990) *The New Islamic Presence in Western Europe*, London: Mansell.

Green, E. and C. Singleton (2007) '"Safe and risky spaces": gender, ethnicity and culture in the leisure lives of young South Asian women', in C. Aitchison, P. E. Hopkins and M.-P. Kwan (eds), *Geographies of Muslim Identities: Diaspora, Gender and Belonging*, Aldershot: Ashgate.

Heater, D. (2001) 'The history of citizenship education in England', *Curriculum Journal*, 12(1).

Hopkins, P. E. (2004) 'Young Muslim men in Scotland: inclusions and exclusions', *Children's Geographies*, 2(2).

Hörschelmann, K. (2008) 'Youth and the geopolitics of risk after 11 September 2001', in R. Pain and S. Smith (eds), *Fear: Critical Geopolitics and Everyday Life*, Aldershot: Ashgate.

James, C. (2005) 'All inclusive – the first Muslim Scout camp', *Scouting Magazine*, August/September.

Jeal, T. (1989) *Baden-Powell: Founder of the Boy Scouts*, London: Hutchinson.

Jessop, B. (2001) 'Institutional re(turns) and the strategic-relational approach', *Environment and Planning A*, 33.

Joly, D. (1990) 'Making a place for Islam in British Society: Muslims in Birmingham', in T. Gerholm and Y. G. Lithman (eds), *The New Islamic Presence in Western Europe*, London: Mansell.

Kadish, S. (1995) *A Good Jew and a Good Englishman: The Jewish Lads' and Girls' Brigade 1895–1995*, London: Valentine Mitchell.

Kay, T. (2007) 'Daughters of Islam, sisters in sport', in C. Aitchison, P. E. Hopkins and M.-P. Kwan (eds), *Geographies of Muslim Identities: Diaspora, Gender and Belonging*, Aldershot: Ashgate.

Kinsman, P. (1995) 'Landscape, race and national identity: the photography of Ingrid Pollard', *Area*, 27.

Kraftl, P. (2006) 'Building an idea: the material construction of an ideal childhood', *Transactions of the Institute of British Geographers*, 31(4).

Kyle, R. (2007) *The Moral Geographies of the Boys' Brigade in Scotland*, Unpublished PhD thesis, University of Glasgow.

Mandaville, P. (2001) *Transnational Muslim Politics: Reimagining the Umma*, London: Routledge.

Matless, D. (1995) 'The art of right living: landscape and citizenship, 1918–39', in N. Thrift and S. Pile (eds) *Mapping the Subject: Geographies of Cultural Transformation*, London: Routledge.

— (1998) *Landscape and Englishness*, London: Reaktion Books.

Matthews, H., M. Taylor, M. Sherwood, F. Tucker and M. Limb (2000) 'Growing up in the countryside: children in the rural idyll', *Journal of Rural Studies*, 16.

Modood, T. (2005) *Multicultural Politics – Racism, Ethnicity and Muslims in Britain*, Minnesota: University of Minnesota Press.

Modood, T., A. Triandafyllidou and R. Zapta-Barrero (2006) *Multiculturalism, Muslims and Citizenship: A European Approach*, London and New York: Routledge.

Neal, S. and J. Agyeman (eds) (2006) *The New Countryside? Ethnicity, Nation and Exclusion in Contemporary Rural Britain*, Bristol: Policy Press.

Nielsen, J. S. (1990) 'Muslims in Britain and local authority responses', in T. Gerholm and Y. G. Lithman (eds), *The New Islamic Presence in Western Europe*, London: Mansell.

Paris, L. (2008) *Children's Nature: The Rise of the American Summer Camp*, New York: New York University Press.

Parmar, P. (1995) 'Gender, race and power: the challenge to youth work practice', in C. Crichter, P. Bramham and A. Tomlinson (eds), *Sociology of Leisure: A Reader*, London: E. and F. N. Spon.

Peek, L. (2003) 'Reactions and response: Muslim students' experience on New York City campuses post 9/11', *Journal of Muslim Minority Affairs*, 23(3).

Phillips, R. (1997) *Mapping Men and Empire: A Geography of Adventure*, London: Routledge.

Philo, C. (1992) 'Neglected rural geographies: a review', *Journal of Rural Studies*, 8(2).

Philo, C. and H. Parr (2000) 'Institutional geographies: introductory remarks', *Geoforum*, 31.

Proctor, T. (1998) '(Uni)forming youth: Girl Guides and Boy Scouts in Britain, 1908–1939', *History Workshop Journal*, 45, Spring.

— (2002) *On My Honour: Guides and Scouts in Interwar Britain*, Philadelphia, PA: American Philosophical Society.

Rosenthal, M. (1986) *The Character Factory: Baden-Powell and the Origins of the Boy Scout Movement*, New York: Pantheon Press.

Sardar, Z. (2008) *Balti Britain: A Journey through the British Asian Experience*, London: Granta.

Scout Association (2006) *Developing Scouting in Minority Ethnic Communities*, Factsheet FS185019, Scout Association Information Centre.

Springhall, J. (1977) *Youth, Empire and Society: British Youth Movements 1908–1930*, Beckenham: Croom Helm.

Springhall, J., B. Fraser and M. Hoare (1983) *Sure and Steadfast: A History of the Boys' Brigade 1883–1983*, London: Collins.

Threadgold, T., S. Clifford, A. Arwo, V. Powell, Z. Harb, X. Jiang and J. Jewell (2008) *Immigration and Inclusion in South Wales*, York: Joseph Rowntree Foundation.

Valins, O. (2000) 'Institutionalised religion: sacred texts and Jewish spatial practice', *Geoforum*, 31

Ward, C. (1990a) *The Child in the City*, London: Architectural Press.

— (1990b) *The Child in the Country*, London: Bedford Square Press.

Warren, A. (1986a) 'Citizens of empire – Baden-Powell, Scouts and Guides and an Imperial ideal', in J. Mackenzie (ed.), *Imperialism and Popular Culture*, Manchester:

Manchester University Press.

— (1986b) 'Sir Robert Baden-Powell, the Scout Movement, and citizen-training in Britain 1900–1920', *English Historical Review*, 101.

Weller, S. (2007) *Teenagers' Citizenship: Experiences and Education*, London: Routledge.

Wilkinson, P. (1969) 'English youth movements, 1908–1930', *Journal of Contemporary History*, 4(2).

Williams, C., N. Evans and P. O'Leary (2003) *A Tolerant Nation? Exploring Ethnic Diversity in Wales*, Cardiff: University of Wales Press.

6 | The utopian space of the Islamic bathhouse or *hammām*

MAGDA SIBLEY AND FODIL FADLI

Some of my earliest and happiest memories, as a child growing up in Algiers, centre on the *hammām* I would visit with my grandmother. Losing the perception of time in the main, steamy washing room with its central marble table; the suns rays filtering through the pierced dome; the smell of fresh oranges and lemons being peeled; the sound of women talking and children playing; the affection and attention of my grandmother scrubbing my body; the fresh and beautiful towels used after the bath; the cool lemonade ordered by my grandmother after the bath and a sense of being reborn. These experiences and memories are still part of me twenty-two years after leaving Algiers and settling in England. They inspired me to research and document *hammām*s, not only in Algeria but throughout North Africa and the Middle East at a time when the names '*hammām*' and 'Turkish bath' are reappearing in advertisements for new spas and wellness centres in European cities such as London, Paris, Madrid and Vienna.

Others share my affection for these places. My co-author, Fodil Fadli, who is also an Algerian-born architect living in the UK, speaks of the *hammām*s of his youth in similar terms.

Until the age of three, I used to go to the public bath of the 'houma', the neighbourhood, with my mother and aunties, as did other kids of my age. After that, my weekly visit to the *hammām* was with my father and brothers, every Thursday evening. One of my striking childhood memories was my fear of the unbearable heat in the hot room and the rough scrubbing of my body. These young-age experiences meta-morphosed into nostalgic happy memories, however, once I became a teenager and then an adult. My adult experience of the *hammām* was with friends bathing and relaxing, at weekends or before major cele-brations such as weddings and Eid festivities after Ramadan. More recently, and after leaving Algeria, I still enjoy going to the *hammām* whenever I am visiting Algiers, my home city.

These childhood memories hint at how the *hammām* is a space in which religious, personal, national, gender and family identities and experiences intermingle. They suggest how, for the authors of this chapter as for many others, the *hammām* brings together Islam, home, childhood memories and family – in no particular order.

In the context of an often depressing and negative portrayal of the Islamic world, this chapter revisits what for many Muslims, but also many others in the West, has long been a utopian Islamic space: the *hammām*. It provides an insight into the *hammām* as a living heritage that survived into the twenty-first century and has managed to reinvent itself to meet the requirements of contemporary society not only in North Africa but also in a number of European cities. So the *hammām* can be a space of hope, both for Muslims in the Islamic world, and for Muslims and others in the West: both as a place in which Muslims can come together, and also as a kind of utopian space that presents a positive picture of Islamic culture to others.

This chapter is based on our research and our own experiences of using the *hammām* in different countries of North Africa and the Middle East as part of fieldwork funded by the Arts and Humanities Research Council in the UK and the European Commission. It is also based on the accounts of European tourists visiting *hammām*s in North Africa and the Middle East and the description of *hammām*s in European cities as sourced from the Web. Historic *hammām*s were visited, surveyed and photographed in Cairo (Egypt), Tunis (Tunisia), Tripoli (Libya) and Marrakesh (Morocco) between 2007 and 2009. Face-to-face structured interviews and informal discussions were also conducted with the owners, managers, workers and users of the *hammām*s. In some cases, overt participant observation has taken place in order to gain an insight into the way the *hammām* spaces are used.

THE *HAMMĀM* OR ISLAMIC BATHHOUSE

The *hammām* or Islamic bathhouse, commonly known as a Turkish bath, is a building type that has evolved from the Roman and Byzantine public baths. It is not of Turkish origin although it flourished during the Ottoman period and spread over a large geographic area under the Ottoman Empire. The period following the rise of Islam witnessed a rapid development in the history of baths and the change from Roman to Islamic bathing habits. Washing by pouring water over the body became the norm as sharing water with another person was considered to be unhygienic. The cold plunge pool, a major feature of the Roman bath, disappeared in the Islamic bath. One of the best examples of early

Islamic *hammām*s is 'Qusair Amra', found in the Jordanian desert. It consists of a large reception hall followed by a series of cold, warm and hot rooms. The bathing spaces are heated by a hypocaust system, a raised floor under which smoke from the furnace travels and heats the hot and warm rooms before being extracted in chimneys located within walls. This heating system remained for centuries one of the most typical features of the Islamic baths in cities throughout the Islamic world.

Ritual purification is common to many religions. Known as ablution or *wudu'* in Islam, the ritual of washing parts or the whole of the body is a compulsory requirement before each of the five daily sessions of prayers representing one of the main pillars of Islam. Cleanliness and purity are of paramount importance. *'Cleanliness is part of faith'*, according to the saying of the Prophet Muhammad. Two forms of ablutions exist: lesser ablutions or *wudu'*, which consist of washing parts of the body (face, hands, arms, mouth, ears, nose, head and feet) and greater ablutions, *ghusl'*, which consist of washing the whole body. Greater ablutions are necessary after sexual intercourse, the end of menstruation, giving birth, before Friday prayer and major religious festivities, and after death.

The need to carry out major ablutions before praying explains the wide spread of public baths in Islamic cities at the time when public bathhouses were disappearing in the West after the fall of the Roman Empire. Located near mosques, souks and in residential centres, their number was very high as they provided an essential facility for the whole urban population. Andre Raymond stated that the average number of *hammām*s in the Islamic medina was one for 4,000 inhabitants (Raymond 1969). It was estimated that in the tenth century, however, Baghdad counted a public bath for every fifty inhabitants and Kairouan in Tunisia counted one *hammām* for every eighty inhabitants. Ecochard and Le Coeur counted sixty bathhouses in the old city of Damascus in 1942 and Edmond Pauty counted forty-seven in Cairo in 1933. Their location within the urban fabric was closely linked not only to the location of mosques but also to the urban water distribution system and ease of access from residential neighbourhoods.

Hammām buildings vary in size and importance, depending on their location within the city. They are frequently part of a cluster of urban facilities such as the mosque, the madrasa (theology college), the neighbourhood oven and the public fountain. They consist most of the time of a single structure, used by men and women at different times of the day. Some *hammām*s located in the centre of a market area, however, are dedicated exclusively to men, whereas others located in the heart of residential areas are exclusively used by women. In some cases a

Figure 6.1 Hammām al-Silsila, Damascus. The ceiling of the bathing space is pierced by light bulbs (*source*: the authors)

Figure 6.2 Hammām Tayrouzi, Damascus, the roofscape (*source*: the authors)

Figure 6.3 Entrance of Hammām Sahib al-Tabaa', Tunis. A cloth is hung over the door to indicate a women's bathing session (*source*: the authors)

twin *hammām* structure can be found, whereby two adjacent structures operate simultaneously for men and women.

Architecturally, *hammām*s present a rich variety of spaces and forms. A composition of domes and vaults, pierced with light bulbs, is a typical characteristic of these buildings (Figures 6.1 and 6.2). Their presence in the urban fabric is usually discreet as they present a blind façade to the street. One notices only their decorated entrance, which displays (at particular times of the day) a cloth hung above it, indicating that the *hammām* is admitting women and acting as a deterrent to men to enter the building (Figure 6.3). The entrance to the first space in the *hammām*, the reception/changing room, is right-angled, an indirect transition space providing a semi-private buffer zone between the public (outdoor) and private (indoor) spaces.

The changing room is one of the largest spaces in the *hammām* and frequently the most decorated space, as illustrated in Figure 6.4. Although it is the access and exit point of the *hammām*, the undressing and dressing space, it is also much more than that. It is the greeting, meeting and farewell space, where both rich and poor, old and young meet: a social hub for women exchanging the latest neighbourhood news; a negotiation space where marriages are discussed; a counselling and support space where personal problems are shared between friends; a business and trading space where goods are sold; a festive space where singing and dancing take place; a catering space where specific drinks, sweets and dishes are brought as part of pre-wedding celebrations; a fashion space where women exhibit their jewellery, clothes and latest lingerie and accessories; a nursery space where kids are looked after while mums are enjoying their bath time. For centuries, the *hammām* used to be the only public social gathering space for women in the Islamic city.

As one moves from the changing room to the bathing spaces, the experience is that of a journey from the outside to the inside, from the public to the private spaces, from light to semi-light to semi-dark spaces, from cold to warm to hot, steamy spaces. The sequence is that of a tortuous itinerary towards the hottest and steamiest space, where the heat from the fire of the furnace is at its fiercest and where the steam from the hot water creates a thick mist. It is a space where bodies are left to relax and sweat for as long as they can stand it before being vigorously scrubbed by the *hammām* attendant using a '*Kassa*', a camel-hair scrubbing glove, then washed with black soap.

The experience of the hot room is more than that of just washing one's body. It is a congregational space where people sit on the marble

Figure 6.4 Hammām Malik al-Thaher, Damascus. Men relaxing and socializing in the changing room (*source*: the authors)

table under a vast pierced dome, with daylight filtering through the steam into the spaces, creating a surreal atmosphere. It is a space of reconciliation with one's body, where people move around in a state of semi-nakedness. It is also a space of social interaction and happy hours spent with family members and friends, and a space where children play freely with water.

The sequence of bathing spaces, their size and configuration and the relation between them, can vary from one country to another and from one historic era to another. The experience of the journey inside the *hammām*, however, remains more or less the same (Sibley 2006). The architecture of the *hammām*s of the Maghreb in general is less monumental than that of the Middle East and Egypt. They are simple utilitarian structures with some displaying outstanding features, such as those built in Morocco during the Merinide dynasty (1258–1465). The architecture of traditional Moroccan *hammām*s is reminiscent of the Roman *balnea* (Nielsen 1993; Al-Habashi 2006) and has remained so up until the present day. The same basic linear organization of three simple consecutive rooms with increasing temperatures – the cold (*frigidarium*), locally called *barrani*, the warm (*tepidarium*), locally called *wastani* (Figure 6.5), and the hot room (*calidarium*), locally called *dakhli* in Morocco or *Bayt al harrara* in Egypt (Figure 6.6) – still survives today and continues to be the prototype adopted for recently built

Figure 6.5 Hammām Sahib al-Tabaa', Tunis, al-wastani (*source*: the authors)

Figure 6.6 A Cairo *hammām*, the hot room (*source*: the authors)

structures. The historic *hammām*s of Cairo, however, present a very different organization of bathing spaces, with a cruciform hot room surmounted by a large pierced dome and one to two raised chambers containing small hot water pools, a feature that has managed to survive only in the Cairene *hammām*s.

The use of the *hammām* was traditionally regulated by firm rules and etiquette. These were observed by generations until the mid-1950s, when the population of the historic cities started to be replaced by families of rural origins migrating to the medinas (the old cities) in search of jobs and better living conditions. There are, however, still innate rules that provide a framework for what is considered as acceptable behaviour. *Hammām* attendants establish the codes for socially acceptable behaviour. As one of the *hammām* attendants in Tunis put it, 'it is not always easy to find a fine balance between the need to control clients and the fact that the *hammām* is a place for relaxation and well-being'. The quality of the service and the long-term relationship with the *hammām* attendants play an important role in the way customers prefer some *hammām*s to others, as expressed by some clients who explained that they have developed an attachment to a particular *hammām* from childhood to adulthood and are still dependent on the services of a particular attendant who has been working in their neighbourhood *hammām* for more than twenty-five years. The *hammām* provides an egalitarian space in the same ways as the mosque does. It receives poor and rich alike. Indeed, some *hammām*s have a flexible entrance fee to cater for those on low incomes. The *hammām* can also be booked by some families for a morning or an afternoon session as part of pre-wedding celebrations.

*Hammām*s are nowadays a major attraction for European tourists visiting Middle Eastern and North African historic cities. They represent a living heritage that is facilitating inter-cultural exchange and under-standing. During the authors' visit to the *hammām*s of Marrakesh in December 2008, European families who live in the courtyard houses in the medina have started to pay regular visits to the traditional *hammām* located in their neighbourhood. When interviewed by the authors, they explained that using the neighbourhood *hammām* was part of their attempt to understand the local Moroccan culture and integrate with local life. Although many touristic *hammām*s are proliferating within the *riad*s (large courtyard houses transformed into five-star lodging facilities within the historic city), these families preferred to share the genuine experience of the *hammām* and were made to feel welcome in mingling with the locals.

THE *HAMMĀM* AND THE WEST

The *hammām* has been a source of inspiration for many European artists, writers, photographers and film-makers. Nineteenth-century orientalist painters were particularly drawn to the *hammām* (Thornton 1992). It has been argued that their representations of the *hammām* pro-jected imperialist and masculinist erotic fantasies, promising to 'uncover and expose to the public gaze inner secrets of the forbidden and sacred' (Macmaster and Lewis 2004: 147). Male European orientalists, denied access to *hammām*s and other women-only spaces, turned to accounts by others, notably European women. In his book on the *Manners and*

Customs of Modern Egyptians (1978 [1860]), Edward Lane relied on his sister Sophia Lane's descriptions of the harem and the *hammām*. On this basis, he portrayed bathing as one of the greatest luxuries enjoyed by the people of Egypt, with between sixty and seventy *hammām*s or baths in Cairo alone (ibid.). Similarly, Ingres painted the famous *Turkish Bath* (1862), which now hangs in the Louvre in Paris, without ever travelling to the East. Instead, he worked from the French translation of Lady Mary Montagu's account of her visit to a *hammām* in the early eighteenth century. She emphasized the fact that there was no impropriety among the large crowd of bathers, but Ingres seems to have ignored this in his voyeuristic and fantastic depiction of sapphism. His other bath scenes also remain sexually suggestive. It is clear from many of these paintings that *hammām*s were misrepresented and misunderstood in a number of ways. In addition to over-sexualization of the *hammām*, distortions and inaccuracies appear in a number of other Western paintings of them. For instance, a large central pool is a recurrent feature displayed in many orientalist paintings such as *After the Bath* by Rudolf Ernest, *Bathing in the Seraglio* by Theodor Chasseriau, *Steam Bath*, the *Great Bath* and *Nargileh Lighter* by Jean-Léon Gérôme. Yet large pools are a rare feature in *hammām*s and, when available, they are much smaller and do not occupy a central position in the spaces. Indeed, large pools disappeared completely from the Roman bath as it was assimilated into the Islamic tradition of bathing.

The European representations were accurate in some respects, however, and are also positive – not just sexual fantasies or orientalist clichés. This is the case, for example, with Jules van Biesbroeck's painting *Entering the Hammām*, depicting the entrance to a *hammām* in Algiers, as experienced by Magda during her childhood. It portrays Algerian women wearing their traditional white veil, waiting with children in the *Skiffa* – the transitional space between the street and the entrance to the changing room. John Singer Sargent's painting *Ambergris Smoke* (completed in Tangiers in 1880) is another example of an accurate representation of a traditional practice linked to the *hammām*. The painting depicts the fumigation of a Moroccan woman, a process of perfuming the body but most importantly warding off the evil eye by stepping over the smoke of a small stove, burning incense. This practice still survives today, as was witnessed by Magda in July 2008 in the changing room of Hammām al-Halga in Tripoli. Similarly, Edward Lane's depiction of *hammām*s in Cairo is in many ways accurate and appreciative:

Many persons go to the bath twice a week: others, once a week, or less frequently ... The women who can afford to do so visit the *hammām* frequently; but not so often as the men. When the bath is not hired for the females of one family, or for one party of ladies, exclusively, women of all conditions are admitted. In general all the females of a house, and the young boys, go together. They take with them their own seggadehs, and the napkins, basins, etc., which they require, and even the necessary quantity of sweet water for washing with soap, and for drinking; and some carry with them fruits, sweet-meats, and other refreshments. (Lane 1978 [1860]: 314)

Europeans not only appreciated the *hammām*; they copied it, albeit through the lens of their own orientalist painters and writers, in the designs of private and municipal bathhouses throughout Europe (Mac-Kenzie 1995: 83). By 1861 small Turkish baths had opened in many towns and cities around the British Isles. Two famous large London establishments, Dr Barter's oriental baths in Victoria Street and David Urquhart's Jermyn Street *hammām*, were built as hybrid establishments with some Roman bath features such the dry hot-air rooms and the cold plunge pools, with the added shampooing and massage of the Turkish baths. It is important to highlight the fact that although they were called 'Turkish baths', only a very small section of these large buildings consisted of one or two components of a real Turkish bath, sometimes limited to a small steam room (www.victorianturkishbath.org).[1]

The European fascination with *hammām*s continued in the twentieth century, resulting in a number of detailed and valuable studies. In the 1930s and 1940s French scholars conducted valuable research on *hammām* architecture and social practices. Studies were carried out in Fez by Edmund Secret (1942) and Henri Terrasse (1950), in Cairo by Edmond Pauty (1933) and Pascal Coste (1839), and in Damascus by Ecochard and Le Coeur (1942). These studies represent a valuable and rare record of the architecture of many *hammām*s that have disappeared today or are in an advanced state of decay, such as Hammām Bashtak in Cairo (Figure 6.7). Later studies were carried out on the *hammām*s of Cairo in the 1960s by Andre Raymond (Raymond 1969) and more recently by Nicolas Warner (2002, 2005) and Martin Dow, who published a book on the Islamic baths of Palestine (Dow 1996).

A new generation of European *hammām*s has been built by and for North African immigrants, who originate in countries and cities in which this bathhouse culture is alive and well. The tradition and practice of going to the *hammām* on a regular basis (once a week) is still very much alive in North African cities, with the exception of Egypt, where

Figure 6.7 Hammām Bashtak, Cairo. The *hammām* is in an advanced state of dilapidation (*source:* the authors)

the tradition has almost vanished. Indeed, new public baths are still being built in almost all new neighbourhoods in cities such as Algiers, Casablanca, Tripoli and Tunis. Newly built *hammām*s are frequently attached to other modern facilities such as hairdressing, beauty treatment and fitness centres. They have become important centres of body treatment and wellness and have inspired the development of new structures in European cities such as Paris, Brussels and Amsterdam. These are not only attracting migrant communities of Moroccans, Algerians and Tunisians, they are also used by an increasing number of Europeans. The process of relaxing in the steam room, washing the body with black Moroccan soap, scrubbing the body with the *Kassa* and massaging it with argan oil, and beauty treatments using natural beauty products (traditionally associated with *hammām*s) such as henna and *Ghassoul* (a clay-based product used for hair and skin) have all become expensive luxuries advertised as part of the services offered in contemporary spas. Furthermore, different versions of the so-called 'Moroccan' *hammām*s are proliferating in five-star hotels, newly built health clubs and beauty salons.

In Europe the culture of bathing and the fashion of 'modern *hammām*s' are flourishing again. In France, Turkish-style baths are spreading in major cities and provide a much-needed break for weary city residents of all income levels. For Parisians, the *hammām* at La Mosquée de Paris in the fifth arrondissement, constructed in 1927, is the ultimate initiation into the seductive world of the *hammām*.

An Englishwoman tried the *hammām* for the first time in her life at the Paris Mosque *hammām*. She comments on her experience as follows:

> The scene that greeted us, however, as we stepped into the large vaulted atrium of the baths, was more like a sensual *Arabian Nights*. The high room, lavishly decorated with mosaic tiles and carved woodwork, filtered sunlight through stained glass and filigreed lanterns. Around the edges of the room, in various states of undress, lay women reclined on beds covered with cushions, sipping mint tea from tiny glasses, nibbling on pastries, laughing, whispering and drifting in and out of sleep. 'I feel like the Sultan may come at any moment.'

Another woman commented as follows:

> By the end of our all-over massages by capable and gentle North African women, we'd been heated, steamed, soaked and drenched. We'd been scrubbed and rubbed and scented with almond-scented oils. Our skin felt like velvet. But even better, we'd experienced just a small piece of Arabic culture in a female-centric atmosphere. As a character in the *Arabian Nights* says, 'Oh my lord! Verily the bath is the Paradise of this world.' (www.traveltowellness.com/parishammam)

The references to the *Arabian Nights* in these quotations indicate the survival of fantasies about the *hammām*, which are in some cases tinged with sexuality and sensuality, but they also admit to genuine admiration and appreciation of these spaces.

Moreover, the Western fascination with these bathhouses is nothing new. So-called 'Turkish baths' proliferated and were very popular in Victorian Britain, for instance, as Malcolm Shifrin has shown (www.victorianturkishbath.org). Few of these baths are still operating today; those that are include the Royal Turkish Baths of Harrogate, which were extensively restored in 2004, and Victoria Baths in Manchester, which include a 'Turkish baths' section and are also currently undergoing restoration. These restoration programmes reflect a broader renaissance of European *hammām*s, from Madrid to Vienna, London and Paris.

DECLINE, REVIVAL AND HOPE

The present revivial of *hammām*s in some countries comes in the wake of a period of decline, which has yet to be arrested in the Middle East, particularly Lebanon, Turkey, Syria, Palestine and Egypt. A number of factors have contributed to this. Threatened by recent interpretations of Islam, the *hammām* is seen as an immoral place, where partial nudity between people of the same gender is forbidden, considered *haram*, despite the role this institution has played for centuries in the conduct of major ablutions before prayer. Another factor is the association of the *hammām* with homosexuality, as depicted in a number of films, such as *Hammām Al Malatyali*, produced in Egypt in the 1970s, and the 1990s film directed by Ozpetek entitled *Hammām: The Turkish Bath*. These have contributed to the closure and rapid decline of a number of historic *hammām*s in Cairo as they become identified as immoral places (Fadli and Sibley 2008a).

The decline of the *hammām* has also been hastened by more practical factors. The introduction of modern bathroom facilities in private dwellings has reduced the need for public bathing. Road-building projects in historic urban centres have also led to the demolition of a significant number of baths throughout North Africa and the Middle East. Across North Africa, *hammām*s are generally in a poor state, and buildings are rarely listed as heritage assets. It is difficult to find any *hammām* that has benefited from a well-informed restoration programme, despite initiatives in a number of cities including Damascus (a private initiative) and Cairo (by the supreme Council of Antiquities) (ibid.).

European interest in the *hammām* is making a difference, though. Through the work of the international HAMMAM consortium, funded by the European Commission, local and international awareness of the importance of safeguarding *hammām* buildings has been raised and initiatives for the restoration and safeguarding of both the tangible and the intangible *hammām* heritage have been on the increase. In Damascus, Hammām Ammuna, a small neighbourhood *hammām* dating back to the fourteenth century, has been saved from closure. It has been bought by a local private investor, restored and reopened for women with new facilities including Jacuzzi, massage, hairdressing and beauty treatment. The *hammām* has become a focal point for the local community; its restoration and reopening have brought new hope and triggered new local initiatives for improving the urban environment of the historic neighbourhood in which it is located. Furthermore, our own work, funded by the Arts and Humanities Research Council in the UK, will provide valuable documentation of historic *hammām*s across the whole of North Africa, contributing to raising hopes for the survival of this valuable Islamic city facility.

The *hammām* continues to be used by different members of society,

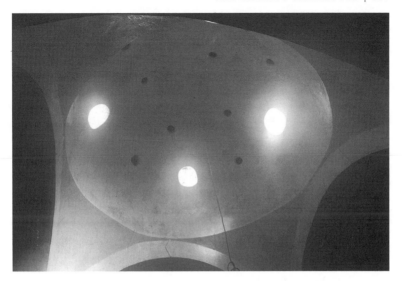

Figure 6.8 Hammām Sahib al-Tabaa', Tunis, the dome (*source*: the authors)

people from different cultures and religions. It has resisted colonization, acculturation and globalization, but at the same time it has proved adaptable, reinventing itself in different times and places. The *hammām* or Turkish bath was and is still a link between European and Muslim societies. It is the perfect expression of a 'democratic' space encapsulating socio-cultural sharing. Hence, it is not only a facility linked to the Islamic city but also a living cultural heritage spanning time, geography, religion and ethnicity. The *hammām* is not simply a place in which Muslims and others come together in a literal sense, but rather a space that both these groups find appealing, and are able to imagine as one of the rare remaining multicultural utopian spaces: a space of hope.

NOTES

This work would not have been possible without financial support from the European Union and the (British) Arts and Humanities Research Council (AHRC), through the following research grants: European Union: 'HAMMAM – Hammam, Aspects and Multidisciplinary Methods of Analysis for the Mediterranean Region', FP6-2003-INCO-MPC-2, Contract Number: 517704, Coordinator: Oikodrom; The Vienna Institute for Urban Sustainability; AHRC: 'The Historic Hammāms of North Africa, and their survival into the 21st century'.

1 Other websites containing useful information on *hammām*s include: www.cyberbohemia.com//pages/Islahammam.htm and www.archnet.org/library.

REFERENCES

Al-Habashi, A. (2006) 'Restoration for site presentation: the ruins of the Idrissid Bath in Volubilis, Morocco', in *Proceedings of Conference: Conservation in Changing Societies: Heritage and Development*, Raymond Lemaire International Centre for Conservation, Katholieke Universiteit Leuven, Belgium, pp. 267–76.

Al-Manawī, A. R. (1987) 'al Nuzha al Zahiya fi Ahkam al Hammām al Shar'iya wa al Tibiya' [Health and religious jurisprudence in *hammām* manners], Cairo: Al-Dar al Misriya al-Lubnaniya.

Benkheira, M. H. (2007) 'Hammām, nudité et ordre moral dans l'Islam médiéval', *Revue de l'Histoire des Religions*, April, rhr.revues.org/document5303.html.

Bouhdiba, A. (1964) 'Le hammām, contribution à une psychanalyse de l'Islam', *Revue Tunisienne des Sciences Sociales*, 1 September, pp. 7–14.

Coste, P. (1839) *Architecture Arabe ou Monuments du Kaire; Mesurés et dessinés de 1818 à 1825*, Paris: l'Institut de France.

Dow, M. (1996) *The Islamic Baths of Palestine*, Oxford and Jerusalem: Oxford University Press for the British School of Archaeology.

Ecochard, M. and C. Le Coeur (1942) *Les Bains de Damas*, Beirut: Institut Français de Damas.

Fadli, F. and M. Sibley (2008a) 'The historic hammāms of Cairo: safeguarding a vanishing heritage', *Journal of Architectural Conservation*, 14(3), November.

— (2008b) 'The restoration of hammāms in Cairo: how sustainable is it?', Paper presented at Heritage 2008 International Conference, Portugal, 7–9 May.

Lane E. W. (1978 [1860]) *An Account of the Manners and Customs of Modern Egyptians: Written in Egypt during the Years 1833–1835*, The Hague and London: East-West Publications.

Lassoued, M. R. (1987) 'Hammāmāt madinate Tarabulss', *a-Tarabulss al-Qadima*, 3, May.

MacKenzie, J. M. (1995) *Orientalism: History, Theory and the Arts*, Manchester: Manchester University Press.

Macmaster, N. and T. Lewis (2004) 'Orientalism: from unveiling to hyperveiling', in H. Moghissi, *Women and Islam: Critical Concepts in Sociology*, London: Routledge.

Mohammed, S. M. (1983) *Al Hamamate al-Islamiya fi al Kahira el Kadima* [Islamic *hammām*s of historic Cairo], Unpublished PhD thesis, University of Cairo.

Nielsen, I. (1993) *Thermae et Balnea: The Architecture and Cultural History of Roman Public Baths*, Aarhus: Aarhus University Press.

Pauty, E. (1933) *Les Hammāms du Caire*, Cairo: L'Institut Français d'Archéologie Orientale du Caire (IFAO).

Raymond, A. (1969) 'Les bains publics au Caire à la fin du XVIII siècle', *Annales Islamologiques*, 8.

— (1978) 'La localisation des bains publics au Caire a l'époque otto-mane', *Bulletin d'Etudes Orientales*, 30, pp. 347–60.

— (2002) 'Les caractéristiques d'une ville Arabe moyenne au XVIII siècle', in *Arab Cities in the Otto-man Period*, Variorum Collected Studies Series, Aldershot: Ashgate.

Saadaoui, A. (2003) 'Les bains pub-lics de Tunis à l'époque ottomane',

Revue Tunisienne des Sciences Sociales, 40(12).

Secret, E. (1942) 'Les hammams de Fès', *Bulletin de l'Institut d'Hygiène du Maroc*, NS 2, reprinted in E. Secret (1990), *Les Sept Printemps de Fès*, Tours: Impression Aps.

Sibley, M. (2006) 'The historic hammāms of Damascus and Fez: lessons of sustainability and future developments', in C. Compagnon, P. Haefeli and W. Weber (eds), *Proceedings of the 23rd International Conference on Passive and Low Energy Architecture (PLEA)*, Geneva: Imprimerie St Paul Fribourg, pp. 81–6.

— (2007) 'Pre-Ottoman public baths of Damascus and their survival into the 21st century: an analytical survey', *Journal of Architectural and Planning Research*, 24(4).

Sibley, M. and F. Fadli (2008) 'The surviving historic hammāms of the medina of Tripoli, Libya: tangible and intangible dimensions', *International Journal of Architectural Research*, 2(3).

Terrasse, H. (1950) 'Trois bains mérinides du Maroc', in *Mélanges offerts à William Marçais par l'Institut d'Études Islamiques de l'Université de Paris*, Paris: Éditions G.-P. Maisonneuve.

Thornton, L. (1992) *Women as Portrayed in Orientalist Painting*, Paris: Art Creation Realisation.

Warner, N. (2002) 'Taking the plunge: the development and use of the Cairene bathhouse', in J. Edwards (ed.), *Historians in Cairo, Essays in Honor of George Scanlon*, Cairo: American University in Cairo Press.

— (2005) *The Monuments of Historic Cairo*, Cairo: American University in Cairo Press.

7 | Making space for Muslims: housing Bangladeshi families in East London

AYONA DATTA

This chapter shifts the focus from public to private spaces and from larger to more intimate Muslim geographies. It argues that homes – including affordable homes for lower-income families – can be refashioned as spaces of hope, which acknowledge and accommodate Muslims in nuanced ways: not simply as one-dimensional figures, but as individuals and communities with complex and multiple identities and positionalities.

Hitherto, debates about multiculturalism and efforts to produce more convivial forms of multiculturalism have revolved largely around streets and other public spaces (Gilroy 2006). The presence of ethnic shops, restaurants and marketplaces, for example, is frequently cited as evidence of cosmopolitanism (see Appiah 2006). In Western countries with multicultural agendas, planning regulations and building permits actively create and celebrate places in which ethnic and racial groups might mix, such as London's Brick Lane, with its curry houses and 'Banglatown' street signage. Meanwhile, narratives of multiculturalism have much less to say about private spaces such as the home, even though these spaces are also crucially important in the production and performance of cultural identities. With the right designs and layouts, homes are capable of accommodating national, ethnic and religious identities, enabling groups to remain distinct – to nurture their own identities and cultural practices – while negotiating the demands placed upon them to participate within multicultural cities and societies. This lays a burden on architects, who must not only respect the architectural histories and values of cities and neighbourhoods, but must also learn to understand and respond to the complex identities of the changing communities, families and individuals they are working for. With respect to Muslims, this means understanding the complex ways in which religious, ethnic, gendered and class-based identities intersect. In East London, for instance, this is crucial since its British Muslims largely belong to one specific linguistic group of Bangladeshis.

The case of one affordable housing scheme largely designed and built for a Bangladeshi tenant population in East London illustrates how architects do take into account some of the positionalities of class and ethno-national origin among British Muslims, even though others, such as those of gender relations, often remain unacknowledged. I shall suggest that the cultural and gender practices of Bangladeshi Muslims correspond to the specificities of their particular spatial locations and geopolitical histories that, while remaining distinct, also presuppose certain Islamic values and ideologies. Thus the intersectionalities of their ethnic, gendered, national and racial identities with a wider British Muslim identity in a multicultural Britain allow them to articulate particular uses of domestic spaces and hence spatial boundaries of private and public within the home, while at the same time articulating how these spaces provide them with a new 'respectability' as British Muslims.

This chapter, an in-depth study of affordable housing tenants in Tower Hamlets, East London, draws upon the findings of a research project. The study was conducted during 2002/03 when East London was experiencing an increase in the building of affordable housing estates. The study incorporated in-depth interviews with the participants living in these estates in three sites, including Pritchard's Road, the subject of this chapter, which is a small development of just eleven terraced houses accommodating tenants decanted from a demolished council tower block. Most of these tenants knew each other from before, and apart from one Somalian family, all of them were Muslims who could trace their roots to the Sylhet district in Bangladesh. The interviews were intended to discuss how these tenant families perceived the new architecture of affordable housing, their sense of belonging, constructions of cultural identity, and notions of differences that were produced from inhabiting these new spaces. Most of these interviews were carried out in Bengali apart from those with second-generation Bangladeshi participants, who spoke in English. As a native speaker of Bengali, I also translated and transcribed these interviews. The narratives of these participants alongside architectural drawings and design reports highlight the fluid ways in which participants used their identities to negotiate the domestic spaces of affordable housing. These identities were not necessarily 'Muslim' per se; rather a more complex nexus of cultural beliefs and practices that drew upon a range of subjectivities – religion, ethnicity, linguistic heritage, class and gender – as they intersected with a variety of spaces and places in East London.

BANGLADESHI/BENGALI MUSLIM IDENTITIES IN BRITAIN AND THE WEST

As many other contributors to this book have stressed, Muslims in Western countries such as Britain are not a homogenous group. Rather, they belong to diverse social, cultural, regional, national, linguistic and ethnic backgrounds, and many can trace their histories to Asia, Africa and the Middle East. The increasing attention to Muslims within debates about multiculturalism is partly due to the ways in which religion has become a key marker of identity in contemporary British society, as well as a wider global politics that sees Muslims across the world as the victims in Western societies. Bangladeshi Muslims too have been drawn into this notion of religious multiculturalism, although they simultaneously practise other aspects of their identities.

Bangladeshi and Bengali are not mutually exclusive categories. Both are also identified loosely under a notion of 'Asian' identity in Britain, as collectives that can trace their roots to the Indian subcontinent (Brah 1996). Bangladeshi and Bengali Muslim identities in Britain are part of multifaceted and context-specific constructs, within class, religion, caste and language, as well as particular colonial and post-colonial histories. Bangladeshis began arriving in UK in the 1950s when men from Sylhet who were working with the British merchant navy started taking low-paid jobs in catering industries (Kabeer 1991). These Bangladeshi immigrants, most of whom were from families of small rural landowners, who spoke the Bengali dialect known as Sylheti, settled mainly in the East London borough of Tower Hamlets, where they found jobs in a range of low-paid sectors, including catering and clothing, and subsequently sponsored their family and members of kinship networks and villages to join them in the UK.

Bangladeshi refers to a national identity that is linked to Bengali ethnic and cultural practices – but these identities are also part of important colonial and post-colonial histories and geopolitics. Formed along religious lines out of the partition of the state of Bengal consequent upon Indian independence in 1947, Bengal's Hindu majority areas were absorbed within India, while the Muslim majority areas that were ceded to Pakistan came to be known as East Pakistan. Over the years, the larger state of Pakistan enacted a series of laws and restrictions that attempted to replace the Bengali language and cultural traditions with what was understood as an 'authentic' Islamic identity. Resistance against such measures in East Pakistan led to state repression and large-scale human rights violations. Bangladesh as it is known now received independence from Pakistan in 1971 and established itself as a secular state. Kabeer (ibid.) argues that it is this problematic relationship between state and religion in Bangladesh which produces ambivalences within the Bengali Muslim collective consciousness. Its separation from Pakistan in 1971 brought about a notion that while its Islamic beliefs and Bengali culture were central to its unique identity in the Indian subcontinent, its geopolitical histories had prevented these two positionalities from being reconciled simultaneously as part of a Bengali identity in Bangladesh. On the other hand, as Bangladeshis arrived in the UK, increased racism during the 1960s and 1970s encouraged them to join faith-based community groups which prioritized religious identities over class and ethnic identities among minorities in British society. Thus, London's Bangladeshi population in Tower Hamlets found a new respectability as Muslims – whereby they increasingly distanced themselves from the earlier syncretic 'folk' versions of Islam in Bangladesh to construct an 'authentic' scriptural identity as Bangladeshi Muslims in the UK (Eade et al. 2002).

For the second-generation Bangladeshis in Tower Hamlets whom Eade (1996) calls 'Cockney Bengalis', these identities are further enacted within the wider cultural politics of race and religion in contemporary Britain, which overlaps with the politics of deprivation in Tower Hamlets. In recent years, second-generation Bangladeshi youth has increasingly identified with a growing Islamic interpretation of Bangladeshi nationalism, global politics of Islam, and a collective consciousness of being Muslims in the West (ibid.). As Modood (2007) notes, this is part of a broader pattern also observed in other groups of Muslims living in the UK.

These complex politics of identification among Bangladeshi Muslims and of differences constructed with non-Muslims from the Indian subcontinent produce particular performances of gender within public and private realms. While traditionally Islamic architecture relied on the strict separation of men and women in public places, in the home this separation was delineated along gendered and family lines. Particularly in the rural areas of Bangladesh, women still practise purdah, which refers not just to the veil covering one's head but also the visual and physical separation of the men's and women's domains in the home – whereby only male family members are allowed to enter the women's quarters. Such separations can be seen to define women as 'transmitters of religious cultural identity and markers of group identity' (Mohammad 1999), which, through their focus on women's bodies and the psyche – visually, spatially and temporally – incorporate them into an architectural language of privacy and domesticity. In the UK, such ideas among South Asian Muslims are reinforced through the notion of an 'others' other' (ibid.), whereby the values and practices of a white English and largely Christian population are seen to be in conflict with the gendered codes inscribed within Islam. These 'Islamic' values of modesty and women's honour are often reinforced by religious leaders in mosques and madrasas (religious schools) and enacted within both public and private realms.

These translations of spatial codes from religious, cultural and largely rural identities from Bangladesh into racialized, working-class and increasingly Islamicized identities in Tower Hamlets have led to ambiguous connections between national origin, religious affiliation and ethnicity in ways that produce particular perceptions and negotiations of domestic architecture among Bangladeshi Muslims in Tower Hamlets.

HOUSING BANGLADESHIS IN EAST LONDON

Long before the Bangladeshis arrived in East London, it had been imagined as a 'place of dreadful danger' where prostitution and sexual danger were rampant on its streets (Walkowitz 1992). East London, with its dockyards, journeymen and smugglers, was constructed as the dark side of London – a place of crime and immorality (Hobbs 2006). Such perceptions were briefly challenged through Young and Wilmott's (1957) depiction of the survival of white working-class communities and kinship within East London – the existence of spaces of hope in terms of solidarities and continuities. Historical discourses of East London, however, have always focused on issues of overcrowding and deviancy in the area.

During the post-war period, programmes of slum clearance received a boost in East London and were implemented by the construction of a large number of council housing estates in Tower Hamlets – one of its most deprived boroughs. During the 1970s and 1980s large-scale deindustrialization saw those among the Bangladeshi population who had been engaged in blue-collar work in the textile industries losing their jobs and depending on state benefits. Although at this time social housing tenants were largely white working-class, the numbers among the Bangladeshi population receiving housing benefits slowly began to increase. The rise in unemployment and poverty in the area required more and more council housing to be built over the subsequent years and it reached a peak of 74 per cent of total housing in the area in 1987 (Tower Hamlets 2002). In the decades after the war, the architecture of council housing (tower blocks) and public perceptions of the 'stigma' of dismal and overcrowded living conditions dominated the landscape of Tower Hamlets.

Council housing in Tower Hamlets and elsewhere in Britain was built as the pinnacle of modernity during the post-war years through an efficient and functional rationalization of spatial layouts (Llewelyn 2004). These were based on modernist architectural principles of healthy, efficient and functional living with adequate light and air in each room, which were legislated through a series of reports produced by the British government (Datta 2006). Such layouts were achieved through the design of independent flats stacked one upon the other, with clearly delineated spaces for kitchen, bedroom, living room and bathroom, which led to the form of tower blocks. These were places where most Bangladeshi families were housed from the 1970s and where they formed strong community networks with other Bangladeshi families.

'A new architectural language' In the late 1990s regeneration fever took hold of Tower Hamlets. In attempts to break from its past and attract a new generation of residents and investors, much of the architecture of the tower blocks began to be dismantled. A large stock of council housing was transferred to Registered Social Landlords (RSLs), and private landlords, and refurbished, or demolished and then rebuilt (Malpass 2001). Although much higher in the past, at present council housing is no longer the dominant tenure (36 per cent compared with nearly 74 per cent in 1987), while the RSLs have increased their stock from 8 per cent in 1987 to 20 per cent in 2000 (Tower Hamlets 2002). Further, fifteen council tower blocks have been demolished since 1986 and their tenants housed in low-density housing estates, many of which have been built by the RSLs. Social housing in London (which includes both council housing and that provided by RSLs), however, has its highest concentration in Tower Hamlets, with 42 per cent of households in this borough living in such accommodation (Goodchild and Cole 2001).

In 1995, one such RSL, the Peabody Trust, and its architects began to explore a framework of 'modular' plan-types for houses, which were meant to be easily adapted to specific projects, and replicated on different scales, thus reducing costs for both the Trust and its tenants. At the heart of the design was the concept of a house with a garden that could range from three-bedroom to five-bedroom units. The design was based on the London terraced houses, which were reworked to 'satisfy contemporary social housing standards and meet the needs and aspirations of the current tenant population' (Peabody Trust, personal communication, 5 August 2002), which was understood to be largely ethnic minority families. One of the main criteria was 'to avoid the mistakes of earlier social housing in failing to cater for the different needs of Asian families which tended to be larger'.[1]

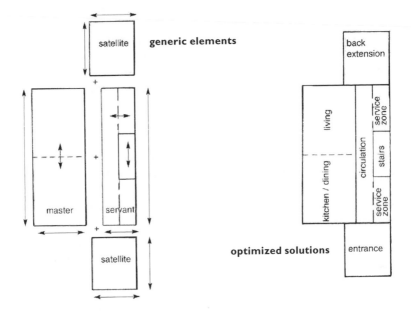

Figure 7.1 Adoption of Georgian layout to new social housing (*source*: Peabody Trust)

The architects based their designs upon model dwellings for 'families', and the 'qualities of traditional Georgian and Victorian terraced houses in urban settings' (HTA Architects 2002). In designing the houses they 'combined optimum space standards, quality materials, and simple elegance to create an aesthetic for social housing which also attracts shared ownership and private buyers' (ibid.). This design distances itself from the functionalist element of earlier council housing to provide for a spatial layout that reinforces the legacy of Georgian and Victorian homes in East London, adapting them to suit the demands of large 'Asian' families. This house crucially also has a garden – an essential component of Victorian 'respectability' (Madanipour 2003).

Georgian and Victorian terraced houses, which form most of the older housing stock in Tower Hamlets, reflect the politics of public and private divisions within the home in the West. Georgian terraced houses usually consist of a front room and a back room connected through a corridor with the stairs on one side of the rear of the plot. This means that on the upper floors the front room can take up the whole width of the plot. These rooms also allow some functional separation between different activities – cooking, eating, socializing and sleeping. This system of stacking rooms made it flexible enough to fit houses to the varying lengths and widths of different plots, which made Georgian layouts so popular until the nineteenth century, and part of the reason why they can be revived in the Peabody Trust housing. Crucially, as Madanipour (2003) notes, Georgian layouts allow for spatial demarcation of different activities on different floors.

Victorian architectural layouts, however, offer much stricter separation between the private and public. They reflect the emergence of nuclear families during the nineteenth century, which produced a strong family ethic. The increasing social hierarchies and economic inequalities during industrialization that set forth clear separations between working- and middle-class areas were also translated into hierarchies within model families – in the order of men as head of households, women as homemakers, children and servants, each obedient to those above them in this domestic social order (ibid.). Spaces within homes were clearly designed to delineate boundaries between the family and servants, between children and parents and between siblings of opposite sexes. These manifested themselves in distinct room functions – drawing room, dining room, kitchen, bedroom, living room and so on, and through these a clear delineation of private and public realms within the home. The architects working for the Peabody Trust thus combined these divisions of public/private in Victorian layouts with the flexibility of the Georgian stacking of rooms and floors. Their sketches (Figure 7.1) illustrate how the zoning of the home through master, servant and satellite areas becomes a metaphor for the hierarchies in the use and function of different rooms.

Pritchard's Road estate was built in 2001 using this modular concept – a series of houses placed along a terrace; their vibrant colours making a visual rhythm along the street, while their front gardens convey an aura of Victorian respectability. The houses accommodate three to five bedrooms in keeping with the requirements of large families. The unusual 'hybridity' of the plan between Georgian and Victorian layouts, though, means that the living room is accommodated on the first floor over the kitchen and corridor. The dining room and kitchen are on the ground floor with the latter at the front of the building, which is meant to allow for visual access to the street while in the kitchen. The utility area is meant to be flexible for use as a bedroom with an en suite bathroom at a later stage for a less able-bodied person.

Thus the architects conceived of Pritchard's Road not simply for British Muslim families but rather as a space sensitive to the changing demands of larger ethnic minority families in Tower Hamlets. The

Figure 7.2 Terraced house on Pritchard's Road (*source*: author)

architectural conceptualization of domesticity in these layouts was varied – gender sensitivity in the provision of a kitchen looking on to the street, flexibility in terms of increasing family needs over time, as well as a sensitivity towards the needs of the elderly, who are often cared for in these families. Of the eleven four- and five-bedroom houses in Pritchard's Road, nine were rented to Bangladeshi Muslim families, while the other two were rented to Afro-Caribbean families.

'RESPECTABLE' CITIZENS

These conceived spaces of Pritchard's Road estate, designed by the architects and built by Peabody Trust, were experienced and negotiated very differently across the Bangladeshi Muslim tenant population. While for most of them the house with a garden made a significant break with their long relationship with tower blocks, much of their move was narrated also as a break from deeply embedded social networks in these tower blocks.

For the first-generation Bangladeshi Muslims, East London had been their home since they had arrived in the UK, but much of their social network had been built around activities and everyday practices that were collectively enacted with other Bangladeshi immigrants they had encountered in the streets, workplaces, mosques and in their tower blocks. Over the years, their transnational connections with Bangladesh and with other Bangladeshis across the world have been strengthened through these networks, which have maintained Bangladesh as the homeland and Tower Hamlets as an immigrant home. This did not mean that they did not maintain local connections – on the contrary, they continued to be involved in local businesses, mosque activities and festivals in Tower Hamlets. Yet this involvement was conducted within a transnational space – through the mobilization of transnational networks from the home to the neighbourhood to the homeland.

For the second generation, though, the connection to Bangladesh was often a cultural one. Many of their networks and friendships were not necessarily through transnational ties to Bangladesh but through their schools, universities and workplaces in Tower Hamlets, where they had significant memories from their childhood. Many of these memories were not pleasant – second-generation participants narrated racist encounters involving being spat at, being escorted home by teachers from school during riots, and insensitive remarks from white English friends after the 9/11 terrorist attacks. Yet parallel to these there were also narratives of hope – of the changes taking place in Tower Hamlets, its multiculturalism, which is now being perceived by the rest of the city as its strength, and the changing nature of architecture in the borough. Thus second-generation participants positioned themselves as being 'at home' in Tower Hamlets.

> It's just you are born here, and you just like the noise, there is something about it. I know there are a lot of bad things happening, but it's home for us. It's my home. My parents don't feel the same way. But with us, like when people ask us where are you from? With my parents they will straight away say Bangladesh, but with me I will say East End, Bethnal Green. (Razia)

Razia, a young Bangladeshi Muslim student living with her parents and siblings in Pritchard's Road, suggests that belonging is complexly connected with national origins and place associations. The differences in belonging between her parents and herself highlight how home is constructed through territorial loyalties that intersect with generation, nationality and ethnicity. As she was a second-generation British Muslim,

Razia's identity was spatially constructed as being 'rooted' in the East End of London; her layering of spatial and social identities relied upon the differential experiences that identity formation brought about. In this context of transformation in Tower Hamlets, the construction of identities forms part of participants' efforts to negotiate through a new architectural language that distances itself from tower blocks. This new language makes a clear break with the past – from the social stigma of high-rise estates and crime to spaces of hope within terraced houses with front and rear gardens. These terraced houses mark them not as social housing tenants but as newly 'respectable' Tower Hamlets citizens. This was even more significant in an area where their neighbouring housing was still largely tower blocks – their physical locations amid this older council housing produced a perception of privilege and pride in their own social positions. As Razia noted,

> You know when people say, 'Oh, you are from Tower Hamlets' and they will think you live in a dump. So when they see your houses like that you feel proud of it. (Razia)

This perception was partly related to the sheer physical appearance of these houses in the ways that they were different from other council housing and partly to the ways in which this design then transformed the 'negative' uses of its architectural spaces. As Kamran notes:

> It's designed like a house which is good which is not an estate. I think it makes a difference that it is not an estate, I don't know why but it does, doesn't it? I think in an estate you would get more people, obviously more children, what have you, whereas this area because it's not an estate there is not any space for children or for people to gather around and make a nuisance of themselves. (Kamran)

For Kamran, a second-generation Bangladeshi Muslim who grew up in Tower Hamlets, the estate's spaces of collective use – the communal stairs and gardens – were reflective of particular types of uses that often lead to teenage crime. The terraced house, on the other hand, does not provide for communal spaces and thus transforms social relationships from the communal to the private scale. The row of terraced houses then represents a 'positive' environment for many participants since it responds to the needs of the family and erases negative uses specifically associated with tower blocks.

Kitchen as an ethnic space A characteristic feature of these homes was the generous size and position of the kitchen within the house, which was meant to respond to the cultural practices of food preparation of ethnic minority families. While the house with a garden symbolized significant transformations in their self-identification, the layout and position of the kitchens in these houses mobilized identification with particular racialized and ethnic identities in relation to the West.

> As an Asian you would like your bathroom big or kitchen big or whatever. So if you go to an older house and see the kitchen they are literally about box size but now they are large. I like that. (Kamran)

For Kamran, as a second-generation Bangladeshi, this preference for a larger kitchen defines his identity as a British Muslim with links to particular cultural practices as an Asian. Kamran does not cook himself – this is a practice enacted by his mother and his wife; but he notes that Asians are different in that they do not prepare 'microwave meals' like the English, and therefore require larger food preparation and cooking areas. Hence the desire for a larger kitchen or bathroom is understood as a distinct 'Asian' preference, which connects to a diverse range of social and religious groups from the Indian subcontinent.

The generous sizes of the rooms in the house were also perceived by the participants as maintaining the spatial boundaries that were desired and expected between family members. This included the more intimate sleeping and relaxation areas for the family. The separation between male and female bodies in space through discrete rooms for each person and for different activities was constitutive of the private space allotted to each family member. The size of the houses, then, was a common topic of discussion when referring to such particularities.

> This is a dream house for us. It's got space, we always wanted a garden and we have our own rooms. We are not living on top of each other like we used to do before. The garden is the pride of my parents; they have done so much to it. We love the kitchen ... it's massive, look at it. We can have a party in it. (Razia)

The suggestion that the entire family 'loved' the kitchen suggests that for both Razia and Kamran, the size and layout of the kitchen were perceived as responding to the ethnic aspect of their identity over a gendered aspect. Although food preparation was primarily enacted by the women in the family, it was also seen by the men as responding to the needs of the family to eat healthy meals. The garden, on the other hand, was often used by first-generation Bangladeshi participants as a place for food cultivation rather than for leisure. Razia's parents noted that this reminded them of their days back in Sylhet, where land was always used to grow food. Razia's mother, like other Bangladeshi women in the Pritchard's Road estate, had started growing food in her garden – tomatoes, chillies and other herbs and vegetables that she used in her everyday cooking.

Kitchen as gendered space While second-generation participants used a variety of identities – Asian, British-Bangladeshi or British-Asian – to reflect their multiple locations and intersectionalities with a larger Muslim subjectivity, they rarely discussed their use and perception of the house through gendered or religious positionalities. Muslim identities were narrated through their relationships with wider urban, national and global spaces – through their political participation in various Islamic organizations, their everyday religious activities in mosques, education in Islamic schools, and membership of various faith-based community collectives. In all of this, it was a 'Bangladeshi' identity which was articulated – one that presupposed a Muslim identity that remained implicit in all conversations. Although none of the participants explicitly discussed religion as affecting their use of domestic spaces, religious values and practices remained relevant, on the basis of which they discoursed gender and ethnic identities within domestic space.

The intersectionalities of Asian, Bangladeshi and Bengali identities with Muslim identities provided participants with ways to articulate spatial boundaries within their domestic space. These boundaries were as much between bodies of different family members in the ways that they appreciated having their own rooms, but more significantly in the separation between men and women, family members and outsiders, in the house. Such boundaries overlapped with perceptions of private and public realms translated from participants' domestic spaces in Sylhet, as well as their memories of previously occupied council housing, where the living room was at the front of the house. This spatial knowledge of the separation of the public and private overlapped with their traditional ideas concerning the separation of gendered realms within the house – a practice that was not possible within the new architectural layouts. The positioning of the living room on the first floor and the kitchen and dining room on the ground floor in the Pritchard's Road houses meant that visitors to these houses had to pass through the food preparation areas and walk through most of the house before they reached the living room. This was noted by Nasir Mia as insensitive to their everyday spatial practices of cooking and entertaining guests.

Design is a bit different. If the front side had the front room and the back had the kitchen then for our practical use, for guests and relatives, everything, it would have been good. We could have sat there in the front room. When the guests come they see her [the wife] cooking, it's a problem. (Nasir Mia)

For Nasir Mia, a first-generation Bangladeshi Muslim from Sylhet, the overt narratives of private and public realms were constructed around the separation between the spaces of food production and entertaining, between the kitchen and living room, and between women's and men's domestic roles. Nasir Mia constructed the home around more traditional and Islamic ideas of separation of men's and women's realms, whereby women in his home would not be in the presence of men unless they were part of the family. While Nasir Mia described the 'public' gaze on his wife as an encroachment into her 'private' act of food preparation, his narrative also suggests a more pragmatic desire of separating guests from women's workspaces in the home. This desire for separation was constructed not simply through his Muslim identity, but also through a more complex cultural link with the practices of gendered domestic privacy in Sylhet.

Such constructions of public and private that corresponded to male and female bodies in particular spaces became critical in the use and negotiation of spatial boundaries within the home. For some women, however, such divisions corresponded to efficiently enacting their gendered domestic roles within the home. A lack of pragmatism in the design of the home was seen as a gendered problem, and significantly also as an ethnic divide between the designers and the users of this home.

I think women will do it [design] more beautiful than men. Because I think women know more about the home than men do. They know better about tidying, and decorating, and about privacy. We would think it's better that dining and living room are together. When children are studying, I can watch while cooking. I would have put the kitchen at the back, and the living room in the front. So that when guests come, then they first enter the living room. As a Bengali it's very difficult. I think men designed this house. They are not aware of how it is to work in a kitchen, what the difficulties are. (Majeeda)

Majeeda, a first-generation Bangladeshi Muslim widow with three children, perceives architecture as a 'masculine' practice at odds with women's 'expert' knowledge of domestic work. Further, Majeeda's articulation of an 'authentic' Bengali desire for a particular type of privacy within the home differentiates between the domestic spatial practices of English and Bengalis. Significant is Majeeda's assertion of her 'Bengali' identity – a positionality that implicitly links Bengali cultural practices and Bangladeshi origins to notions of privacy relating to Muslim women's bodies and spaces within the home. These intersectional positionalities of Nasir Mia and Majeeda are reflective of the perceptions of the nature of boundaries that should exist between kitchen, living room, dining room and other areas within the house.

SPACES OF HOPE?

Pritchard's Road housing illustrates the complex relationships between Bangladeshi Muslims and architecture; how spatial divisions, especially of public and private, are constructed by inhabiting the new domestic architecture; and how meanings and values associated with a diversity of Muslim positionalities are mapped on to architectural layouts to produce new perceptions of domestic space and of themselves. The architecture of Pritchard's Road was produced by its architects and Social Landlords from particular assumptions of domestic life in Tower Hamlets, which established links with the architectural history of the area, and the perceived spatial practices of a largely Bangladeshi Muslim tenant population. The designers repeated, relocated and translated earlier built forms and layouts in such ways that the domestic spaces of East London could be appropriated, transformed, rehistoricized and read anew. The designs, however, provided a new language of respectability for the tenants as British Muslims and as residents of East London. Through the transformation of architectural layouts (such as the terraced façade, the kitchen, the garden and the living rooms) in relation to each other, the negotiations of the Muslim subject in occupying these spaces, and the articulation of multiple Muslim identities, the architecture of affordable housing made Bangladeshi Muslims optimistic about their future in Tower Hamlets – a place that had earlier been pathologized in public imagination.

On the other hand, the perceptions of public and private separations inside the house produced more complex constructions of Muslim identities. As they negotiated through their newly acquired houses, as they moved from tower blocks to large family houses, as they used the gardens for growing food, as they enacted their everyday domestic practices, the participants perceived the unusual layouts of the houses through differences between a range of equally significant identities – as men and women, as mothers and young adults, as Asians, Bengalis and Bangladeshis. Muslim identities were implicitly woven into these through the insistence on the separation between male and female bodies, and consequently the separation between food preparation and guest reception areas. Yet the appreciation of other domestic spaces such as the large kitchen and the kitchen garden, and the perceived aesthetic qualities of the home, also drew upon other positionalities of race, ethnicity, class and their own geopolitical histories.

Thus the public/private tensions perceived by Bangladeshi participants, I argue, is not based on religious practice so much as on a notion of ethnic or diasporic difference that Bangladeshi Muslims constructed with reference to the 'other' that is the English. This reinforces the nature of difference that exists between categories of male and female among Muslim families from Bangladesh, but from a position of ethnic preference. This difference presupposes a Muslim identity; but in the discourses of everyday spatial practices and interactions with domestic spaces, it is the self-which-is-Bengali that precedes the self-which-is-Muslim. Through its attention to the Bangladeshi community in the UK, this challenges essentialist perceptions of Muslim identities and suggests that religion is only one part of their identity, which also includes gender, ethnicity and race. This architecture of affordable housing also invites residents to feel and continue to negotiate spaces for themselves, from where they are able to construct a sense of belonging and feel 'at home' in cities such as London.

NOTES

I am infinitely grateful to the participants of Pritchard's Road estate in Tower Hamlets who gave time to answering my questions. I am also grateful to the Peabody Trust for providing me with all the background information about the design conceptualization.

1 The average size of Asian families in Tower Hamlets is 4.3 members as against white families with 1.8 members.

REFERENCES

Appiah, K. A. (2006) *Cosmopolitanism: Ethics in a World of Strangers*, London: Penguin.

Brah, A. (1996) *Cartographies of Diaspora: Contesting Identities*, London: Routledge.

Datta, A. (2006) 'From tenements to flats: gender, class, and modernisation in Bethnal Green Estate', *Social and Cultural Geography*, 7(5).

— (2009) 'Places of everyday cosmopolitanisms: East European construction workers in London', *Environment and Planning*, 41(2).

Eade, J. (1996) *Living the Global City: Globalization as a Local Process*, London: Routledge.

Eade, J., I. Fremeaux and D. Garbin (2002) 'The political construction of diasporic communities in the global city', in P. K. Gilbert (ed.), *Imagined Londons*, New York: Suny Press.

Gilroy, P. (2006) 'Multiculturalism in times of war', *Critical Quarterly*, 48(4).

Goodchild, B. and I. Cole (2001) 'Social balance and mixed neighbourhoods in Britain since 1979: a review of discourse and practice in social housing', *Environment and Planning D*, 19.

Hobbs, D. (2006) 'East Ending: dissociation, de-industrialisation and David Downes', in T. Newburn and P. Rock (eds), *The Politics of Crime Control: Essays in Honour of David Downes*, Oxford: Oxford University Press.

HTA Architects (2002) *Report on Standard House-Types for Peabody Trust*, London: Peabody Trust.

Kabeer, N. (1991) 'Quest for national identity: women, Islam, and the state in Bangladesh', *Feminist Review*, 37.

Llewelyn, M. (2004) '"Urban village" or "White House": envisioned spaces, experienced places, and everyday life at Kensal House, London in the 1930s', *Environment and Planning D*, 22.

Madanipour, A. (2003) *Public and Private Spaces of the City*, London: Routledge.

Malpass, P. (2001) 'The restructuring of social rented housing in Britain: demunicipalization and the rise of "Registered Social Landlords"', *European Journal of Housing Policy*, 1(1).

Modood, T. (2007) *Multiculturalism: A Civic Idea*, Cambridge: Polity.

Mohammad, R. (1999) 'Marginalisation, Islamism and the production of the "Other's" "Other"', *Gender, Place and Culture*, 6(3).

Parekh, B. (2000) *Rethinking Multiculturalism: Cultural Diversity and Political Theory*, London: Palgrave Macmillan.

Tower Hamlets (2002) *People and Profile Fact Files 1–9*, London: Tower Hamlets Borough Council.

Walkowitz, J. (1992) *City of Dreadful Delight: Narratives of Sexual Danger in Late-Victorian London*, Chicago, IL: University of Chicago Press.

Young, M. and P. Wilmott (1957) *Family and Kinship in East London*, London: Penguin.

THREE | ECONOMIC AND POLITICAL EMPOWERMENT

8 | Muslim economic initiatives: global finance and local projects

JANE POLLARD, HILARY LIM AND RAJ BROWN

In the Middle East, South-East Asia and elsewhere, Islamic charitable institutions like *awqaf* (singular, *waqf*) are able to incorporate land, to collect and distribute economic assets, absorb and coordinate capital flows, and create vibrant sub-economies linking diasporic Muslim merchant networks with global markets. This chapter explores the potential for such Islamic charitable organizations to contribute to economic activity and empowerment in Muslim communities in the East End of London, home to over 30 per cent of the UK's Muslim population. In so doing, however, we are concerned not only to be open to models and institutions of philanthropy practised in different parts of the globe, but also to acknowledge the transnational, relational and hybrid economic, social and legal elements that constitute Islamic philanthropy in London. Exploring these networks of philanthropy disrupts simple East/West, North/South binaries and hints at more complex geographies of empowerment for Muslims in London.

More broadly, it is true that the economic and social exclusion of different groups of Muslims in the UK generates considerable concern for the UK government and a range of social, cultural and financial agencies and religious non-governmental organizations (NGOs). While acknowledging this context, this chapter is designed to contribute to a broader 'politics of hope' for British (and other) Muslim communities. As Metcalf (1996: xii) notes, without wishing away the deprivation, prejudice and racism that affect many Muslims, these communities also have reserves of cultural strength, creativity and inventiveness.

The chapter is organized in three parts. Part I provides an outline of the *waqf* and discusses the theoretical significance of such institutions in a Western context. Part II establishes the empirical context by considering recent evidence describing the economic and social realities of life for diverse groups of Muslims in London. In Part III, we consider the role of Islamic charities in London, the reception of/place of Islamic law in England and its relevance with respect to the *waqf*.

PART I: ISLAMIC ECONOMIC PHILANTHROPY AND *AWQAF*

An oft-noted feature of Islam is its strong emphasis on charity and self-sufficiency; indeed, Ariff (1991: 3) argues that 'the significance of the voluntary sector in the Islamic order can hardly be overemphasized'. In Islam, charitable obligation finds its most obvious expression in *zakat* – one of the five pillars of Islam – which is a levy on Muslims for distribution to the poor and needy. The emphasis on charity within the Koran also inspires further discretionary charitable donations (*sadaqa*) towards economically dependent family members, community and society as an act of goodness and piety. One of the most significant post-Koranic Islamic institutions managing such charitable donations is a *waqf*. A *waqf* is a legal arrangement under which an owner settles property and other assets in perpetuity for the use of beneficiaries for specific purposes (Sait and Lim 2006). As such, *awqaf* take on the character of endowments in which ownership of assets like property and land are 'arrested' or 'detained' (ibid. 2006: 150) for charitable purposes. Three types of *waqf* can be identified: *waqf ahli* (where property is held for a family or other specified individuals until the death of all their descendants, at which point it is diverted to a charitable purpose), *waqf khairi* (permanent endowment of property for public interest) and *waqf mustarak* (quasi public, wherein property provides for a particular family but also some public interests such as a mosque) (see ibid. 2006; Tyabji 1991).

Research in South-East Asia and the Middle East has revealed *awqaf* with considerable physical assets in the form of land, property, madrasas (schools), burial grounds, orphanages and mosques. Singapore in particular provides a rich source of material detailing the activities and potential of *awqaf* (Tyabji 1991; Brown, R. 2008). Given that a *waqf*'s assets of land and properties were to be held in perpetuity, transfers could be made only for assets of similar or higher value. Such exchanges (*istibdal*) also had to be permitted within the original deeds of the foundation. Among Sunni Muslims, there are four main *madhahib* (singular *maddhab*) jurisprudential schools: *Hanafi*, *Maliki*, *Hanbali* and *Shafi'i*. These *madhahib* were named after their leading jurists and each is the dominant authority in different parts of the world. Singapore Muslims are mainly Shafi'i and perpetuity and continuity of endowment assets were insisted upon. The Hanbali school, known for its strictness in terms of ritual, which is not as popular as the other schools, but is the official doctrine in Saudi Arabia, asserted that ownership is transferred to beneficiaries but still persevered with the perpetuity of assets. The Hanafi and the Maliki schools were the first to develop and correspondingly became the most geographically widespread. Hanafis too adhered to the same principle of perpetuity of assets. The Maliki school, however, which grew out of the city of Medina, spreading through North Africa and into Sudan, accepted that while ownership rested with the endower and is inherited by legal heirs, the *waqf* could be subject to alterations or variations in the assets. Even among their adherents, however, temporality was not accepted if the land had a mosque or a cemetery.[1] A large proportion of *waqf* land in Singapore had a mosque or cemetery and thus transfers had to be carefully negotiated. Nevertheless, the concept of perpetuity of *waqf* was often open to reinterpretation by *ijtihad* or personal reasoning. This was translated into social need or *maslahah*. Hence *istibdal* could be practised but it was still a fraught process to evaluate the specifics of sharia compliancy.

Two examples of *waqf* in Singapore are the Alsagoff *waqf* (the Sayyid Muhammad bin Ahmad Wakaff Fund, existing since 1885) and the Alkaff *waqf* (founded in 1888). The former was dedicated to the maintenance of a mosque, burial sites, schools in Singapore and Yemen, and in assisting pilgrims to Mecca (Sia 1987). The latter financed schools, hospitals, religious centres and road-building in Tarim and Seyu (Freitag 2003). By some commentators, however, *awqaf* have been critiqued for hampering the development of market forces and private land ownership; the attachment to perpetuity restrained the use and sale of land and locked resources into unproductive channels for the preservation of family interests and charitable purposes (Kuran 2004; Goldstone 2003). Kuran (2007), for example, argues that the *waqf* inhibited Islamic entrepreneurship by limiting flexibility and innovation. In Singapore, legal challenges to perpetuity in the vesting of properties were pervasive between 1954 and 1984, corresponding with the introduction of the legislation on the compulsory acquisition of land.

The Singapore state, both in the colonial and the independent phases, introduced legislation to justify compulsory acquisition of land for the public good, and this included *waqf* land. British colonial legislation shaped the implementation of perpetuity in Singapore. The English Accumulation Act of 1826 (which opposed perpetuity and the increasing accumulation of land) was amended in 1905 legislation through the creation of the Mohamedan and Hindu Endowment Board, whereby the *waqf* was exempted from this anti-perpetuity principle. The 1911 *Waqf* Prohibition Enactment and an Amendment in 1935 preserved the inalienability of *waqf* lands but introduced restrictions on the creation of new *waqf*. Further legislation on the *waqf* in the 1950s and 1960s imposed greater centralization and administration through the Majlis Ugama Islam Singapura (MUIS)[2] and *waqf* trustees, acting in consultation with the Singapore state. The rigid interpretation of the perpetuity clause was relaxed to ensure that perpetuity appealed to the aim and purpose of the bequeathing of land and properties within the *waqf*, rather than the physical assets themselves. This liberal response is seen in the fatwas issued in South-East Asia, revealing flexibility in the application of the legal doctrine to actual circumstances. The *waqf* in Singapore and throughout South-East Asia thus exemplifies an institution that responds, adapts and opts for pragmatism. While in some cases, the public *waqf* could be exploited for private gain (Kuran 2001), it could also be argued that the *waqf* afforded land security and protected the assets of a Muslim minority from a state intent on urban land development; compulsory acquisition of land presented a greater threat to the *waqf* and its ability to mobilize land assets for higher commercial value and use than its Islamic precepts. In the face of this threat, static perpetuity did provide some freedom of opportunity for the *waqf* to identify and undertake regeneration on its own terms. The *waqf* also protected wealth from feuding families.

Across the Muslim world, there is a resurgence of interest, promotion and rethinking on the *waqf* (OIC 2000) as an embodiment of the principles of self-sufficiency and egalitarianism. Although in many Muslim countries the *waqf* as an institution has declined – abolished, nationalized and mismanaged – the idea of the *waqf*, as an integral part of Islamic philanthropy, remains deep rooted. *Awqaf* have developed Islamic banking and halal funds and used Islamic financial contracts to transform land and real estate assets into higher-value commercial assets. Islamic charities in Thailand, Singapore, Malaysia, Indonesia and the Philippines have used *awqaf* to promote local, regional and global links and to tie down regional and international flows of Islamic funds to support economic growth. Similarly, cash *waqf* in South-East Asia, fuelled by moneylending and remittances between South-East Asia and the Middle East, have been a significant source of income for different groups of Muslims, supplying money to traders and Islamic teachers and maintaining mosques and madrasas. What is attractive about (some) models of *awqaf* is their potential as an inclusive, responsive, locally focused and authentic economic institution capable of considerable resource mobilization and redistribution.

The economic significance of *awqaf* in South-East Asia raises a host of empirical, political and theoretical questions. Theoretically, the role and performance of *awqaf* resonate with heterodox literatures on diverse or 'alternative' economies that stress the need to pluralize analyses of what 'counts' as 'the economy'. Building from influences that include feminism, post-colonialism, queer theory and poststructuralism, these heterodox approaches have challenged prevailing understandings of the economic by acknowledging and valuing the practices (market and non-market, semi- and non-capitalist, formal and informal) that shape the livelihoods of different groups (Gibson-Graham 1996, 2006; Leyshon et al. 2003). In addition to recognizing the diversity of practices that constitute 'economy', these literatures push researchers to recognize a broader spectrum of sites that produce the economic, including community, household and family.

More than this, however, a second theoretical (and also political) concern is Chakrabarty's (2000) call for Western scholars to 'provincialise' their understandings of economic practices and knowledges. Post-colonial theory has, thus far, made relatively few inroads into the disciplines of economics (Zein-Elabdin and Charusheela 2004) or the sub-discipline of economic geography (Pollard and Samers 2007; Pollard et al. 2009). Nevertheless, it offers a number of important challenges to the putatively universal language, categories and tools of economic geography and development studies. Post-colonial critiques highlight the enduring Eurocentrism of European and North American knowledge production that normalizes the historical experiences and categories of the West as the basis for knowing, measuring and understanding other parts of the globe. European experiences of 'development' have often been transposed to other regions of the world, where religious authorities and faith-based organizations have played major roles in economic development. A second post-colonial contribution is the critique of Western historicist narratives of transition, or what Chakrabarty (2000: 7) describes as the 'first in Europe and then elsewhere' structure of (Western) global historical time. This narrative has the effect of converting history into a 'waiting room', from which non-Western economies are expected, eventually, to emerge as they achieve Western capitalist modernity. The recognition of multiple pathways (and 'destinations') cautions against any simple dismissals of institutions like *awqaf* as anti-modern or 'relic' institutions that are destined either to fade into insignificance or instead 'progress' to the point of resembling Western institutions (see Pollard and Samers 2007). Finally, post-colonial critiques, alongside other more recent relational strains of economic geography, problematize the spatial metaphors invoked in Western discourses, notably the relationship between the 'there' and the 'here'. More recent research in economic geography has illuminated the transnational and relational presences that mean that 'the distant is implicated in our "here"' (Massey 2004: 10; see also McEwan et al. 2005). If 'the other' is always already 'inside the core', then it becomes important, in this context, to explore the transnational networks of Islamic assets that flow through the East End of London. As Amin (2007: 107) argues, 'Harnessing exteriority is crucial for a progressive politics of place'; it is thus important to explore flows of people, commodities, remittances and so forth that constitute the East End of London (McEwan et al. 2005, Henry et al. 2002).

To what extent are/could such assets be turned to local economic regeneration in London? Empirically, we know very little about flows of Islamic charitable donations. Other research on remittances, however, suggests that London supplies about half of the estimated £1.5 billion in remittances sent from the UK in any one year (GLA Economics, cited in Mayor of London 2006).[3] Flows of Islamic charitable assets could be significant in a UK context. London has a growing presence as an international centre of Islamic finance (FSA 2007), and the development of Islamic finance plays to discourses about London's eminence as an international financial centre and also to the Labour government's commitment to a social inclusion agenda. Yet research has thus far found little evidence to suggest that Islamic banking is addressing the needs of the 'poorest of the poor'[4] (Dar 2004; Pollard and Samers 2007). For this reason, there is growing academic and policy interest in the development of Islamic microfinance initiatives (Ferro 2005), as these offer the possibility of community-centred financial initiatives that draw upon Islamic principles of risk-sharing, entrepreneurship and participation of the poor. A *waqf* could be used to guarantee Islamic microfinance projects, including housing microfinance. As defined by Islamic law, a *waqf* also has potential for wealth creation by creating interlocking circuits of capital – including land, property, commodities – and by collecting and distributing flows of *zakat* and *sadaqa* (see Siddiqi 2002).

PART II: THE EMPIRICAL CONTEXT

The empirical and political context for our interest in the *waqf* is the growing corpus of academic and policy research that documents some common elements of the economic, social and political lives of the UK's Muslim population. While noting some points of commonality, however, it is important to recognize at the outset the ethnic diversity of UK Muslims, and especially those living in London (see Table 8.1). With recent improvements in data collection by religious faith, there is now a significant body of work that demonstrates various elements of social exclusion for UK Muslims.[5] In what follows, however, we are interested primarily in some of the key economic dimensions of Muslims' lives.

In the UK context, Muslims are disproportionately represented in

TABLE 8.1 Proportions of Muslims by ethnic group, England and Wales and London, 2001

	England and Wales		London	
	Muslim population	Ethnic group of Muslims (%)	Muslim population	Ethnic group of Muslims (%)
White	179,773	11.62	116,292	19.16
British	63,042	4.08	32,888	5.42
Irish	890	0.06	452	0.07
'Other White'	115,841	7.49	82,952	13.66
Mixed	64,262	4.15	28,310	4.66
White and Black Caribbean	1,385	0.09	530	0.09
White and Black African	10,523	0.68	6,088	1.0
White and Asian	30,397	1.97	11,258	1.85
Other Mixed	21,957	1.42	10,434	1.72
Asian	1,139,065	73.65	353,312	58.2
Indian	131,662	8.51	40,497	6.67
Pakistani	657,680	42.52	130,653	21.52
Bangladeshi	259,710	16.79	142,931	23.54
'Other Asian'	90,013	5.82	39,231	6.46
Black or Black British	106,345	6.88	80,098	13.19
Black Caribbean	4,477	0.29	2,713	0.45
Black African	96,136	6.22	73,851	12.16
Other Black	5,732	0.37	3,534	0.58
Chinese	752	0.05	324	0.05
Other ethnic groups	56,429	3.65	28,747	4.74
Total	1,546,626	100	607,083	100

Source: ONS 2001 Census Tables ST104, cited in Mayor of London (2006: 21)

TABLE 8.2 Economic activity of men and women aged 16–24, London, 2001

	General population (%)	Muslim (%)
Men		
Economically active	62.3	46.5
Economically inactive	37.7	53.5
Women		
Economically active	58.1	36.7
Economically inactive	41.9	63.3

Source: ONS 2001 Census Tables ST153, cited in Mayor of London (2006: 52)

some of the most deprived urban areas in the UK, more likely than other faith groups to live in social housing, have no educational qualifications and have a long-term illness (Annual Population Survey, OSI 2004; TUC 2005; Mayor of London 2006). In the labour market, Muslims have the lowest employment rate of any faith group (ONS 2001, cited in Mayor of London 2006) and are less likely than other faith groups to be working in managerial and professional occupations (Mayor of London 2006). Muslims are more likely to be in unskilled occupations than other religious groups, with one in ten Muslim men working as taxi drivers or chauffeurs and 37 per cent employed in distribution, hotel and catering industries (ONS 2004). Some of these figures may also reflect the relatively young age profile of UK Muslims; half of the UK's 1.8 million Muslims are under twenty-five years of age (TUC 2005).

London is home to 14 per cent of the UK population and more than 33 per cent of the UK Muslim population. London's Muslim population is more ethnically diverse than is the case nationally (Table 8.1) and has the youngest age profile of all religious groups in London (Mayor of London 2006). Many of the UK economic statistics regarding Muslims' representation in the labour market are mirrored in London. Tables 8.2, 8.3 and 8.4 document the relatively low economic activity rates[6] for Muslims in London that persist across age groups and for both men and women. Moreover, Muslims are more likely to be economically inactive than Jews, Sikhs, Hindus and Christians (ibid.).

Refining the geographical focus further, Muslims in London are most concentrated in Tower Hamlets (over 71,000, 36.4 per cent of the borough's population) and Newham (over 59,000, 24.3 per cent of the population), followed by the boroughs of Waltham Forest, Hackney,

TABLE 8.3 Economic activity of people aged 16–24, London, 2001

	General population (%)	Muslim (%)
Economically active	60.1	41.6
Employee part time	4.6	5.2
Employee full time	34.3	14.0
Self-employed	1.5	0.7
Unemployed	5.7	6.8
Full-time student	13.7	14.7
Economically inactive	39.9	58.4
Retired	0.1	0.1
Student	31.7	43.6
Looking after family/home	3.4	7.2
Permanently sick/disabled	0.7	0.9
Other	4.0	6.7

Source: ONS 2001 Census Tables ST153, cited in Mayor of London (2006: 51)

TABLE 8.4 Economic activity of people aged 25 and older, London, 2001

	General population (%)	Muslim (%)
Economically active	69.1	51.0
Employee part time	9.4	8.7
Employee full time	44.3	24.8
Self-employed part time	2.5	1.8
Self-employed full time	7.9	6.5
Unemployed	4.1	7.7
Full-time student	0.9	1.6
Economically inactive	31.0	49.0
Retired	11.7	5.8
Student	1.7	3.6
Looking after family/home	7.9	19.7
Permanently sick/disabled	5.3	7.8
Other	4.4	12.0

Source: ONS 2001 Census Tables ST153, cited in Mayor of London (2006: 54)

Brent and Redbridge (all with populations of more than 10 per cent Muslim; ONS 2001). Tower Hamlets remains one of the most deprived areas of the UK (DCLG 2007). Despite significant development around Canary Wharf and the City fringe, Tower Hamlets is characterized by high levels of unemployment and the lowest economic activity levels of any London borough. Tower Hamlets also has the lowest level of owner occupation in London[7] and over a quarter of its population has no qualifications[8] (ONS 2006/07). Other East End boroughs share this deprivation. Newham and Hackney, like Tower Hamlets, are ranked in the top six of the government's index of multiple deprivation (DCLG 2007).

These national and regional statistics paint a familiar and rather depressing picture. Optimists could argue that the situation may improve in the near future; between the London 2012 Olympics and the New Deal for Communities regeneration projects, there are numerous schemes under way to generate new jobs and housing in the East End. We are interested here, however, in the practices and possible further mobilization of specifically Islamic networks and resources that are directed at improving the lives of Muslim communities in London. This involves exploring some dimensions of Muslims' economic lives that are not reflected in official statistics; these embrace a range of Islamic philanthropic institutions able to harness local, and often transnational, flows of donations, endowments and business information to support economic growth. In what follows, we consider some of the possibilities and challenges facing Islamic philanthropic and charitable institutions in London.

PART III: *AWQAF* AND ECONOMIC REGENERATION IN LONDON?

As we have established, London's Muslims are ethnically diverse, although well-established communities reside in highly localized areas. Particular boroughs and wards are distinctive in their active reconstitution of Muslim ways of life in parts of the Arab world, South Asia, Turkey, Iran and so on. In East London, for instance, substantial Turkish and Kurdish Muslim groups are found in Stoke Newington and Hackney, while the Muslim population in Tower Hamlets and Newham is predominantly Bangladeshi, specifically Sylheti. The origins of such local settlement are described by Yilmaz (2005: 56) in terms of Muslims arriving in Britain often as 'connected individuals', in 'cascading chains along well-worn paths of kinship and friendship', for which a former geographical location was the key factor. These men, and (later) women, did not throw away their religious and cultural values, but maintained their networks of relational links with Muslim communities elsewhere and re-created relatively self-contained traditional 'trans-local' diasporic settings, a home away from home (*desh bidesh/desh pardesh*, Urdu/Bengali) (Pearl and Menski 1998; Shah 2005). The manifestation of these trans-local identities for the non-Muslim population takes the form of mosques, shops, community centres, cultural organizations and branches of South Asian, Arab and Turkish banks on London's streets.

Muslim charities vary in size, purpose, source and distribution of funds, but operate within, and play an integral part in, the physical and psychological reconstruction of traditional communities and particularistic identities. Reflecting the Islamic charitable obligation for Muslims everywhere, there are long-established institutions, including mosques, which are a key focus and point of connection for London's Muslim communities, providing welfare, educational, counselling and other services largely funded through donations. Other organizations, such as community centres, also supply a variety of services, including those for women, children and older people, often directed towards Muslims in a particular borough, which depend on funding through grants from public bodies. Zokaei and Phillips (2000: 54) regard this as a cause of concern, commenting that,

> sadly, mosques and community organizations have sometimes served the specific needs of the particular communities they represent and associate themselves ... only with a small group where all they have in common is a shared language or local regional background.

From the perspective of developing strategies to unlock Islamic philanthropy, a tradition with such a narrow cultural focus may present a barrier. Recognition of these particularistic trans-local identities and their institutionalization may serve, however, to disrupt essentialist views of Muslims as an alien Other. Nevertheless, they do not begin to capture the enormous range of British Muslim identities, or the economic geography of philanthropy for Muslims living in Britain, not least because many are not closely linked to such local community structures.[9] It must also be recognized that British Muslim identities are inevitably intertwined with indigenous Western practices, 'actively produced, reproduced and transformed' (Kahani-Hopkins and Hopkins 2002: 289) and therefore produced and reproduced from sites of contestation.

There is much that unites Muslims, and local or trans-local identities are accompanied by a transnational 'superordinate collective identification' (Hopkins and Kahani-Hopkins 2004a: 44). Muslims see themselves as a universal community (*umma*), which displaces space and territory as the means of identification (Brown, K. 2006: 7–8), generating an abstract but 'inclusive domain' of shared faith and experience, the 'Household of Islam' (Zokaei and Phillips 2000: 54; Kahn 2000: 37–8) and a 'collective cross-cultural Islamic consciousness' (Mohammed 1999: 224).

The *umma* is more than a community of the faithful; it is embodied in shared Islamic obligations, including *salat* (prayers) and *zakat* (charity) (Kahn 2000: 37–8). The *umma*, this superordinate community identity, is construed as 'a political category of belonging', and a clear alternative to the nation-state and a challenge to the notion that political power is territorially based (Hopkins and Kahani-Hopkins 2004a: 50). It has been widely argued that, in response to globalization processes, but also marginalization and exclusion from mainstream Western society, there has been a self-conscious articulation of a revitalized or revived idea of the *umma* among Muslims, particularly young British Muslims (Brown, K. 2006; Eade 1997; Kandiyoti 1987; Werbner 2004).[10] This is connected to the 'movement of many young people towards a more "pure" or orthodox form of Islam based [in part] in a rejection of their parents' "traditions"' (Husain and O'Brien 2000: 9), yet it does 'not necessarily coincide with increased piety among Muslims' (Brown, K. 2006: 6). The Salman Rushdie affair is particularly cited as having encouraged Muslims to re-examine 'the nature and significance of their Islamic identifications … to address their contemporary location, identity and interests' (Hopkins and Kahani-Hopkins 2004b: 344), emphasizing that the *umma* is both a residual Islamic identity and 'negotiated within … local as well as global contexts' (Brown, K. 2006: 6). As Kahn (2000: 38–9) suggests, with reference to the predominantly South Asian Muslims in Britain, 'whether [such] minorities manifest a need to articulate religious, national or ethnic identities may be influenced by their particular historical experiences, and the situation of their societies of origin on the Indian sub-continent'. He suggests further that younger Muslims are 'more likely to rationalize Muslim presence and experience in Britain within a global, historic and colonial framework' (ibid.: 41). The activities of some Muslim charities, such as Islamic Relief and Muslim Aid, which undertake extensive fund-raising in the UK but whose spending supports projects overseas, can perhaps best be understood against a backdrop of mobilization on specific Muslim needs and issues which transcend territorial and national boundaries.

Islamic charities in London According to the Charity Commission's Faith and Social Cohesion Unit (FSCU) there are 486 registered Muslim charities in Greater London, recognized and regulated by the state, together generating over £69 million per annum. In order to achieve recognition and formal registration, the documented purposes of these institutions must be accepted by the Charity Commissioners, who have central registration, supervision and monitoring functions, as falling exclusively within the legal definition of charity[11] and being for the public benefit.[12] Until recently charitable status had four principal 'heads' – the relief of poverty; the advancement of education; the advancement of religion; and other purposes beneficial to the community. Without departing in any fundamental way from this meaning, or disrupting the status of existing charitable bodies, developed by means of analogy over centuries on a case-by-case basis, the definition has now received statutory clarification within the Charities Act 2006. In particular, Section 2(2) lists twelve charitable purposes, which in effect offer a fuller and more detailed description of purposes under the fourth head, including the advancement of citizenship or community development; the advancement of human rights; conflict resolution or reconciliation; or the promotion of religious or racial harmony or equality and diversity.

The most obvious motivation for any organization in seeking legal charitable status is financial. Charities earning income from dividends and rents do not, for example, pay income tax or corporation tax on this money if it is applied for charitable purposes.[13] To acquire charitable status Muslim institutions, like other charities, must be shaped into an accepted legal form, usually a charitable trust or a registered corporation,[14] managed by persons designated as trustees or directors, with substantially similar roles and duties.[15] Charitable trustees and directors must, with the exception of charities with an annual income and expenditure of less than £10,000, supply annual accounts and an annual report detailing the charity's activities for that year to the Charity Commissioners. These reporting and accounting mechanisms can provide rich records of individual charities.

Muslim charities and the 'living law' The terms *waqf* and trust are evident in the registered names of a small number of contemporary registered Muslim charities. With respect to some charities, these terms can be perhaps explained in terms of trans-local associations and familiarities. In contrast to colonial and post-colonial histories in parts of the Muslim world, the *waqf* has, for instance, flourished in Bangladesh, where *waqf* estates include mosques, educational institutions, medical centres and even a shopping centre.[16] It may also be an effect of increasing Muslim pride in the survival and revival of the *waqf* as an institution. It may also hint at legal diversity and a continued, if partially hidden, deeper observance of unofficial Islamic norms, concepts and institutions. Registration of charitable bodies with the Charity Commissioners inevitably entails an engagement with the official legal system and its regulatory networks. Yet just as Muslims in Britain did not dispose of their cultural baggage, but re-created diasporic trans-local communities and transnational links, so they also reconstructed 'Muslim laws in England as a post-modern response to legal modernity' (Yilmaz 2005: 49) and an 'ongoing multiple conflict scenario' (Pearl and Menski 1998: 52).

For British Muslim individuals and communities there is on the one hand the modern Western legal system, claiming to be blind to 'social conventions' and 'cultural practice' and expecting assimilation in return for legal protection. Muslims do not want to transgress official norms and may indeed want to utilize them, but the English legal system often appears to offer them only grudging, inconsistent and piecemeal legal recognition of, or adaptation to, their ways of life.[17] On the other hand there is Islamic law (sharia), which binds the conscience of Muslims wherever they are living, shaping their experiences whether or not the state 'officially' implements it. As is well documented, what has emerged from, or been created by, the seemingly 'unbridgeable conflict' (Pearl and Menski 1998: 52) is *angrezi shariat* (Urdu, *ingreji shariyot* Bangla/ Sylheti), 'hybrid rule systems' and dispute forums 'developed to satisfy the requirements of both official English law and unofficial Muslim law' (Yilmaz 2005: 59; see also Shah 2005). Instances of such 'normative fluorescence' (Bowen 2003) are not uncommon and have been referred to as 'deep legal pluralism' (Woodman 1998).

Some Muslims did formulate demands in the 1970s and 1980s for explicit recognition of Muslim personal or family law, governing matters of marriage, divorce, maintenance, inheritance and so on, by the English legal system. The demand reflected the widespread South Asian and South-East Asian experience, as already discussed in Singapore, both in the colonial and post-colonial contexts, of sharia law applying to Muslims with respect to family matters, including recognition of the *waqf*, although not necessarily other social and legal issues (Bradney 2000: 187; Pearl and Menski 1998: 73). These requests were dismissed, however, at least until much more recently. Instead, individuals and communities have 'built the requirements of English law into their traditional legal structures' (Pearl and Menski 1998: 75), initially it seems haphazardly but more recently in a much more conscious process involving informal Muslim dispute settlement by Islamic Sharia Councils. Muslims have become 'skilled cultural navigators', 'subtly, often imperceptibly to the outsider', reasserting their cultural, religious and legal values (ibid.: 55), finding ways to avoid official law where possible or accommodate it where unavoidable or necessary. One striking feature of *angrezi shariat* is that there is considerable local diversity within these internal regulatory frameworks, often reflecting pre-existing distinctiveness in Islamic law as a consequence of particular trans-local connections, specific community customs and values and concepts of honour (Yilmaz 2005: 61). A further aspect is the fairly widespread deployment of the legal technique of *talfiq* (patchwork), the combining of approaches or principles from different Islamic schools of law and even drawing on scholarly opinion from outside the four main Sunni schools (ibid.: 63). Thus, the interests of social actors are marked by support from informal norms coupled with the use of formal rules, procedures and institutions (Razzaz 1998), negotiated 'internally' but often unobserved on the official plane. The constraints of functioning within the space 'permitted' by official norms have produced a flexibility and creativity which manifest themselves differently but resonate with the Singapore experience of a minority Muslim population. Unlike in Singapore, where sharia law is institutionalized by the state, in Britain 'ownership' of Islamic law and values has remained largely with Muslim communities, although this should not be taken to suggest that it is therefore easy to be British and Muslim.

Since 2007, a degree of official status has been accorded to some sharia 'courts'. Muslim Arbitration Tribunals were set up in several major British cities, including London, Birmingham and Manchester, under the Arbitration Act (1996) and within the British alternative dispute resolution framework, to decide upon civil cases relating to matters such as inheritance disputes, religious divorce, neighbour disputes and domestic violence, where the parties concerned agree to abide by the tribunals' resolution. These tribunals consist of a Muslim legal scholar sitting with a solicitor or barrister registered to practise in England and Wales and their decisions are enforceable within the civil courts. Their existence led to a flurry of interest in the newspapers in September 2008, following comments by the Shadow Home Secretary, Dominic Grieve, expressing concern at what he regarded as a quiet or secret sanction given to sharia courts by the government (Hickey 2008; Stote 2008; Taher 2008).

Within the first year, it was widely reported in British newspapers that the five Muslim Arbitration Tribunals in England had between them heard 100 cases. The extent to which the unofficial sharia councils are utilized by Muslims or particular Muslim communities to settle their disputes is less clear, but there are lessons to be drawn from outside Britain. Legal systems throughout the Muslim world exhibit considerable variety owing to their specific historical and colonial contexts, the state ideology and the extent to which Islamic law is able to trump secular or customary laws. Saudi Arabia and Iran are exceptional countries which have largely resisted Western legal influences and profess exclusivity of Islamic laws. Other Muslim countries, however, represent a greater hybridity of legal cultures. The practice of Islamic law in the Muslim world involves potentially complex and difficult relationships between particular brands of Islamic law and other forms of law, whether state or customary. The existence of a variety of different legal spaces and normative orders can be the cause of conflict, yet, as Rosen (1999: 93) has suggested, that does not have to be the case. He points to the existence in Moroccan society, for instance, of seemingly incompatible institutions, 'Maliki Islamic law, Berber and Arab customary practices, former colonial laws, confessional laws, and contemporary Moroccan codes', which are not treated as mutually contradictory. Instead, individuals shuttle among them, making choices about forums and treating them as resources. As Bowen argues with reference to Indonesia, 'in the practice of reasoning about cases and justifying decisions reached, Muslim authorities and ordinary Muslims always have found themselves having to tack among competing values, norms and commands' (2003: 9–10). From the perspective of participants, even in Britain, with its quite widespread ad hoc unofficial sharia courts, more recent officially sanctioned Muslim tribunals and the official court system, choices will be made about the forum for a dispute, based upon, for instance, efforts to shape lives in an Islamic way, nostalgia for Islamic law ('Abd Al-Fattah 1999: 161), embracing the 'purity' of Islamic law, local and trans-local norms and traditions of particular cultural communities. This is not a passive legal pluralism, but as N. J. Brown (1997: 202–9) has suggested in the context of Egypt, people choose between formal and extralegal bargaining opportunities, deploying tools offered by law as a complement to a range of problem-solving strategies.

Analysis of the creation and development of *angrezi shariat* has been largely confined to discussions about family law, demonstrating how English law mechanisms are used where practical, and new techniques developed to satisfy official legal requirements and those of religious law (Yilmaz 2005: 80).[18] Although the *waqf* is often considered as a part of Muslim personal law, it has not been a point of analysis of the 'living law' of British Muslims, nor has the extent to which the *waqf* survives, either in concrete terms or as an 'idea', within the mechanism of the formal trust, been explored.

The aims and activities of Muslim organizations may have been transformed by the required formulations of official state law, in order to acquire charitable status. There are, however, few noteworthy areas of obvious conflict between the 'shell' of the charitable trust and the *waqf* (Thompson n.d.). As is well documented, the *waqf* shares many features with the English charitable trust, which is often the mainstream 'legal sleeve' for Islamic philanthropy in England and Wales.[19] On the surface at least it shares most of its essential characteristics with the trust, including the division between 'administration' and 'beneficial enjoyment' of property and as a legal device for the renunciation of ownership of property and its dedication in perpetuity. One difference is that the *waqf khairi* has always maintained its connection with the religious precept of charity, but most Muslim charities will have as part of their list of charitable purposes the carrying out of religious work, so again this can be 'accommodated'.[20]

Legal pluralism can lead to tense relations and conflicts between systems, or relatively peaceful cohabitation, compromise and adaptation. The latter is less likely to be highlighted, but it does not mean that the *waqf* is not alive, albeit hidden from outside view, within the informal legal culture, influencing how the donation of funds, their management and distribution are 'thought through'. It is evident from trustees' reports and accounts of some East London Muslim charities, deposited with the Charity Commissioners, that while meeting the requirements of English law, they operate within a distinctively Islamic framework and a legal culture pertaining to philanthropic activity. One of the largest trusts in East London is the London Mosque Fund, with a substantial income which, in addition to a mosque, is concerned with a wide range of activities, including schools, legal advice, healthy living and schools attendance projects. The trustees' report for the year ending March 2006 meticulously covers all the information required by the Commissioners and is unremarkable in that regard. The relevant accounts list as incoming resources, however, *zakat* and *fitra* collection, and collections at Friday prayers, as well as *zakat* and *fitra* distribution. Perhaps more strikingly, a repayment of *Qard-e-Hasanah*, a specifically Islamic benevolent interest-free loan (often used to help fund those in the poorer sections of society to acquire an education or start a business), is listed and explained, in 'official' terms, as a private loan. The Islamic framework surrounding resources and expenditure is also clearly evident in the financial report for the same year of the Alhuda Cultural Centre and Masjid, in the Mile End Road, yet the United Kingdom Turkish Islamic Association, which is focused on the Azizya mosque in Stoke Newington, provides no such evidence in its equivalent accounts. Moreover, the overlapping legal spaces and economies in which such charities operate are complex. The London Mosque Fund, like several other East London Muslim charities, uses two conventional banks,

HSBC and Barclays Bank plc, as its 'main banks', and the UK Turkish Islamic Assocation also banks with another East London branch of Barclays Bank, despite the presence of several Turkish banks within the vicinity of the mosque. There is no evidence in the reports to suggest that specifically Islamic banking windows within these conventional banks are being utilized.

As the UK government has become interested in the character and extent of Islamic philanthropy and institutions, as well as the promotion of entrepreneurship and inclusion in 'hard to reach' communities (DCLG 2008), it raises a question as to whether the *waqf* should remain within the informal internal regulatory mechanisms of the Muslim community, or whether, given the resurgence of interest in this institution within the Muslim world, it could be a better explicit vehicle for the Islamic charitable ethos. If the *waqf* form gained recognition within the English legal, financial and regulatory systems, even if there were few obvious 'legal' advantages, would it be a better model for soliciting and managing funds, and might those funds be used more readily for a broader set of regeneration and welfare purposes, within the UK, than is currently the case?

CONCLUSION

This chapter has outlined some elements of Islamic charitable organizations that contribute to economic activity and empowerment in Muslim communities in some of the most deprived parts of London. In so doing, it has learned from research undertaken in South-East Asia and elsewhere on the Islamic institution of the *waqf*. Although debate continues regarding the role and performance of *awqaf* in different regional, religious and political contexts, there are examples of *awqaf* able to manage land and property and collect and distribute other economic assets and link diasporic Muslim merchant networks with global markets (Ariff 1991; Sait and Lim 2006). In the legal context of England and Wales, the *waqf* resembles the English charitable trust, and there is some evidence that elements of the *waqf* are alive, if often hidden, in London. The idea of the *waqf*, as a charitable vehicle, is deep rooted and retains its appeal as an institution that houses key Islamic principles of philanthropy and egalitarianism and one capable of very considerable resource mobilization and redistribution.

Although much more research is needed on the nature and extent of Islamic philanthropy in the UK, the possibilities for development of *awqaf* in London are intriguing – economically and politically – because of the size of the Muslim population, its strong ethic of charitable donation and the growing policy interest in the UK in producing legal, regulatory and political spaces in which Islamic financial and charitable tools can mobilize assets for Muslims in need. Evidence from models of Islamic philanthropy from around the globe suggests that, for all the economic marginalization faced by many Muslims, there are Islamic institutions and practices able to pool and mobilize assets to create spaces of hope for Muslims.

NOTES

1 With burial tombs and cemetery sites, appropriation was forbidden, although this inviolability was broken by the urban planning ambitions of the PAP government of Singapore from 1968 (see Powers 1999).

2 A statutory body with powers to oversee *waqf* and religious education, collect and distribute *zakat* and to appoint religious officials (see Tyabji 1991).

3 South Asia is a key destination, with Bangladesh receiving 6 per cent and Pakistan 13 per cent (Mayor of London 2006).

4 Although the advent of sharia-compliant mortgages is allowing for home purchase among middle-income Muslims. Increased home equity may, in turn, support further entrepreneurial activities.

5 The OSI (2004), for example, identified three domains of social exclusion: economic exclusion, exclusion through violence, and political and public exclusion.

6 Where 'economic activity' is defined as either in employment or unemployed and looking for work.

7 Twenty-nine per cent compared with 55 per cent in London as a whole and 68.8 per cent for England and Wales (Halifax 2008).

8 Compared to 13.8 per cent of the national population.

9 A recent study for the Joseph Rowntree Foundation found that housing aspirations for younger white and South Asian British women were similar; in particular both groups expressed a desire to live in 'mixed neighbourhoods', as opposed to homogeneous neighbourhoods, in terms of race, religion or trans-local connections. This preference was said to be in part because women wished to avoid outside interventions into their private family lives. White and South Asian women aspired to owner occupation; interestingly Muslim women were in the main not attracted to Islamic mortgages, regarding them as costly, not necessarily sharia compliant and inflexible (Harries et al. 2008).

10 K. Brown (2006: 6) points to a report in the *Guardian* that in 2002 41 per cent of younger (under thirty-five) Muslim respondents to an ICM poll preferred to self-describe only by religion, as opposed to ethnicity or ethnicity and religion.

11 There are a small number of charities which do not require registration.

12 In a strengthening of the law, under s3 of the Act charities, whatever their purpose, are required now to *demonstrate* that they are 'for the public benefit'.

13 Gifts to charities where the donor has made a covenant through

the Gift Aid scheme permit the reclamation of tax by the charity concerned. Charities are also exempt from capital transfer tax and inheritance tax (on donations), capital gains tax, stamp duty and 80 per cent of non-domestic (business) rates on buildings that the charities occupy, with some religious buildings wholly exempt.

14 The choice of incorporation is widely regarded as beneficial for larger charities with considerable assets, since it affords limited liability to the directors and the advantage of the corporate body having a legal personality. A possible disadvantage of incorporation is that it carries two accounting and reporting obligations – as a company as well as a charity – and two initial registrations, with the Charity Commissioners and Companies House. A new mechanism is being introduced by the Charities Act 2006 called the CIO (Charitable Incorporated Organization), which will give the benefits of incorporation but which will no longer require separate registration at Companies House and which will require charities only to report/submit audited accounts to the Charity Commissioners.

15 A small number of charities are exempt from registration, such as higher education corporations. Mutual societies are registered under the Industrial and Provident Society Act 1965 and can receive charitable status from HM Revenue and Customs (not the Charity Commissioners). Some mutual societies, particularly housing associations, have a particular Muslim or Islamic affiliation, such as the North London Muslim Housing Association (est.

1986), which operates in East and North London.

16 Estimates of *waqf* estates in Bangladesh stand at over 150,000, including the Baitul Mukarram shopping centre in Dhaka, as well as 8,000 educational institutions (Sadeq 2002).

17 One recent such adaptation was with respect to the tax changes to accommodate sharia-compliant mortgages.

18 In many cases, such as divorce and marriage, this may mean performing legal events twice, in order to meet both informal and formal norms. Or choosing to perform only one of the two events to meet the needs of the parties and families concerned, while meeting religious requirements and community recognition.

19 Cattan (1955), in his close analysis of the two institutions, described the similarities between the *waqf* and the trust as 'striking', both as institutions and with regard to their respective technical legal frameworks. Cattan also takes the view that the English trust was derived from the Islamic *waqf*, as a consequence of cultural exchanges in the thirteenth century, by which time the *waqf* was already a thriving and well-developed legal device. See also Lim (2000).

20 The colonial engagement produced an encounter between legal cultures, and specifically between the trust and the *waqf*, which may be termed legal orientalism, whereby legal culture became an object of colonization (Strawson 1996; Lim 2000), with the *waqf* designed as responsible for the lack of economic development in the Muslim world.

REFERENCES

'Abd Al-Fattah, N. (1999) 'The anarchy of the Egyptian legal system: wearing away the legal and political modernity', in B. Dupret, M. Berger and L. al-Zwaini (eds), *Legal Pluralism in the Arab World*, The Hague: Kluwer Law International.

Amin, A. (2007) 'Rethinking the urban social', *City*, 11(1).

Ariff, M. (ed.) (1991) *The Islamic Voluntary Sector in South East Asia*, Singapore: Institute of South East Asia Studies.

Baer, G. (1969) *Studies in Social Histories of Modern Egypt*, Chicago, IL: University of Chicago Press.

Bowen, J. R. (2003) *Islam Law and Inequality in Indonesia*, Cambridge: Cambridge University Press.

Bradney, A. (2000) 'The legal status of Islam within the United Kingdom', in S. Ferrari and A. Bradney (eds), *Islam and European Legal Systems*, Aldershot: Ashgate.

Brown, K. (2006) 'Realising Muslim women's rights: the role of Islamic identity among British Muslim women,' *Women's Studies International Forum*, 29(4).

Brown, N. J. (1997) *The Rule of Law in the Arab World*, Cambridge: Cambridge University Press.

Brown, R. (2008) 'Islamic endowments and the land economy in Singapore: the genesis of an ethical capitalism 1830–2007', *Journal of South East Asia Research*, 16(3).

Cattan, H. (1955) 'The law of *waqf*', in M. Khadduir and H. J. Liebsney (eds), *Law in the Middle East*, vol. 1: *Origin and Development of Islamic Law*, Richmond: William Byrd.

Chakrabarty, D. (2000) *Provincialising Europe: Postcolonial Thought and Historical Difference*, Princeton, NJ: Princeton University Press.

Dar, H. (2004) *Demand for Islamic Financial Services in the United Kingdom: Much Ado about Nothing?*, London: Institute of Islamic Banking and Insurance.

DCLG (2007) *Indices of Deprivation*, London: Department for Communities and Local Government.

— (2008) *Supporting Faith Communities: Framework for Partnership*, London: Department for Communities and Local Government.

Eade, J. (1997) 'Identity, nation and religion: education and young Bangladeshi Muslims in London's East End', in J. Eade (ed.), *Living in the Global City: Globalisation as Local Process*, London: Routledge.

Ferro, N. (2005) *Value through Diversity: Microfinance and Islamic Finance and Global Banking*, Milan: Fondazione Eni Ennoco Mattei.

Fraser, N. (1989) *Unruly Practices*, Minneapolis: University of Minnesota Press.

Freitag, U. (2003) *Indian Ocean Migrants and State Formation in Hadramaut: Reforming the Homeland*, Leiden: Brill.

FSA (Financial Services Authority) (2007) *Islamic Finance in the UK: Regulation and Challenges*, London: FSA.

Gibson-Graham, J. K. (1996) *The End of Capitalism (As We Knew It): A Feminist Critique of Political Economy*, Oxford: Blackwell.

— (2006) *A Postcapitalist Politics*, Minneapolis: University of Minnesota Press.

Goldstone, J. A. (2003) 'Islam, development and the Middle East: a comment on Timur Kuran's', in *USAID, Institutional Barriers to*

Economic Change: Cases Considered,
Washington, DC.

Halifax (2008) *Record Fall in
Owner-Occupation in England*,
Press release, 13 February,
www.hbosplc.com/economy/
includes/130208Record_fall_
in_%Owner_Occupation.doc,
accessed October 2008.

Harries, B., L. Richardson and A.
Soteri-Proctor (2008*) Housing
Aspirations for a New Generation:
Perspectives from White and South
Asian British Women*, Coventry:
Chartered Institute of Housing.

Henry, N. D., C. McEwan and J. S.
Pollard (2002) 'Globalisation from
below: Birmingham – postcolonial
workshop of the world?', *Area*,
34(2).

Hickey, M. (2008) 'Islamic *Sharia*
courts are now legally binding',
Daily Mail, 15 September

Hopkins, N. and V. Kahani-Hopkins
(2004a) 'The antecedents of
identification: a rhetorical analysis
of British Muslim activists,
constructions of community and
identity', *British Journal of Social
Psychology*, 43.

— (2004b) 'Identity construction and
British Muslims' political activity:
beyond rational actor theory',
British Journal of Social Psychology,
43: 339–56.

Husain, F. and M. O'Brien (2000)
'Muslim communities in Europe:
reconstruction and transformation', *Current Sociology*, 48(4).

Kahani-Hopkins, V. and N. Hopkins
(2002) 'Representing British
Muslims: the strategic dimension
to identity construction?', *Ethnic
and Racial Studies*, 25(2).

Kahn, Z. (2000) 'Muslim presence
in Europe: the British dimension
– identity, integration and com-

munity activism', *Current Sociology*,
48(4).

Kandiyoti, D. (1987) 'Emancipated
but unliberated? Reflections of
the Turkish case', *Feminist Studies*,
13(2).

Kuran, T. (2001) 'The provision of
public goods under Islamic law:
origins, impact and limitations of
the *Waqf* system', *Law and Society
Review*, 35(4).

— (2004) 'Why the Middle East is
economically underdeveloped:
historical mechanisms of
institutional stagnation', *Journal of
Economic Perspectives*, 18.

— (2007) 'The scale of entrepreneurship in Middle Eastern history:
inhibitive roles of Islamic institutions', Unpublished paper.

Larner, W. and R. Le Heron (2002)
'From economic globalisation to
globalising economic processes:
towards post-structural political
economies', *Geoforum*, 33.

Leyshon, A., R. Lee and C. C.
Williams (eds) (2003) *Alternative
Economic Spaces*, London: Sage.

Lim, H. (2000) 'The *Waqf* in trust', in
S. Scott-Hunt and H. Lim (eds),
*Feminist Perspectives on Equity and
Trusts*, London: Cavendish.

London Development Agency (2005)
*Sustaining Success: Developing
London's Economy*, London: LDA.

Massey, D. (2004) 'Geographies
of responsibility', *Geografiska
Annaler*, 86.

Mayor of London (2006) *Muslims in
London*, London: Greater London
Authority.

McEwan, C., J. S. Pollard and N. D.
Henry (2005) 'The "global" in
the city economy: multicultural
economic development in Birmingham', *International Journal of Urban
and Regional Research*, 29(4).

Menski, W. (2006) *Comparative Law in a Global Context*, Cambridge: Cambridge University Press.

Metcalf, B. D. (1996) Preface and Acknowledgements, in B. D. Metcalfe (ed.), *Making Muslim Space in North America and Europe*, Berkeley: University of California Press.

Mohammed, R. (1999) 'Marginalisation, Islamism and the production of the Other's Other', *Gender, Place and Culture*, 6(3).

OIC (Organization of Islamic Conference) (2000) *Promoting Waqfs and Their Role in the Development of Islamic Societies*, Report of the Secretary-General to the Twenty-Seventh Session of the OIC Conference, Kuala Lumpur, 27–30 June.

ONS (Office for National Statistics) (2004) *Annual Population Survey*, London: ONS.

— (2006/07) *Annual Population Survey*, London: ONS.

OSI (Open Society Institute) (2004) *Muslims in the UK: Policies for Engaged Citizens*, London: OSI.

Pearl, D. and W. Menski (1998) *Muslim Family Law*, London: Sweet & Maxwell.

Pollard, J. S. and M. Samers (2007) 'Islamic banking and finance and postcolonial political economy: decentring economic geography', *Transactions of the Institute of British Geographers*, 32.

Pollard, J. S., N. Laurie, C. McEwan and A. Stenning (2009) 'Economic geography under postcolonial scrutiny', *Transactions of the Institute of British Geographers*, 34(2): 137–42.

Powers, D. S. (1999) 'The Islamic endowment (Waqf)', *Vanderbilt Journal of Transnational Law*, 32.

Razzaz, O. M. (1998) 'Land disputes in the absence of ownership rights: insights from Jordan', in E. Fernandes and A. Varley (eds), *Illegal Cities*, London and New York: Zed Books.

Robinson, J. (2003) 'Postcolonialising geography: tactics and pitfalls', *Singapore Journal of Tropical Geography*, 24(3).

Rosen, L. (1999) 'Legal pluralism and cultural unity in Morocco', in B. Dupret, M. Berger and L. al-Zwaini (eds), *Legal Pluralism in the Arab World*, The Hague: Kluwer Law International.

Sadeq, A. M. (2002) '*Waqf*, perpetual charity and poverty alleviation', *International Journal of Social Economics*, 29(1/2).

Sait, S. and H. Lim (2006) *Land, Law and Islam: Property and Human Rights in the Muslim World*, London: Zed Books.

Shah, P. (2005) *Legal Pluralism in Conflict: Coping with Cultural Diversity in Law*, London: Glasshouse Press.

Sia, L. L. (1987) *The Arabs of Singapore: A Sociographic Study of Their Place in the Muslim and Malay World of Singapore*, BA thesis, Department of Sociology, National University of Singapore.

Siddiqi, M. N. (2002) *Problems and Prospects of Islamic Banking and Finance*, www.anderson.ucla.edu/zone/clubs/mbsa/future.htm, accessed 31 October 2008.

Siti, M. M. (2006) *Waqf in Malaysia: Legal and Administrative Perspectives*, Kuala Lumpur: University of Malaya Press.

Stote, M. (2008) 'Muslim courts have heard 100 cases in Britain', *Daily Express*, 15 September.

Strawson, J. (1996) *Encountering Islamic Law*, Research Publications no. 1, University of East London.

Taher, A. (2008) 'Revealed: UK's first official *Shari'a* courts', *Sunday Times*, 14 September.

Thompson, H. A. (n.d.) *The Best Legal Structure for Islamic Charities*, www.aml.org.uk/-charitable/trusts/php, accessed October 2008.

TUC (2005) *Poverty, Exclusion and British People of Pakistani and Bangladeshi Origin*, London: Trades Union Congress.

Tyabji, A. (1991) 'The management of Muslim funds in Singapore', in M. Ariff (ed.), *The Islamic Voluntary Sector in South East Asia*, Singapore: Institute of South East Asia Studies.

Werbner, P. (2004) 'Interventions in pure space: honour, shame and embodied struggles among Muslims in Britain and France', Paper presented at conference entitled 'The constructions of minority identities in Britain and France', Bristol University.

Woodman, G. (1998) 'Ideological combat and social observations: recent debate about legal pluralism', *Journal of Legal Pluralism and Unofficial Law*, 42.

Yilmaz, I. (2005) *Muslim Laws, Politics and Society in Modern Nation States: Dynamic Legal Pluralisms, England, Turkey and Pakistan*, Aldershot: Ashgate.

Zein-Elabdin, E. O. and S. Charusheela (eds) (2004) *Postcolonialism Meets Economics*, London: Routledge.

Zokaei, S. and D. Phillips (2000) 'Altruism and intergenerational relations among Muslims in Britain', *Current Sociology*, 48(4).

9 | Muslims and the anti-war movements

RICHARD PHILLIPS AND JAMIL IQBAL

While some Muslim individuals and communities have empowered themselves through investments in property and industry, in ways that Ziauddin Sardar and Jane Pollard, Hilary Lim and Raj Brown have described in this book, others have done so through other means, including through political activism and organization. This chapter examines one particular way in which Muslims have mobilized and acted politically, and argues that, while immediate goals have not always been achieved, some longer-term benefits have resulted. It focuses upon resistance to the so-called war on terror, which was a catalyst for political cooperation between Muslims and non-Muslims in a number of Western countries. This chapter charts the rise and fall of this relationship, as it unfolded in the UK, recognizing some of the problems with its conception and practice – not least, its alleged tendency to advance a narrow and simplistic conception of Muslim identities and politics – but also arguing that it brought together groups and individuals who had previously had little contact, energizing and widening the horizons of both. Looking back on the UK anti-war movements through interviews with activists who were or are close to the Muslim Association of Britain, the Muslim organization that played the biggest role in the mainstream anti-war movements there, through its partnership with Stop the War Coalition, this chapter throws new light on relationships between Muslims and others, both as they have been conceived, and as they might be in the future. Doing so, it identifies a series of spaces in which these relationships have been conceived and constructed, and it thereby not only describes 'spaces of hope', it also argues that geographical imagination and material geographies are fundamentally productive in opening up new political relationships and possibilities, new contours of hope.

ISLAMOPHOBIA AND RESISTANCE: BRIDGING EAST AND WEST

Italian Prime Minister Silvio Berlusconi was quick to speak, in the wake of the September 11th attacks, of a clash of unequal civilizations and of Islamic otherness: 'We must be aware of the superiority of our civilisation, a system that has guaranteed well-being, respect for human rights and – in contrast with Islamic countries – respect for religious and political rights.'[1] Though characteristically undiplomatic and denounced as 'dangerous' by the EU presidency, and also by then British prime minister Tony Blair, the Italian leader spoke through a broader discursive structure, rearticulated by successive generations of politicians, journalists, artists and intellectuals, including Samuel Huntington, whose *Clash of Civilisations* (1996) encapsulated this new-but-familiar orientalism. In this context of heightened Islamophobia (Halliday 1999), people from many walks of life – including Muslims and people of other faiths and none – saw the importance of building bridges between communities, contesting the social divisions that were being opened up by those who proclaimed the war on terror.

This reference to 'bridges' begins to open up questions about the ways in which geographies – both material and metaphorical – can be mobilized within anti-Islamophobic and related forms of progressive politics. References to connecting spaces can be set against their opposites, including walls and barriers, which were also cited by activists. For instance, a prominent Muslim anti-war leader, to whom I return later in the chapter, declared that his community would not be 'intimidated into creating our own ghettos and building our own walls around ourselves'.[2] These references to bridges and walls are essentially metaphorical, though they also relate to material spaces: to the streets, parks and other public spaces in which demonstrations take place, to the everyday places such as schools and shops in which Muslims may be and/or feel visible to non-Muslims, and to the organizational and institutional geographies in which members of these groups may encounter each other and interact.

It was not clear what form the new bridges should take in the UK anti-war movements. Whether, for instance, they should involve formal working arrangements or more personal engagements and friendships; direct joint action or indirect cooperation; partnerships between organizations or looser forms of affiliation; the assertion and mobilization of Muslim political identities, or their suspension in the interests of broader projects; and whether these relationships should be temporary or permanent. These questions were raised by Muslims, contemplating the place they might take in the wider anti-war movements, as well as by others, particularly the leaders of Stop the War Coalition (StW), who became convinced of the need to work with Muslims.

This chapter traces attempts to build bridges between Muslims and others, and more specifically between Muslim-identified and left-led anti-war groups. It does so through interviews – designed and conducted in autumn 2006 and spring 2007 by Richard Phillips, Naima Bouteldja and Jamil Iqbal – with leaders, members, supporters and observers of the Muslim Association of Britain (MAB). The emphasis, then, is on how MAB activists themselves understood their working relationships with other anti-war groups, including StW – why they entered into and finally withdrew from these relationships. Though it begins in the past, this chapter looks to the future, considering the lessons and legacies of collaboration, and explaining why joint action is sometimes remembered as a 'beautiful thing'[3] – a space of hope. This hope is illustrated in the way Anas Altikriti, a former MAB spokesperson, has described the demonstrations that took place in London, Rome, Madrid and other cities around the world on 15 February 2003 against the impending war on Iraq. Referring specifically to the London demonstration, Altikriti described people from all walks of life – Muslims and others – standing together politically:

> We had Muslims standing by non-Muslims, we had Muslim women in their hijab leading the demonstration, and the shouting and megaphones and people repeating after them. We had people of all ages, of all classes, standing together; it was a historic day and the anti-war movement, I believe, was part of creating that kind of unity and unanimity.[4]

According to Altikriti, this demonstration channelled the will of the grass roots to bridge cultural divides that had been opened up by the war on terror, though he also attributes its success to the efforts of organizations and their leaders. 'Everyone predicted that this anti-war movement was a marriage of convenience, that it would break up and that Muslims would never share a platform with atheists, and that gays would never stand together with a Muslim. It was all proven to be wrong.' This, he argued, was due to the 'leaderships of the three enti-ties' – MAB, StW and the Campaign for Nuclear Disarmament (CND), which worked together to organize anti-war protests. These individuals and groups 'recognized that we had our differences, we recognized that ideologically we all were entitled to our own opinions and views but that there were far greater objectives that we agreed on and those were the issues of peace, of justice, of freedom'.[5] In other words, collaborative politics were fostered by organizations representing the various anti-war constituencies, in particular the two original and, according to some, senior partners in this project: StW and MAB.

The partnership between MAB and StW was a specific relationship between two organizations, and should not be mistaken for a broader relationship between Muslims and non-Muslims, or more narrowly between Muslims and the left. These communities were and are large and disparate, and neither could be represented by any one organization, however inclusive it may claim or have claimed to be. Nevertheless, as Altikriti asserted, this partnership spoke to broader relationships between Muslims and 'non-Muslims'.

STOP THE WAR COALITION AND THE MUSLIM ASSOCIATION OF BRITAIN

In the weeks after 11 September 2001, with the prospect of a US-led war in Afghanistan, the Stop the War Coalition was founded in London, bringing together a number of organizations, the largest of which was the Socialist Workers Party (SWP). None of the larger or more mainstream Muslim organizations was formally involved in these initial meetings, even though some of their members attended in private capacities. Ruhul Tarafder, then a campaign officer with the 1990 Trust anti-racist organization, found it 'disappointing at the start that there weren't many Muslims' at early StW meetings.[6] Most of those interviewed also recalled that the earliest of the anti-war demonstrations seemed to have not involved Muslims in any large numbers. Atif Nazar, an anti-war activist, remembers that 'white people' represented 'more than 98–99 per cent of the demonstrations' and that 'the participation of the Muslims or ethnic minorities was really less ... Muslims played a part, but it wasn't a very big part and it wasn't a significant part'.[7] On the other hand, Ruhul remembers there being large numbers of Muslims at one of the first anti-war demonstrations, which took place in London in November 2001.

An early attempt to respond to the absence of any mainstream Muslim organizations within, or in partnership with, StW was Just Peace, an ad hoc anti-war organization founded by a group of young Muslims. Naima Bouteldja remembers that the formation of Just Peace was, in part, a response to there being, until then, very few Muslim organizations in the anti-war movement.[8] Shaheed Salem and Shahedah Svawda of Just Peace became two of StW's seven officers, along with Asad Rehman of the Newham Monitoring Project, a secular anti-racist campaigning group.[9] But Just Peace was a fringe organization and there remained an absence of mainstream Muslim organizations in StW.

At this time the Muslim Association of Britain was still a new organization, barely four years old, and with fewer than four hundred

to be 'led by the left'.[24] They would remain a distinct and autonomous bloc, able to shape the agenda. To this end, MAB's leaders accepted some compromises: 'These are ten per cent of things that we possibly disagree on but which we amicably arrive at a particular resolution, either in our table or theirs.'[25] For example, they had wanted the 28 September 2002 demonstration to be exclusively about Palestine, which they regarded as 'the cause of all problems in the Middle East'; but they agreed to broaden the agenda to include opposition to the invasion of Iraq.[26] The demonstration's slogan conveyed this pragmatic compromise, 'No war in Iraq, justice for Palestine'. Unable to agree completely on priorities, MAB decided that its leaflets would have 'Freedom for Palestine' above 'Stop the war in Iraq', while StW's leaflets put the slogans in the opposite order. MAB had also wanted to call the joint demonstration the 'One million march' but accepted StW's objection to this, that a turnout of less than a million would have been humiliating.[27] StW made concessions, too, and the partnership was fruitful to both parties. At the helm of the growing national anti-war movement, they took joint decisions with each other and then with the third partner, the Campaign for Nuclear Disarmament (CND): as to who, for instance, would be admitted on the platform at demonstrations and thereby granted audiences in the hundreds of thousands, even millions.[28]

Having emerged as the chosen vehicle for Muslim participation in anti-war politics, MAB was elevated from a relatively obscure group to one with a national profile. It gained considerable influence, punching well above the weight suggested by its limited membership and narrow formal constituency. MAB helped mobilize thousands of Muslims, encouraging them to get involved in the anti-war movement. At demonstrations, protesters from many different religious and political backgrounds carried its placards.[29] MAB assumed an unprecedented significance both for British Muslims and for the anti-war movement. Its membership rose from 400 to 800 or 1,000 – still small, of course, but twice its original size (Leiken and Brooke 2007; Hamed 2007).[30] Some of the organization's leaders and members were already politically experienced but others were not and the anti-war campaign gave them opportunities to learn political skills and form political relationships, both of which they drew upon in the following years.

CRITICS OF THE COALITION

In general, members of MAB did not enter the anti-war movement lightly. One of the reasons for this was that they were hearing, and having to contend with, arguments from other political trends within the wider

Muslim community, that political engagement with non-Muslims was haram (religiously illicit). As Reza Kazim, a volunteer with the Islamic Human Rights Committee (IHRC), put it: 'Standing on a platform with people who weren't Muslim was an issue for some people.' (Not, he stressed, for himself.)[31] Arguments against working with non-Muslims or, more precisely, within a non-Islamic framework were advanced most loudly by groups such as Hizb ut-Tahrir (HT). HT's relationship with the wider anti-war movement was at best lukewarm. There were a number of reasons given for this, including a rejection of some of the political compromises of such a grand coalition (which included groups who were less categorical about their opposition to war) and, if not an outright hostility to working with non-Muslims, a preference for working within the Muslim community.[32] HT's basic position on British politics is that 'voting in the Western democratic process to elect someone in the government is prohibited'.[33] Warning against togetherness for its own sake, one HT activist commented: 'It's our observation that some Muslim organizations put so much emphasis on the engagement side; the very nature of that sort of cooperation means that ultimately the message becomes more and more diluted.'[34] He and others commented on the risk of working together: the perception that Muslims could be assimilated by their political partners. As he put it, HT was not worried about 'engaging with the left' or 'engaging with non-Muslims per se'. Rather, concerns were raised by 'some statements that we'd come across in which a section of the anti-war movement and the left talked about assimilating Muslims into a secular and socialist politics'.[35] As HT member Nazmul Hoque put it, the ideal was to be – and to remain – independent rather than isolationist: 'We cannot rely on other people to do our work for us.'[36] As a result of these arguments, some were persuaded to avoid engaging politically with non-Muslims,[37] though others within HT denied any 'principled objection' to doing so.[38]

Shamiul Joarder, a member of MAB, recalls the dilemma he faced as a student, after participating in mixed demonstrations and then hearing Muslims argue that 'you shouldn't go to demonstrations, it's not halal to go to demonstrations, don't mix with these people who are telling you to do these kind of activities'.[39] Many members and supporters of MAB who decided they were comfortable working with non-Muslims in principle continued to be troubled by aspects of doing so in practice: attending meetings in which men and women mixed, or demonstrations with confrontational or carnival atmospheres that seemed alien and inappropriate to their purpose. Nor did they wish to bury these cultural differences. 'Once you start doing that too much,'

Moazzam Begg suggested, 'I think that you may have lost something that was specifically or exclusively part of your identity, which is what a lot of the Muslims feel also.'[40]

Though British Muslims have increasingly politicized their religious identities, there remain many different ways to be a political Muslim. Some prefer to keep their religion private, others to work primarily through other identities and/or organizations – approaching politics as socialists, Asians or Bangladeshis, for instance, and/or as British citizens, Welsh or Scottish nationals, Londoners or Liverpudlians (Peach 2006; Eade et al. 1996; Hopkins 2007; Marranci 2007).[41] Many of these Muslims have been frustrated by the assertiveness and success of religiously defined political organizations in the anti-war movement and of the open arms with which these groups have been received by socialist leaders of StW. Ansar Ahmed Ullah, an activist in the Bangladeshi community in East London, regretted that 'the anti-war coalition, in order to work with the Muslim community, has decided to work with Islamists'.[42] Many older Bangladeshi Britons and some of their younger relatives are drawn towards the secular nationalist politics of the Bangladeshi national movement and are opposed to Islamist forms of politics. Ullah criticizes leaders of StW for failing to engage with secular groups that include Muslims but are not defined primarily or singularly as Muslim. He says that there did not seem to have been 'any effort on their part to engage with many secular groups that exist within the Muslim community'. He speculated that this reflected 'a lack of … understanding or naivety' on the part of StW. This has not all been StW's doing, of course, since Muslims who have worked with them *as Muslims* have effectively presented themselves (or allowed themselves to be presented) in essentialized terms, which sacrifice some of the balance between competing desires for recognition as a group, on the one hand, and as a differentiated series of communities and identities, on the other.

One of the important lessons here is that political relationships between Muslims and non-Muslims cannot be forged through self-appointed representatives of either position. Rather, a more nuanced understanding of who Muslims and non-Muslims are, and how the two might work together, ought to be promoted. The diversity as well as the unity of Muslims must be kept in sight at all times and those who do not wish to identify politically as Muslims have to be acknowledged. As Massoud Shadjareh, chair of IHRC, put it: 'Muslims were almost expected to be all under one umbrella and usually the real world is not like that.'[43]

THE END OF THE PARTNERSHIP

In the end, the fatal blow to MAB's partnership with StW did not come from a fear that political or religious identity would be diluted. Rather, some within MAB felt that the organization's anti-war activities had pitted it too publicly and forcefully against the British establishment, taking it away from what they considered its primary purposes – religious and cultural. By joining the anti-war movement and favouring street activism, MAB's leadership had shifted the political culture of the organization, breaking away from the traditional forms of lobbying undertaken during the previous decade.[44] But a more conservative and traditional faction, made up, predominantly, of 'the old, who came from outside the country',[45] had been unhappy with MAB's new-found political activism. MAB activist Mohammed Sawalha explains that members of the older generation – including immigrants from Egypt and Iraq – were not apolitical but had seen comrades jailed and exiled and perhaps suffered this themselves.[46] Following the 7 July 2005 bombings in London, and the heightened tensions they provoked, the arguments of this faction came to greater prominence. According to Tamimi: 'What led to MAB falling into a big crisis was the objection that we, the leaders of MAB, myself and my other colleagues, who were at that time in MAB, had over-politicized MAB and put MAB on a crash course with the government, with the establishment.'[47] Another source close to MAB, speaking anonymously, described a trend within the organization which thought MAB was putting itself 'in jeopardy' by opposing the government – 'that trend has probably won over'.

Those who led MAB into partnership with StW, including Tamimi and Altikriti, lost control of the organization in December 2005, when a new president and, by extension, a new executive board were elected. According to Tamimi:

> There were others within MAB who were also in the leadership – but they were the minority in the leadership – who were travelling up and down the country talking to our grass roots, convincing them that we are a danger to MAB, derailing the project, because what MAB is supposed to be – it's supposed to be about social issues, taking care of the individual, spirituality – all this nonsense that they were talking. And we were so busy [campaigning], we were not doing something similar. A gap was growing between the leadership and the grass roots because of this.[48]

The new leaders persuaded members that as 'a small minority we cannot afford to oppose the establishment; this is too dangerous'.[49] MAB's new leaders effectively – albeit implicitly and gradually – dissolved the organization's relationship with StW. There does not appear to have been a formal dissolution of the relationship but both organizations saw that their formal partnership had ended.

This returned MAB to what its new leaders and some of its members considered less uncomfortable political ground. The organization was steered away from direct political action, though the more politicized individuals within MAB continued undeterred, both as individuals and as members of other and new organizations. According to Massoud Shadjareh, the relationship between StW and MAB revolved around personal connections 'and that relationship has continued with those individuals' but not with 'MAB let alone with the community as a whole'.[50]

By February 2006, the individuals who had led MAB into partnership with StW formed a new organization, the British Muslim Initiative (BMI), which effectively took the place vacated by MAB in relation to StW.[51] A source close to BMI, who preferred to remain anonymous, said: 'The brothers and sisters that were involved in the anti-war stuff went and set up BMI because they saw that relationship with the left and Stop the War as unique, as something which needs to be nurtured and in fact needs to be spread globally as well as within the UK.' The relationship between MAB and BMI was not clear. Some saw the latter as a wholly new organization, not warmly regarded by MAB's leadership.[52] For others, BMI is effectively – though not officially – a branch of MAB, its principal members drawn from the membership and former leadership of that organization.[53] In any case, BMI took over where MAB left off in many respects, meeting StW to negotiate campaign strategies and sharing costs equally. But BMI is a smaller organization with more limited support,[54] lacking MAB's national and grassroots presence.[55]

The model of collaboration between Muslim organizations and the left continued not only in the anti-war movement but also in other spheres, such as with the formation of the Respect Party. Building on the energy of the anti-war movement in 2003/04 and aiming to occupy the political space opened up by the Labour Party's shift to the right, Respect contested the 2005 general election, winning a parliamentary seat in Tower Hamlets and coming a close second in Birmingham Sparkbrook. Glyn Robbins, a former chair of Respect in Tower Hamlets, attributed the ongoing relationship there between Muslim organizations and the left to shared interests and problems. For example, he explained, 'there's a lot of poor housing in this borough' and 'the people who are suffering some of the worst effects of that are Muslim'.[56] Shahed Yunus, an activist within the Bangladeshi community in Tower Hamlets, regarded Respect as 'the biggest achievement of the anti-war movement'.[57] Others on the left made similar claims about their ongoing collaboration with Muslims, some adding that collaboration was actually increasing. An anti-war activist we spoke to in Glasgow claimed (anonymously) that the establishment of a local branch of StW in 2006 had increased Muslim involvement in the anti-war movement there, something she felt that the Scottish Coalition for Justice not War (the CND-led coalition that dominated the anti-war movement north of the border between 2001 and 2005) had failed to achieve.

 An increasingly hostile environment for Muslims after July 2005, however, meant that many Muslims were fearful of acting politically outside their own communities.[58] Scrutinized from all sides, 'scared now just to show their faces', they kept a low political profile.[59] Asad Khan, StW coordinator in Bury, said that he had 'found great difficulty in getting the Muslim community interested' in anti-war activities: 'One thing they say is that we don't want to get into trouble, so it's best to keep our head down and get on with our lives. And you can see that, on the demonstrations, they're mainly white people.'[60]

LEGACIES AND PROSPECTS

Looking back on the MAB–StW collaboration, some MAB activists felt that they were exploited by what they saw as the 'secular white left' – by which they generally meant the SWP, which has dominated the leadership of StW nationally and in many local branches.[61] One Muslim activist felt that the SWP had approached StW much as it had done other movements and political processes: going in to the situation to 'feed'.[62] Others suspected 'certain elements of the socialist parties exploiting the Muslims' to make political capital.[63] Many others came to feel that these relationships were either counterproductive or no longer appropriate. Shahed Yunus argued that the coalition between Muslim organizations and the left, including the SWP, worked for a time but did not work later.[64] Azzam Tamimi said that he had no regrets about leading MAB into partnership with StW but realized that he may have run ahead of the organization's grass roots, to whom he was returning. 'My friends in the left – we have a very good relationship, I don't mind attending one or two of their conferences. But personally I feel the emphasis has to shift elsewhere. I need to speak more to the Muslims.'[65]

At the very least, the partnership between StW and MAB held for a time, demonstrating that it is possible for two such organizations

to work together when they really need and want to. According to
Shahed Yunus, 'the marriage between the Socialist Workers Party and
the Muslim community – it basically doesn't work but, the thing is, on
this occasion it did. ... We came together with one purpose, one goal
and that was to campaign against the war which we felt was illegal
and it was very successful.' By entering the alliance at a time of their
own choosing, doing so on terms they could live with, and distancing
themselves when they felt the time was right – when the mass anti-war
movement lost some of its momentum and began to be transformed into
a different kind of project, the Respect Party – some Muslim activists
felt that they retained political self-possession and avoided assimilation.
An anonymous member of HT seems to have spoken for a number of
Muslim activists in arguing that, while specific and limited projects with
the left could sometimes be contemplated, 'permanent coalitions' could
not.[66] Catherine Hossain, of the Muslim Public Affairs Committee,
a media lobby group, argued that allegiance to Respect might leave
Muslims marginalized and politically boxed in.[67] Massoud Shadjareh
felt that, through a strategically timed disengagement, he was helping
to keep resistance to war in focus as a cross-party issue.[68] By generally
avoiding settling into a fixed coalition, Muslim activists may have laid
the basis for a more inclusive politics that is sufficiently fluid to keep
Muslim identities in play.

The partnerships between Muslims and non-Muslims, which played
such an important part in the anti-war movement, may yet have an
important legacy: political capital that remains to be channelled and
political and human relationships that remain, in some latent form, for
when they are wanted and needed.[69] This was the note of optimism
sounded by Osama Saeed in his description of the relationships between
Muslims and other veterans of the anti-war movements: 'We all get
along like we're one big family.'[70] For Shahed Yunus, the memories of
joint action seemed to offer similar hope for the future. Discussing how
Muslims coped with demonstrating during the month of Ramadan by
arranging for lorry-loads of halal food to be delivered, he remembered
how this was shared:

> It wasn't just Muslims there ... A lot of human rights movements, the
> Socialist Workers Party, the Labour Party – everyone was there and
> the food was provided for everyone. Everyone joined in and it was
> like – this is how we see the future ... while the Muslims are breaking
> fast, everyone joined in, everyone broke fast with them, which was a
> beautiful thing.[71]

NOTES

The research referred to in this
article, funded by the Economic
and Social Research Council (Grant
RES-000-22-1785), involved
interviews with leaders, members,
supporters and critics of MAB and
other organizations involved in the
anti-war movement.

This chapter is a revised and
extended version of an earlier publication, which appeared in *Race &
Class* (Volume 50, October–December
2008, pp. 101–13). I am grateful
to Arun Kundnani and the editors
of this journal for their comments
on an earlier draft of this chapter.
Permission to reproduce is gratefully
acknowledged.

1 Belgian Prime Minister Guy
Verhofstadt, whose nation held the
EU presidency, said Berlusconi's
'remarks could, in a dangerous
way, have consequences'. Source:
BBC News Europe 27 September
2001, news.bbc.co.uk/1/hi/world/
middle_east.
2 Anas Altikriti, Muslim Association of Britain (MAB), NB, 25 April
2007. (In this and the following
references, interviews are identified
with details of: the interviewee's name
and affiliation or position, when the
interview took place, who did the
interview – where Naima Bouteldja
is NB, Jamil Iqbal JI and Richard
Phillips RP – and the date on which
the interview took place.)
3 Shahed Yunus, founding member of 1990 Trust, JI, 8 March 2007.
4 Anas Altikriti, MAB, NB,
25 April 2007.
5 Ibid.
6 Ruhul Tarafder, Campaign
Officer, 1990 Trust, NB, 22 February
2007.

7 Atif Nazar, member of Marxist
International, StW activist, JI, 11 February and 9 March 2007.
8 Naima Bouteldja, personal
communication, March 2007.
9 Ibid.
10 Osama Saeed, MAB spokesperson in Scotland, Scottish National
Party candidate 2003, NB, 23 February 2007.
11 Ibid.
12 Anas Altikriti, MAB director of
media and public relations 1997–2003,
president 2003–04, NB, 25 April 2007.
13 Ibid.
14 Ibid.
15 Shahed Yunus, founding member of 1990 Trust, JI, 8 March 2007.
16 Osama Saeed, MAB/SNP, NB,
23 February 2007.
17 Azzam Tamimi, former MAB
president, RP/NB, 17 February 2007.
18 Alladin Fida, former MAB
spokesperson, NB, 16 May 2007.
19 Mohammed Sawalha, MAB/
IslamExpo, NB, 26 April 2007.
20 Azzam Tamimi, MAB, RP/NB,
17 February 2007.
21 Anas Altikriti, MAB, NB,
25 April 2007.
22 Ibid.
23 Alladin Fida, MAB, NB,
16 May 2007.
24 Anas Altikriti, MAB, NB,
25 April 2007.
25 Ibid.
26 Alladin Fida, MAB, NB,
16 May 2007; Anas Altikriti, MAB,
NB, 25 April 2007.
27 Ibid.
28 Azzam Tamimi, MAB, RP/NB,
17 February 2007.
29 Alladin Fida, MAB, NB,
16 May 2007.
30 Mohammed Sawalha, MAB/
IslamExpo, NB, 26 April 2007.

31 Reza Kazim, IHRC volunteer, NB, 5 April 2007.

32 Nazmul Hoque, member of HT, JI, 19 February 2007.

33 Nazrul Islam, member of HT, JI, 11 March 2007.

34 Anonymous member of Hizb ut-Tahrir executive, NB, 15 May 2007.

35 Ibid.

36 Nazmul Hoque, member of HT, JI, 19 February 2007.

37 Azzam Tamimi, MAB, RP/NB, 17 February 2007; Shamiul Joarder, MAB, NB, 5 April 2007.

38 Anonymous member of Hizb ut-Tahrir executive, NB, 15 May 2007.

39 Shamiul Joarder, member of MAB, NB, 5 April 2007.

40 Moazzam Begg, ex-Guantánamo detainee, RP/NB, 21 May 2007.

41 Mehdi Hassan, Respect, RP, 13 November 2006.

42 Ansar Ahmed Ullah, Nirmul Committee, JI, 10 January 2007.

43 Massoud Shadjareh, IHRC chair, NB, 19 April 2007.

44 Naima Bouteldja, personal communication, December 2007.

45 Mohammed Sawalha, MAB/IslamExpo, NB, 26 April 2007.

46 Ibid.

47 Azzam Tamimi, MAB, RP/NB, 17 February 2007.

48 Ibid.

49 Ibid.

50 Massoud Shadjareh, IHRC chair, NB, 19 April 2007.

51 Mohammed Sawalha, MAB/IslamExpo, NB, 26 April 2007.

52 Osama Saeed, MAB/SNP, NB, 23 February 2007.

53 Belgacem Kahlalech, MAB, NB, 22 February 2007.

54 Mohammed Sawalha, MAB/IslamExpo, NB, 26 April 2007.

55 Azzam Tamimi, MAB, RP/NB, 17 February 2007.

56 Glyn Robbins, chair of Tower Hamlets Respect Party, RP, 4 October 2006.

57 Shahed Yunus, 1990 Trust, JI, 8 March 2007.

58 Moazzam Begg, ex-Guantánamo detainee, RP/NB, 21 May 2007.

59 Elias Mohammad, StW Glasgow, RP, 10 February 2007.

60 Asad Khan, Bury StW co-ordinator, JI, 22 June 2007.

61 Massoud Shadjareh, IHRC chair, NB, 19 April 2007.

62 Mahir Sayar, Islamic Forum for Islamic Dialogue volunteer, JI, 16 February 2007.

63 Catherine Hossain, MPAC, JI, 13 February 2007.

64 Shahed Yunus, 1990 Trust, JI, 8 March 2007.

65 Azzam Tamimi, MAB, RP/NB, 17 February 2007.

66 Anonymous member of Hizb ut-Tahrir executive, NB, 15 May 2007.

67 Catherine Hossain, MPAC, JI, 13 February 2007.

68 Massoud Shadjareh, IHRC chair, NB, 19 April 2007.

69 Julian Goss, former chair of StW South Wales and SWP member, RP, 21 December 2006. He recalls how StW forged an activist network in South Wales that could be used at a later date, if required, to avoid a repeat of the 'dead period that we had after 9/11'.

70 Osama Saeed, MAB/SNP, NB, 23 February 2007.

71 Shahed Yunus, founding member of 1990 Trust, JI, 8 March 2007.

REFERENCES

Eade, J., T. Vamplew and C. Peach(1996) 'Bangladeshis: the encapsulated community', in C. Peach (ed.), *The Ethnic Minority Populations of Britain*, vol. 2: *Ethnicity in the 1991 Census*, London: HMSO.

Halliday, F. (1999) 'Islamophobia reconsidered', *Ethnic and Racial Studies*, 22(5).

Hamed, S. (2007) 'Islamic political radicalism in Britain: the case of Hizb ut-Tahrir', in T. Abbas (ed.), *Islamic Political Radicalism*, Edinburgh: Edinburgh University Press.

Hopkins, P. (2007) 'Young, male and Scottish: a portrait of Kabir', Paper presented at the annual meeting of the Association of American Geographers, San Francisco, CA.

Huntington, S. P. (1996) *The Clash of Civilisations and the Remaking of World Order*, New York: Simon and Schuster.

Leiken, R. S. and S. Brooke (2007) 'The moderate Muslim Brotherhood', *Foreign Affairs*, 86(2), March/April.

Marranci, G. (2007) 'From the ethos of justice to the ideology of justice: understanding radical views of Scottish Muslims', in T. Abbas (ed.), *Islamic Political Radicalism*, Edinburgh: Edinburgh University Press.

Peach, C. (2006) 'Islam, ethnicity and South Asian religions in the London 2001 Census', *Transactions of the Institute of British Geographers*, NS 31.

10 | Liberalizing Islam: creating Brits of the Islamic persuasion

SARAH GLYNN

This chapter explores the responses of Western governments to the politicization of their Muslim citizens. The immediate aim of current policies is to pre-empt the growth of 'Islamic extremism', but they also build on developments in the incorporation of faith groups into new forms of partnership governance. While I share governmental concern about the risks of young Muslims being attracted by those who advocate violent interpretations of Islam, I argue that current policies will only make this more likely. I argue that the increasing role for faith groups within Western political structures encourages division along faith lines, and that government attempts to promote a 'moderate' Islam from above are more likely to alienate those they seek to reach. And I argue that the rise of political religion of all kinds has to be understood as a consequence of the decline of an effective left movement through which to channel frustrations with local and international inequalities. With socialism, even of the social democratic variety, off – and deliberately removed from – the agenda, some of those who once looked to socio-economic solutions are now turning to other ideologies. I argue that the only way for Western nations to prevent this, and open up real spaces of hope, is to return to addressing those basic socio-economic issues and concentrate on increasing equality both within their own borders and in their foreign policy.

While these arguments can be applied to Western governments in general, some differences of approach have been highlighted, and the chapter focuses on a case study of government-sponsored attempts to promote the development of a liberal version of Islam among British Muslims.

I have described the rise of political religion as a response to in-equalities. The British government does itself talk about 'addressing the grievances that ideologues are exploiting';[1] this, however, is not reflected in their actions. They continue with a foreign policy that has been widely criticized for taking a neocolonial approach and for bringing more

problems to the areas in which it has intervened. They have also introduced anti-terror laws that encroach on long-established civil liberties,
and, because these are more often targeted at Muslims, encourage Muslim alienation from the political system; just as the old stop-and-search
on suspicion, or 'sus', laws alienated a generation of young blacks. And,
most importantly – but least discussed in relation to this subject – they
are following the hegemonic neoliberal agenda. This acts to increase
inequality, and (like other so-called centre-left parties) New Labour has
gone out of its way to eliminate socialist ideas of wealth redistribution
from its ranks, and therefore from mainstream British politics.

ISLAM AND ISLAMISM

In common with other religions, Islam has always generated debate
and dispute over what constitutes 'true' religious belief and practice,
and produced movements for reform and renewal. Such developments
arise within their specific historical and political contexts and are influenced by events beyond the confines of religious thought and custom.
Increasingly, for over a century, religious debate has focused on Islamic
responses to modernity and to the Western liberal tradition. Arguments centre on what makes up the unquestionable core of Islam and
what is open to reinterpretation in response to different historical and
geographical circumstances. Many different modernizing movements
have evolved, both in Muslim majority countries and among immigrant
communities, and these have interacted with each other and with other
streams of Islamic reformism.

Increasingly prominent have been various kinds of Islamism. The
definition of this term has been the subject of much debate, but I am
using it here to refer to all those different forms of Islam in which people
believe that it is not possible to separate a private religion from public
action because religion bears on every aspect of life, and that to be a
Muslim is a matter of politics as well as of faith. In popular debate, the
term Islamism has tended to become demonized – as 'fundamentalism'
was before it – to suggest an unacceptable and dangerous form of Islam,[2]
and Islamists of all kinds are often popularly regarded as potential terrorists. But, however much we may disagree with someone's political ideas,
or with the concept of a system in which the ultimate frame of reference
is interpretation of scripture, this does not make the person who holds
those ideas a terrorist, and political ideology should be debated with, not
outlawed. This last point is crucial for all ideologies and for a healthy
society. Practically, too, driving an ideology underground (as has been
suggested with respect to Hizb ut-Tahrir)[3] can encourage the develop-

ment of violent protest, and is also unnecessary: we already have laws in place to deal with incitement to violence. This chapter uses the term Islamism to mean any version of Islam that argues for the impossibility of separating religion and politics, and it acknowledges that Islamists, like those of other political ideologies and faiths, or of none, can be, and often are, active members of wider civil society.

In response to the growth of various forms of Islamism, recent years have seen a new factor impacting on developments within Islam, as Western governments and their agents attempt to engage with and influence core debates in Islamic thought. Although there are many colonial precedents for government involvement with Islam,[4] government approaches towards Islam today appear to be more deliberately and essentially interventionist.

STATES OF SECULARISM

Inevitably, government responses to Islamism vary from nation to nation. So, for example, British pragmatism can be contrasted with French policies that are built on an assertively secular republicanism and on an imperial tradition that aimed to incorporate its colonies politically and culturally into a greater France. Even in France, however, Nicolas Sarkozy has been attempting to redefine the principle of *laïcité* – the hard-won separation of state and religion that has been enshrined in French law since 1905. In 2003, as interior minister, he promoted the establishment of the French Council of the Muslim Faith (*Conseil Français du Culte Musulman*) as the official representatives of French Muslims on religious matters; this, however, only gave them a similar official voice to that already in place for Catholics, Protestants and Jews. Then, in 2004, he published a book, *The Republic, Religions, Hope* (*La République, les religions, l'espérance*) that broke with established principles. This argues for a public role for faith-based organizations, and for a change in the law to allow the state to help fund the establishment of mosques, so making them independent of foreign influence and allowing French Muslims to catch up with better-resourced religious groups. Sarkozy explains that 'a humiliated identity is a radicalised identity, and therefore dangerous', and the proposed mosques are presented as providing the alternative to clandestine meetings in basements and garages. The aim is to promote an 'open-handed' French Islam, and avoid the Islam of the 'closed fist'. Sarkozy uses the language of rights and responsibilities, and in exchange for its rights French Islam must submit to the values of the republic. It was also Sarkozy who instigated the debates that resulted in the ban (from 2004) on the wearing of conspicuous religious symbols in schools, which was especially targeted at the hijab. His response to the riots that took place in 2005 in the *banlieues* (suburban estates), where much of France's immigrant population live, demonstrated little empathy with those who have endured severe socio-economic marginalization; and the arguments in his book that religious authorities are needed to instil moral order can be seen as an example of conservative authoritarianism, in line with some of his other views that have invited parallels with the American right.[5]

In the USA, despite the legal separation of Church and state, politicians make public display of their religion, and religious groups take an active part in election campaigns and in pushing their moral agenda. 'In God we trust' first appeared on US coins in 1864, and was declared the national motto by Congress in 1956.[6] There has always been a strong reliance on faith organizations to play an important role in civil society, and from 2001 this was supported by Bush's Faith-based and Community Initiative.[7] As in the British case that is the focus of this chapter, recent American policy has promoted 'moderate' Islam, both internationally and nationally. *Building Moderate Muslim Networks*, a policy monograph produced by the Rand Corporation in 2007, although generally critical of actual achievements so far, argues that lessons can be learnt from the way the USA and its allies built up 'democratic networks' during the last great 'battle of ideas' in the cold war. The authors propose that the most effective route to wider geographic influence would be to concentrate on working with Muslim intellectuals, activists and leaders in the Muslim diaspora, and to try to reverse the flow of ideas so that these chosen moderates can impact on Islam in the Middle East.[8] These are all common themes in the anti-Islamism literature described below (Kundnani 2008), and the substitution of a new enemy to replace the old communist bloc feeds the needs of the powerful military-industrial complex.

Recognition of the wider importance of religious developments in the Muslim diaspora is shared by Tariq Ramadan, who many have regarded as a key example of an influential, moderate, diaspora Muslim. He argues that 'Western Muslims will play a decisive role in the evolution of Islam worldwide because of the nature and complexity of the challenges they face, and in this their responsibility is doubly essential' (Ramadan 2004: 225). Ramadan is currently Professor of Islamic Studies at Oxford; he has been a member of the EU High Level Advisory Group on Dialogue between Peoples and Culture, and has spoken at meetings organized by the British-government-backed Radical Middle Way. He has also had his US visa revoked – shortly after taking up an academic post in Indiana – and has been briefly banned from France, demonstrating the confused and contradictory thinking that afflicts political responses to Islam.

The developments in Western liberal thought that have provided the intellectual backing for these confused governmental interactions with Islamism have been explored by Arun Kundnani. He argues that, unlike the neocons, who subscribe to the view put forward by Bernard Lewis and Samuel Huntington that Islam is intrinsically antipathetic to Western civilization, influential Western writers of a more liberal tradition have discovered a new ideological enemy in a generic Islamism. Any Islamic political engagement, without further qualification, is taken to be 'analogous to Stalinism or fascism' and 'regarded as an appropriation of modern European totalitarianism that is basically alien to "traditional Islam"' (Kundnani 2008: 42). Kundnani (ibid.: 47–52) gives special attention to Paul Berman's 'best-selling' *Terror and Liberalism*, published in 2004, which he describes as a 'major source' for such thinking, and shows to be based on a frightening mix of decontextualized, half-digested facts and shoddy argumentation.

MUSLIM BRITONS

Confusion and contradiction haunt governmental responses to the growth of political Islam, as politicians everywhere are trying desperately to learn their way. A rapid turnover of policy initiatives could be said to be a general characteristic of Britain's New Labour government, but Britain's Muslims have found themselves at the centre of an exceptional whirl of policy experiments. Many of these can be understood as government-sponsored attempts to promote the development of a liberal version of Islam.

In some ways – as my subtitle suggests – comparisons can be drawn with the situation around a hundred years ago, when established Anglo-Jewry attempted to encourage East European Jewish immigrants to become Englishmen of the Mosaic persuasion. Assimilated middle-class Jews were concerned not only to promote greater integration, but also to ensure that their co-religionists became the right sort of Englishmen and did not integrate instead into international socialism. They were anxious to tame overtly foreign religious and cultural practices; however, the radicalism that they were afraid of was distinctly secular. Today, though, it is religion that is providing the inspiration for revolutionary movements; and the concern of the establishment – including sympathetic Muslim organizations – is that British Muslims should not only consider themselves British but also embrace the 'right sort' of Islam.

The most important spur for government involvement in this is clearly the wish to pre-empt the growth of 'Islamic extremism', and most explicitly of Islamic-inspired terrorism; their various new schemes and approaches, however, build on developments in forms of governance already taking place across the Western world. Partnership structures play an important part in neoliberal political systems, and faith groups are being brought in to take on partnership roles. Even before recent developments, this had generated a need for Muslim partners that governments could do business with.

MULTICULTURALISM, FAITH ORGANIZATIONS AND NEOLIBERAL GOVERNANCE

Official recognition of faith groups can be seen as developing out of the institutionalization of ethnically defined groups that was encouraged by policies of multiculturalism. The historical shifts of personal and political identity formation that have taken place over the last few decades have been the subject of considerable study (Glynn 2002). Black–white dualism of the 1960s and 1970s gave way in the 1980s to multicultural 'new' – and not so new – ethnicities and the celebration of difference. These, in turn, have increasingly morphed into an emphasis on religious identities, which has been encouraged by international politics and was well advanced before 9/11.[9] Government recognition of religious identity as a primary organizing principle responds to, but also reinforces, the increasing emphasis on religious identity within ethnic minority groups. The prioritizing of 'community' and faith-based interests can be used to cut across class loyalties and discourage the development of a more class-based politics that might threaten elite interests; and multicultural policies can also be used to provide an administration with a progressive veneer without the need to address fundamental socio-economic structures. The turn towards faith groups also allows governments to promote more socially conservative forces that are in tune with currently dominant political thinking. While individual 'community' or faith groups may support progressive as well as more conservative ideas, multiculturalism as a system distracts political attention from fundamental socio-economic problems and divisions, and holds back progress towards greater social equality.

This is an argument with which the main proponents of multiculturalism seem reluctant to engage. So, for example, Tariq Modood acknowledges that the effects on life chances of parental class and education 'are usually much greater than the effects of race or ethnicity' (Modood 2007: 58) but dismisses the view that class identities are a primary form of political mobilization that should not be divided by 'assertions of race, political femininity, gay pride politics and so on' (ibid.: 69). No reference is made to the achievements of those who have addressed multiple inequalities through a unified socio-economic perspective, and instead class-based politics is simply relegated to a past that 'soon gave way to an understanding that these [other] positions were a genuine and significant part of a plural centre-left egalitarian movement' (ibid.: 69). Meanwhile, Will Kymlicka presents a teleological view of the evolution of liberal democracies in which forty years of multiculturalism have 'often helped deepen democratic citizenship and created more just and free societies' (Kymlicka 2008: 280). While there have clearly been huge changes in racial and ethnic relations, this seems rather too complacent when describing a period for almost three-quarters of which the gap between rich and poor has been widening; a period that has led us into a recession where, in the absence of a significant left alternative, social frustrations will increasingly turn towards scapegoat politics and intolerance of all kinds. Even Arun Kundnani's article in *Race and Class*, which provides such a strong critique of dominant views of Islamism, only finds it necessary to quote Shivanadan's rhetorical defence of black anti-racism (and mention the left-wing past of key anti-Islamist liberals) before welcoming, as unproblematic, the possibilities for a new political engagement in progressive British politics mediated through a Muslim identity (Kundnani 2008: 58).

Pragmatic politicians have always recognized and exploited community leaders and organizations for their own ends, but under new systems of governance, some community groups and structural hierarchies are being openly bolstered and given official recognition. Incorporation of community organizations into partnership structures helps neoliberal governments impose their pro-business agenda, and it is no accident that Britain appears to be following a US model in increasing the role of faith groups in the maintenance of civil society. Local government has been reduced to little more than strategic management, and a growing critical literature has shown how partnership mechanisms are being used to incorporate, control and contain possible sources of conflict, tying potential activists into preset systems and strengthening those organizations more ready to comply with government policy (see, for example, Allen 2008; Collins 2007). Mike Geddes has described how scope for real political debate is being restricted, and the state is able to 'maintain tight control over local institutions and actors who might challenge the hegemony of neoliberalism' (Geddes 2006: 93). While only very limited control is conceded to community groups, as important decisions are made elsewhere, these structures do impact on power dynamics within 'communities', strengthening groups seen as more favourable to government policies at the expense of those that could be regarded as more critical. Under this system, the link between the British government and its Muslim citizens is being increasingly mediated through the mosque and other faith-based organizations.

Western governments have always preferred to deal with more conservative forces than encourage the development of alternative groups that might challenge elite interests, and this is true at all levels. What we are seeing here is a less dramatic example of those same political practices that have resulted in the promotion of traditional tribal and religious leaders in Afghanistan and Iraq. Indeed, the resurgence of Islam internationally, as a political force, cannot be understood without looking at the decline of those secular left forces that once attracted many Muslims who wanted to oppose existing political hegemonies. And this decline has been a long-term aim of Western foreign policy. Anyone tempted to doubt the deep-seated resistance that has been deliberately built up towards left ideas only had to listen to the horror that greeted the suggestion, during the US presidential election campaign, that Barack Obama might introduce redistributive taxation. And Europe is not immune. In 2006 Seumas Milne reported in the *Guardian* newspaper that the Council of Europe's parliamentary assembly had 'voted to condemn the crimes of totalitarian communist regimes', linking them with Nazism and complaining that communist parties are still 'legal and active in some countries'. He added: 'Demands that European ministers launch a continent-wide anti-communist campaign – including school textbook revisions, official memorial days and museums – only narrowly missed the necessary two-thirds majority.'[10]

The prominent role being given to 'faith communities' at all levels can be seen to be a tactical choice for those who wish to preserve existing structural hierarchies – even if it is not presented that way. Recognition of 'faith communities' has also been encouraged by coordinated lobbying by different faith groups – including through the Inter Faith Network[11] – but the lobbying has fallen on receptive ground (and not just because of the personal faith of Tony Blair as prime minister). A report for the Home Office Faith Communities Unit in 2004 observed that 'Some areas of policy are now routinely recognised by Departments as requiring the input of the faith communities, for example as partners in urban regeneration', and it put forward recommendations 'designed to make [existing] processes even more effective across government'.[12] The promotion of faith schools is probably the most high-profile – and controversial – example of these policies in action, but they take many forms, some more readily obvious than others. In the London borough of Tower Hamlets, where over a third of the population is Muslim, the borough council holds regular discussions with the local Council of Mosques, which it helped establish in 2001, and the 8,000-square-metre London Muslim Centre, built beside the East London Mosque in 2004, received funding from the borough council, the London Development Authority, the European Development Fund and the government's Surestart programme. The centre is used as a channel for the provision of local facilities by authorities ranging from the health service to the jobcentre, and the mosque's imam has been personally involved in visiting homes as part of the Improving School Attendance Partnership. At the same time, youth groups and holiday projects run by enthusiastic young Islamists have received funding from the borough council and other secular bodies. This is all in line with the observation in the Home Office document quoted above that 'Central Government is increasingly exploring ways of using the experience and resources of faith communities "on the ground" to deliver services' (Home Office Faith Communities Unit 2004: 8).

SEARCHING FOR THE RIGHT PARTNER

If government is to work through faith organizations, this naturally raises questions about exactly which groups it should choose to work with. There are numerous organizations representing different Islamic traditions, but there have also been many attempts to bring them together into wider representative bodies, both locally and nationally. An important local example is provided by the Bradford Council of Mosques, founded in 1981 to cut across Muslim sectarianism and provide a vehicle for interaction with the public authorities on issues such as education. It received grant funding from the city council and (from 1983 to 1988) its community workers were supported by central government (Lewis 2002). Increasingly, attempts were also made to create a national organization – especially following 1988 and the Muslim mobilization generated in response to the publication of Rushdie's *Satanic Verses*. By the mid-1990s, Philip Lewis was able to observe that 'There is now a plethora of bodies presuming to speak for all British Muslims' (ibid.: 207).

By the late 1990s, with the active support of the Conservative Home Secretary, Michael Howard, the Muslim Council of Britain (MCB) had emerged as the most significant link between British Muslims and the British government.[13] The product of years of negotiations, it was officially inaugurated in 1997, six months after the election of the Labour government, with which it developed a strong working relationship.

This umbrella group has brought an impressive number of Muslim organizations under its cover, but is by no means representative of all branches of Muslim opinion. Unlike its critics, however – who were unhappy with the Islamist approach of the leadership and their links with groups such as Jamaat-e-Islami in Pakistan and Bangladesh – the MCB proved a well-organized lobbyist. It seemed all set to take on a role similar to that of the Board of Deputies of British Jews.

But the question of whom the government should choose as an appropriate Muslim partner has been put under the spotlight by the growing fears of 'Islamic terrorism'. Ruth Kelly, as Secretary of State for Communities, made the government's position very clear when she spoke to an invited audience of British Muslims on 11 October 2006:

> It is not good enough to merely sit on the sidelines or pay lip service to fighting extremism. That is why I want a fundamental rebalancing of our relationship with Muslim organisations from now on ... In future, I am clear that our strategy of funding and engagement must shift significantly towards those organisations that are taking a proactive leadership role in tackling extremism and defending our shared values.[14]

The MCB's high profile, and criticism of government policies, had inevitably attracted negative media attention – including John Ware's documentary entitled *A Question of Leadership*, which the BBC transmitted in August 2005 – and by 2006 the tables had turned. Kelly's speech made clear, through its reference to those who boycotted the Holocaust Memorial Day commemorations, that the MCB was no longer regarded as an appropriate organization for the government to work with.

This came three months after Kelly had given a speech at the Westminster launch of the anti-Islamist Sufi Muslim Council,[15] whose claim to represent the silent majority of British Muslims has been met with considerable scepticism.[16] Islamists – who regard public political action as inseparable from their religious beliefs – are out, and instead the government seeks to make political links with religious groups that are nominally non-political. In their response to Kelly's October speech, the MCB accused her of 'engaging in a merry go round to find Muslims who agree with you'.[17]

The Sufi Muslim Council is made up of traditionalists, and their first core principle is to adhere strongly to 'the classic Quranic teaching: "Obey God, obey His Prophet and obey those in authority over you"'. 'This', they explain, 'is a fundamental principle to uphold the laws of the country in which one resides, with its safety and security in mind.' They oppose 'radicalised Islamist strains' and despite talking of 'tolerance', their condemnation of terrorism extends to 'all its forms, whether political, cultural, intellectual or ideological'.[18] Concepts such as 'intellectual terrorism' suggest alarming images of thought police.

Less than two years after the launch of the Sufi Muslim Council, British Muslims gained another high-profile government-approved organization in the form of the Quilliam Foundation, launched to much fanfare in the British Museum. Speakers at the event even included the socialite Jemima Khan, whose lifestyle hardly conforms to any sort of Islamic model, a choice perhaps not best calculated to win over potential radicals. The Foundation describes itself as a 'counter extremism think tank' founded by reformed ex-'extremists', and it includes among its advisers some well-known names of the liberal (and less liberal) establishment: Paddy Ashdown (former leader of the Liberal Democrats), Timothy Garton-Ash (academic, journalist, atheist and self-confessed 'secular liberal'), the director of Demos, the editor of *Prospect*, the director of Civitas and the Conservative MP Michael Gove.[19] This project follows on from the widespread attention given to *The Islamist*, the book by the Foundation's deputy director, Ed Husain, which chronicles his personal religious and political journey. Husain has alienated many Muslims, who regard him as an apologist for the Iraq war, in light of his comment that 'Saddam Hussein effectively invited the US army to invade Iraq' (Husain 2007: 216). More worryingly, inspired by his own experience, and his re-found spiritual Sufism, Husain sees a potentially dangerous causal link between Islamism of all kinds and extremist violence carried out in the name of Islam. He argues that Islamism dehumanises non-Muslims and that 'extremist rhetoric' is 'the preamble to terrorism' (ibid.: 264, 278). His conflation of critical ideas and political dissidence with their expression in violent political action encourages a dangerously authoritarian response. This is the 'all forms of Islamism are unacceptable' argument – and it could easily be extended to attack other critical ideologies. It will have found echoes in sections of government and media that are already familiar with such views, and which have promoted the increasing curtailment of civil liberties in the name of the 'war on terror'.

Although the Foundation claims to be privately funded, it has clearly been given considerable practical support by government and, as its detractors point out, extraordinary access to important figures around the world. Shortly before the Foundation's launch, Inayat Bunglawala, who acts as a spokesperson for the MCB, noted in an article in the *Guardian*:

Some representatives of various UK Islamic groups were invited to see senior officials at the Department of Communities and Local Government recently to discuss the work they were doing with young people. Strong hints were dropped that they could obtain financial support from the government, but only if they were prepared to work with – and thereby help lend credibility to – Ed Husain's soon to be launched Quilliam Foundation.[20]

The MCB is, though, too important to be totally excluded from the government loop, and the draft constitution of the Mosques and Imams National Advisory Body was publicly welcomed by the new Communities Secretary, Hazel Blears, in October 2007, although its four-member steering committee included representatives from both the MCB and the MCB-affiliated Muslim Association of Britain.[21] The MCB leadership is walking a difficult tightrope between not upsetting government and not alienating their own base. Official recognition can bring power and resources, but also pressure to conform, and condemnation through association with unpopular policies. The different roles of helping Islamic organizations and representing Muslims to the outside world can also prove difficult to combine. Groups such as (the now defunct) Al-Muhajiroun have always attempted to denigrate the MCB for their government links,[22] but if the Council are thought to be bending their principles in any way so as to conform with government expectations, they will lose much wider support. Public statements are received very differently by young working-class Muslims and the mainstream press, and Internet blogs from all viewpoints are ready to pick up and spread every possible innuendo.

Meanwhile the merry-go-round has continued to turn, as government officials promote and nurture newly emerging groups or even put together groups of their own; and the search for those who can speak for the 'silent majority' has become a source of satire.[23] The strategy document *Preventing Violent Extremism*, produced in May 2008, makes the government position clear:

> Violent extremists distort Islam in an attempt to justify their actions. We will facilitate debate and amplify mainstream voices against them. Government can help credible individuals to speak out. It can promote discussion and recognise and support people and organisations who speak authoritatively about Islam.[24]

Key activities mentioned in the document include, among others, supporting the Radical Middle Way project, establishing a Young Muslims'

Consultative Group and supporting the establishment of a board of leading Muslim scholars. The accompanying 'Guide for Local Partners in England' explains how local authorities and others should also help appropriate individuals and groups to develop their skills in organization and communication, and provide them with platforms for their views. The examples of local projects that have already been supported include an imam training programme, Islamic study circles and leadership programmes for young Muslims.[25]

The Radical Middle Way was started in 2005. It aims to reach young British Muslims through discussions and speaking tours with international Muslim scholars, and through an up-to-the-minute Internet presence, including on Facebook and YouTube. Although it describes itself as 'a Muslim grassroots initiative' and 'fiercely independent', it is largely funded by the Foreign Office and the Department for Communities and Local Government.[26]

The Young Muslims Advisory Group was launched by the government in October 2008. In the government press release, the twenty-two young Muslims officially appointed to represent, empower and inspire their community are described by Hazel Blears, then Communities Secretary, as 'the next generation of Muslim community leaders'.[27]

'PROPER' ISLAM

The authors of *Preventing Violent Extremism* state, 'We are clear that it is not the role of Government to seek to change any religion.' But they go on,

> However, where theology is being distorted to justify violent extremist rhetoric or activity and threaten both Muslims and non-Muslims, Government should reinforce faith understanding and thereby build resilience.[28]

The search for appropriately 'moderate' Muslims does not stop at the selection and promotion of sympathetic partners. If there are not enough 'moderates', the government is ready to help create more; and if the government does not seek to change Islam directly, it seems ready to help others to do so. Already, since 2004, immigration law has been used to ensure that all ministers of religion coming to Britain from abroad meet a minimum English-language standard; and in July 2008, the BBC reported that the government 'is to fund a board of Islamic theologians in an attempt to sideline violent extremists'. Twenty 'leading thinkers' will be brought together at Oxford and Cambridge universities to 'focus on examining issues relating to Islam's place in Britain and [a Muslim's] obligations as a citizen'.[29] I would not, of course, want to criticize the idea of government funding for academic research, but there has been a growing tendency across the social sciences to direct that research into providing support for government policy (Glynn 2008: 166). Reactions to the proposal were mixed. The BBC reported qualified support from Sheikh Ibrahim Mogra, a prominent MCB member, but opposition from Muhammad Abdul Bari, the MCB's secretary-general. The Islamist scholar Azzam Tamimi, interviewed on BBC Radio, called it a 'naive initiative', explaining, '… credibility is something that people decide, not governments. The government actually erodes the credibility of people by naming them as members of such government-appointed commissions.' Hazel Blears, defending the government's plans, refused to engage with the idea that government involvement might put off just those people whom they most wanted to reach. Instead she claimed that what they were doing was bolstering the Muslim mainstream, and that 'People really do want – especially the young people – to get a *proper* interpretation of a *peaceful* Islamic faith.'[30] This (which chimed with the Home Secretary's earlier references to ideology based on 'a misrepresentation of religion')[31] did indeed suggest a certain naivety, not least in the idea that it is possible to reach a single correct, or 'proper', interpretation of any religion.

HOPES AND FEARS

So, what are the wider impacts of all this? First, the political promotion of faith groups of all kinds, and the emphasis on a person's religious affiliation, is helping to consolidate the power of religious organizations and foreground religious identity. The official argument that the incorporation of faith-based bodies contributes to 'social cohesion' (Home Office Faith Communities Unit 2004: 3) and that 'Muslim identity politics can support and encourage integration' (Choudhury 2007: 5) seems, at best, ingenuous, if not dangerously sophistic. Religious mobilization may, indeed, encourage participation in the political process, and many Islamic groups do encourage their followers to become exemplary members of civil society. However, they become involved first and foremost as Muslims and the government approach seems designed to perpetuate and institutionalize their religious difference. Faith groups may see a mutual benefit in such a system (and this lies behind the Archbishop of Canterbury's ill-fated support for greater recognition of Sharia law)[32], but anything that highlights Muslim difference, and especially which appears to be giving special support for Muslims as Muslims, is likely to generate a negative reaction in the wider population, where there is already considerable anti-Muslim feeling. More broadly, too, as already noted, the promotion of religious organizations is being used by neoliberal regimes as an important method of social control, through a combination of encouraging social conservatism and strong hierarchical organization, and through the old colonial practice of divide and rule. This must be of concern to anyone hoping for the development of a more progressive opposition to neoliberalism.

And what about the attempts to create a more 'liberal' or 'moderate' Islam as a counter to Islamic radicalism? There are clearly huge practical difficulties here. There are problems in the defining of terms and drawing of boundaries – one person's 'moderate' may be another's 'dangerous radical'; there are problems in addressing the vast diversity of Islamic tradition and practice, and there are problems arising from the mere fact of government or other forms of 'outside' involvement putting off the very groups that that involvement was intended to help. But, beyond this, we need to ask whether a 'liberal' Islam could, anyway, provide a successful counter-attraction. To do this we need to understand why young Muslims may be attracted to Islamic radicalism. These are not necessarily people for whom religion is already of overriding importance; indeed, it has been argued that 'a lack of religious literacy and education appears to be a common feature among those who are drawn to extremist groups' (Choudhury 2007: 6). This has, of course, been used as an argument for promoting 'moderate' Islam, but would 'moderate' Islam provide the opportunity for fundamental change that most of these people are looking for? Like radicals of all kinds, they are in search of an ideal – of a better world-view, and a better code for living and plan of action – something that can provide a real, even dramatic, alternative to the inequalities and decadence of capitalist consumerism. Can a more liberal Islam provide this? Even Tariq Ramadan's carefully argued and theologically grounded approach, which many might find religiously bold, seems too politically timid to inspire. His socially responsible Islam would attempt to resist neoliberal capitalism by stages through an ethical business approach that is similar to that adopted by socially concerned church groups (Ramadan 2004: 174–99).

In January 2002 I attended a meeting of Al-Muhajiroun in Ilford, where I observed first hand how idealistic young British Muslims were persuaded to take action on behalf of their Muslim brothers and sisters. Tony Cox, who was with me and who worked for the far-left Militant Tendency in the 1980s, observed that, despite the obvious differences – especially in the proposed solutions – it reminded him of Militant meetings. It was not just the young men in their working clothes in the stark hall, but the serious and focused class-based rhetoric and the promise of being part of a structured resistance. In the paper I published later that year I wrote: 'In his condemnation of hoarding money, his denouncement of interest as the "ball and chain of economic enslavement" and his repeated references to Muslim oppression, the speaker at Al-Muhajiroun's East London meeting appealed to a radical instinct for a fairer society' (Glynn 2002: 985). I argued in that paper that whether they chose the way of practical grassroots action and reformism offered by the Young Muslim Organization or opted for a more revolutionary path, those who turned to Islamism were looking for a sense of purpose in an alienating world that offered them little hope for the future. And, crucially, I linked the turn towards political Islam to the weakness of the socialist movement, and its inability to provide a force that working-class Muslim youth would recognize as a credible channel for their anger and frustrations. It may be contended that this does not account for the large number of middle-class Muslims attracted to Islamist movements, but radical and revolutionary movements always attract a section of middle-class support, especially among students, and this is particularly true for minority groups facing a level of discrimination that cuts across the classes – as exemplified by the high number of Jews in Russian revolutionary movements in 1917. That radical Islamic groups appeal to many of the same sources of discontent as radical socialists is nicely illustrated by the leaflet distributed by Hizb ut-Tahrir at the big anti-war march in London in 2003. The main focus of its attack is capitalist colonialism, and it is not until the final sentence that it invites the reader 'to study the Islamic Ideological solution'.

Philip Lewis, in *Young, British and Muslim*, quotes an interview with the writer Hanif Kureishi from 1995, in which he observed the big change among British Pakistanis in further education colleges from when he had been a student twenty years earlier: 'In my day we were mostly leftists of some variety, but the collapse of Eastern European Communism has made that very difficult. Now they are turning to religion.'[33] It is not just Eastern European communism (which had its own problems) that has collapsed, but an effective left movement of any kind.

Besides this example, though, the linking of the rise of Islamism with the decline of the left is an argument that few people who do not themselves support left politics seem prepared to engage with. I noticed, for example, that the review of research into Muslim political mobilization that was commissioned by the government and produced in 2007 includes long quotes from my 2002 paper, but makes no allusion to its main argument (Choudhury 2007). The liberal establishment, and not least the New Labour government, does not want to accept that people are looking for major structural changes and that with the absence of a left alternative people may turn to other ideologies. (This situation encourages far-right nationalism as well as Islamism, and these different radicalisms can each be boosted by the growth of the other.) An extreme example of the blinkered establishment approach is provided by Will Hutton, who argued in a British newspaper that some strands of Islamic thought were simply provoked into being by the 'self-evident superiority' and success of modern Western values.[34] In contrast, radical Muslims have long been aware of the potential competition from left ideas, especially from practical experience of Middle Eastern politics and the writings of men such as Sayyid Qutb and Ali Shari'ati (1980).

If we want to address the causes that attract young Muslims to radical, and even violent, Islamist groups, we need to look not only at British foreign policy (and at persuading the government to stop being in denial as to its impact), and not only at the alienating effects of authoritarian anti-terrorism policies. We need to look at the deliberate suppression of any effective secular left alternative to the materialism and inequalities of free-market capitalism. Liberal politics cannot provide that alternative, but what the current political system has done is suppress left opposition and leave space for the rise of other radical forces. If we want to create real spaces of hope, then we need organizations prepared to campaign on structural socio-economic issues. These are the issues that have to be addressed in order to bring hope to everyone.

NOTES

1 HM Government, *The Prevent Strategy: A Guide for Local Partners in England*, 2008, p. 6.

2 The *Concise Oxford English Dictionary* (2004) reduces Islamism to 'Islamic militancy or fundamentalism'.

3 Tony Blair proposed a ban following the London bombings in 2005, but was ultimately dissuaded by the Home Office and police, who argued that a ban 'would serve only as a recruiting agent if the group appealed against the move'. *Observer*, 24 December 2006.

4 Such as the support given by the British imperial government to Aligarh Muslim University and the limitations imposed on the scope and practice of Muslim family law under the Raj.

5 BBC News, 28 October 2004; Patrice de Beer, 'Sarkozy and God', opendemocracy.net, 2008; *L'Express*, 1 November 2004, '*Religions, République, intégration: Sarkozy s'explique*'. This last (from which I have taken the quotes) is a long interview with Sarkozy following the publication of his book. It not only explains his views but, in the questions asked, helps illuminate the French secularist context.

6 www.ustreas.gov/education/

fact-sheets/currency/in-god-we-trust.
shtml, accessed November 2008.

7 *The President's Faith-based and Community Initiative in 50 States: A Report to the Nation*, White House, June 2008. Under Obama, the White House Office of Faith-Based and Community Initiatives has been replaced by the White House Office of Faith-Based and Neighborhood Partnerships.

8 Angel Rabassa, Cheryl Benard, Lowell Schwartz and Peter Sickle, *Building Moderate Muslim Networks*, Rand Corporation, Santa Monica, CA, 2007, www.rand.org/pubs/monographs/MG574, accessed 5 November 2008. The Rand Corporation is a research foundation originally founded by the US Air Force, and especially associated with defence policy.

9 Western responses to Palestine and Bosnia have been important factors in the development of British Muslim political identities.

10 *Guardian*, 16 February 2006.

11 www.interfaith.org.uk, accessed April 2008.

12 Home Office Faith Communities Unit, *Working Together: Co-operation between Government and Faith Communities*, 2004, p. 8.

13 Hansard, 19 July 2007, Column 169WH.

14 www.communities.gov.uk/archived/speeches/corporate/values-responsibilities, accessed 12 November 2008.

15 www.communities.gov.uk/speeches/corporate/sufi-muslim-council, accessed 27 March 2008.

16 See, for example, Shehla Kahn, 'From another shore – New Sufis for New Labour', *Muslim News*, 25 August 2006.

17 Letter from Muhammad Abdul Bari, secretary-general of the MCB, to Ruth Kelly, 14 October 2006, downloaded from www.mcb.org.uk, accessed March 2008.

18 Sufi Muslim Council Core Principles, www.sufimuslimcouncil.org/aboutus.php, accessed 5 November 2008.

19 www.quilliamfoundation.org, accessed 31 March and 8 November 2008.

20 *Guardian*, 17 April 2008.

21 Blears's speech to Preventing Extremism Conference, 31 October 2007, www.communities.gov.uk/speeches/corporate/preventing extremism, accessed March 2008.

22 An Al-Muhajiroun press release dated 22 September 2001 described them as a '*Sect* set up by the British government'.

23 *Guardian*, 16 May 2008.

24 HM Government, *Preventing Violent Extremism*, 2008, p. 4.

25 HM Government, *The Prevent Strategy: A Guide for Local Partners in England*, 2008.

26 www.radicalmiddleway.co.uk/about_us.php, accessed 29 March 2008; www.fco.gov.uk/en/fco-in-action/casestudies/young-muslims-uk, accessd 12 November 2008.

27 www.communities.gov.uk/news/corporate/987399, accessed 12 November 2008.

28 HM Government, *Preventing Violent Extremism*, p. 4.

29 news.bbc.co.uk/1/hi/uk/7512 626.stm, accessed 13 November 2008.

30 BBC Radio 4, *Today*, 18 July 2008 (her emphasis).

31 Jacqui Smith's speech at the First International Conference on Radicalisation and Political Violence, January 2008, press.homeoffice.gov.uk/Speeches/sp-hs-terrorism-keynote-jan-08, accessed 14 November 2008.

32 Rowan Williams, Archbishop of Canterbury, put forward his ideas in a lecture, entitled 'Civil and religious law in England: a religious perspective', at the Royal Courts of Justice on 7 February 2008, www.archbishipof canterbury.org/1575, accessed March 2008.

33 Kureishi, interviewed by *Newsweek*, 29 May 1995, quoted by Lewis (2007: 129).

34 *Observer*, 17 June 2007.

REFERENCES

Allen, C. (2008) *Housing Market Renewal and Social Class*, London and New York: Routledge.

Choudhury, T. (2007) *The Role of Muslim Identity Politics in Radicalisation*, Paper commissioned by the Department for Communities and Local Government, London.

Collins, C. (2007) '"The Scottish Executive is open for business": the Royal Bank of Scotland, and the intensification of the neo-liberal agenda in Scotland', in A. Cumbers and G. Whittam (eds), *Reclaiming the Economy: Alternatives to Market Fundamentalism*, Glasgow: Scottish Left Review Press.

Fishman, W. J. (1975) *East End Jewish Radicals 1875–1914*, London: Duckworth.

Geddes, M. (2006) 'Partnership and the limits to local governance in England: institutionalist analysis and neoliberalism', *International Journal of Urban and Regional Research*, 30(1).

Glynn, S. (2002) 'Bengali Muslims: the new East End radicals?', *Ethnic and Racial Studies*, 25(6).

— (2008) 'Soft-selling gentrification?', *Urban Research and Practice*, 1(2).

Husain, E. (2007) *The Islamist*, London: Penguin.

Kundnani, A. (2008) 'Islamism and the roots of liberal rage', *Race and Class*, 50(2).

Kymlicka, W. (2008) Reply to review symposium on 'Multicultural odysseys', *Ethnicities*, 8.

Lewis, P. (2002) *Islamic Britain: Religion, Politics and Identity among British Muslims*, London: I.B. Tauris.

— (2007) *Young, British and Muslim*, London: Continuum.

Modood, T. (2007) *Multiculturalism: A Civic Idea*, Cambridge: Polity.

Ramadan, T. (2004) *Western Muslims and the Future of Islam*, Oxford: Oxford University Press.

Shari'ati, A. (1980) *Marxism and Other Western Fallacies: An Islamic Critique*, trans. R. Campbell, Berkeley, CA: Mizan Press.

FOUR | INTEGRATION AND RESISTANCE

11 | British Muslims and 'community cohesion' debates

CLAIRE DWYER AND VARUN UBEROI

This chapter reflects on the emergence of 'community cohesion' as a policy framework in Britain since 2001 and explores how ideas about British Muslims have been integral to the construction and contestation of this policy framework. While there has already been much critical reflection on the concept, discourse and practice of community cohesion, some of which we draw on here, our particular focus is distinctive because it draws on interviews conducted with politicians and policy-makers who were all actively involved in the evolution and execution of the policy framework. This analysis is part of a wider project which asks how questions about Muslim belonging are shaping wider public debates about British national identity, citizenship and questions of ethnic, religious and cultural 'difference'.[1] As Modood (1992, 2005, 2007) has shown, over the last twenty years Muslims have emerged as central to debates about multiculturalism in Britain. In the 1980s and 1990s existing ways of framing racism or of organizing identity politics were challenged by groups that emphasized a faith identity. Thus Modood (1992) argued that understandings of 'cultural racism' and Islamophobia challenged binary understandings of 'black/white' racism. More recently, and in the context of global political conflict, Muslim identifications in Britain have emerged as so central to public policy debates that there is a danger that Islam is 'privileged' (Lewis 2007) in the analysis of a wide variety of different social issues. Our interest is both in how Muslims continue to be constructed as the most threatening 'Other', but also how a focus on Islam is part of a wider public debate about the place of religion within civic society.

Our broader research asks how Muslims are positioned in public discourse and whether they are seen as different, and perhaps particularly problematic, compared with other minority ethnic or minority religious groups. The broader project focuses on three policy areas: faith schools, the wearing of the hijab (see Meer et al. 2008; Dwyer 2008) and the subject of this chapter, the UK government's policy of community cohesion. In this chaper we begin by sketching out a brief introduction to the evolution of the community cohesion policy framework. We then draw on the findings from our interviews to flesh out this discussion, highlighting both the complex and sometimes contradictory ways in which the policy framework emerged and exploring the ways in which 'Muslims' were positioned in this debate.

COMMUNITY COHESION: A NEW APPROACH TO MULTICULTURAL POLICY?

The concept of 'community cohesion' has become a central theme in British policies towards local government and social and ethnic relations. Prior to 2001 community cohesion 'was not present in the lexicon of either urban theory or public policy' (Flint and Robinson 2008: 3). The policy emerged as an outcome of the reports produced by Ted Cantle (2001) and John Denham (2002) in the wake of the disturbances in Bradford, Burnley and Oldham in the summer of 2001. In his report Cantle warns of different ethnic groups living 'parallel and polarised lives'. In contrast to this construction of separation and encapsulation emerges an alternative conception of 'cohesive community', which is first referenced in the Cantle Report and subsequently becomes established as a principle of policy, officially defined in a guidance document for local authorities (LGA 2002) and then developed both through the

---

COMMUNITY COHESION

Our vision of an integrated and cohesive community is based on three foundations:

- People from different backgrounds having similar life opportunities
- People knowing their rights and responsibilities
- People trusting one another and trusting local institutions to act fairly

And three key ways of living together:

- A shared future vision and sense of belonging
- A focus on what new and existing communities have in common, alongside a recognition of the value of diversity
- Strong and positive relationships between people from different backgrounds.

Source: DCLG, response to CIC Report, February 2008

Home Office and in the Office of the Deputy Prime Minister. In 2006 the new Department for Communities and Local Government (DCLG) was established with central responsibility for delivering the policy. The government had appointed a Commission on Integration and Cohesion, whose report *Our Shared Future* was published in 2007. In February 2008 the DCLG published its response to the Commission's report, which rearticulated the government's definition of community cohesion (see box).

Tracing the intellectual origins of the discourse of 'community cohesion', there are links to previous debates, such as the report of the Commission on the Future of Multi-Ethnic Britain (CMEB 2000). This discourse, however, was also shaped by Robert Putnam's influential theory of 'social capital' (Putnam 2000) – that cohesive societies require strong links and associations across and between groups to produce 'bridging' rather than the more inward-looking 'bonding' social capital. McLaren (2005) also emphasizes the influences of political communitarianism (Etzoni 1995), which seeks to revalue and remobilize civil society. As Margaret Wetherell (Wetherell et al. 2007: 5) concludes:

> Community Cohesion offers, like any policy framework, a particular diagnosis and interpretation of UK Society. This is a reading, we saw, which finds civic alienation, decreasing social interaction and a disintegrating 'social glue' and suggests as a solution the rebuilding of solidarity, the re-vitalizing of communities and measures to break down separateness.

Academic commentators have been heavily critical of the theoretical underpinnings of community cohesion policy, not least because of the ways in which the policy shifted over time to encompass different social concerns from the urban disturbances in 2001, to those in the Lozells district of Birmingham in 2005, to the London bombings in 2005, to concerns about new immigration from EU accession states. As Flint and Robinson (2008: 3) argue: 'community cohesion reflected an empty vessel into which a variety of public policy concerns (social exclusion, race relations, national identity, immigration, law and order) were poured and re-articulated'.

Critique has focused in particular on how definitions of community cohesion do not address sufficiently the structural basis for inequality and disadvantage rooted in economic processes. Instead there is a shift from focusing on economic and social class divisions to ethnic and cultural dimensions and, as Flint and Robinson (ibid.: 5) argue, certain forms of cohesion (in particular, racial and religious) are prioritized over others (such as gender and class). Another ambiguity is how the goal of commonality in diversity is achieved. Critics have warned of the dangers of returning to 'assimilationist models of integration based around publicly enforced allegiance to British values, fearing and rejecting the supposed disruptive power of multiculturalism' (Wetherell et al. 2007: 5; see also Crowley and Hickman 2008). It is argued that there is a depoliticized focus on unity and avoidance of conflict rather than a recognition that community conflict needs to be brought into productive dialogue in the public sphere. Alexander (2007) suggests that community cohesion policy discourse places greater onus on citizens but allows governments to escape their own responsibilities. Focus on the rights and responsibilities of citizens is also seen as a means by which particular ethnic groups, notably Muslims, are pathologized (Abbas 2007; Fekete 2004; Brighton 2007; Burnett 2004; Kalra 2002; Khan 2007).

Critical analysis of the concept of community cohesion policy also rests on the conceptual categories used. While the policy is directed at 'local communities' there is no clear and consistent understanding of scale and how community cohesion problems might be defined or ameliorated at different, and interrelated, scales. Geographers and others have been critical of some of the assumptions about increasing ethnic segregation underlying the earliest formulations of community cohesion discourses, suggesting (Dorling 2005; Simpson 2004) that they reflect insufficient understanding of the demographics underlying current patterns and underplay the structural disadvantages and racisms that continue to shape housing markets (Phillips 2006, 2008). There is also critical reflection about the underpinning of community cohesion policy by 'contact theory' (Hewstone 2005), which posits that physical proximity and interaction will foster local inter-group solidarities. Reflecting on the assumptions implicit in contact theory, Valentine (2008: 332) emphasizes the importance of 'meaningful contact' and suggests that a 'politics of connectivity' (Amin 2004) requires an understanding of the intersectionality of multiple identities and how encounters are embedded within intersecting grids of power. Finally more critical engagement is urged with the concept of 'community', a highly suggestive but also contested, contradictory and elusive concept (Dwyer 1999). Some of these critiques are echoed in recent empirical work exploring the complexities of 'community cohesion' within different localities (see, for example, Wetherell et al. 2007; Flint and Robinson 2008; Jayaweera and Choudhury 2008; Keith 2008).

In this chapter we use interviews with policy-makers involved in the policies to explore the evolution of community cohesion policy and particularly how British Muslims are positioned in these debates. Interviews with policy-makers themselves offer critical reflection on policy evolution and provide evidence for some of the criticisms discusssed above. We begin by tracing how a somewhat diffuse and even contested conception of community cohesion emerged as a basis for public policy. We then explore the complex and multiple ways in which Muslims were positioned in policy debates, drawing out some of the tensions that emerged in political and policy arenas. Our analysis does not necessarily contradict some of the findings discussed above – but it does illustrate some of the complexities of policy negotiations. In our conclusion we put these findings in the wider context of how religious and ethnic differences are framed in contemporary British policy debates.

THE EMERGENCE OF COMMUNITY COHESION POLICY

Between September 2007 and April 2008 we conducted seventeen interviews with a range of politicians and policy advisers selected because of their involvement with the emergence, definition and operationalization of community cohesion policies.[2] In wide-ranging interviews we asked about the evolution of community cohesion policies, how these key actors understood community cohesion and broader questions concerning policies on national identity and definitions of Britishness. The interviews were conducted in tandem with a detailed analysis of policy documents and speeches which focused on similar themes. Some of the findings from this analysis, particularly the question of national identity, have been reported elsewhere (Uberoi et al. 2008; Uberoi and Modood 2008).

From the interviews it was clear that government ministers did not necessarily all agree or offer identical accounts; instead we gained insights into disagreements about the causes of particular social problems or how these perceived causes, or their amelioration, should be framed in policy documents. Reflecting on the origins of the government's policy of community cohesion in response to the urban unrest in Bradford, Burnley and Oldham in 2001, interviewees drew parallels with previous urban conflicts and their underlying causes. As Mark Carroll, former Director General for Communities at the DCLG, commented, the unrest illustrated that: 'We have people within our communities who are feeling as disenfranchised and alienated and marginalised as the African Caribbean community of 1981.' His predecessor, Trevor Hall, put it more bluntly: 'We were within central government taken by surprise that the hitherto peaceful Muslim communities were rioting. ...

*we didn't allow for the deep concerns and anxieties that many Muslim communities felt then.'

While interviewees acknowledged the complex and multiple causes of the urban conflicts (Bagguley and Hussain 2008) there was an emphasis on deprivation and social exclusion and the potential for these issues to become racialized, particularly through the activities of far-right political parties. As Mark Carroll explains, for the then Home Secretary, David Blunkett, the causes of the conflict needed to be understood in a way that recognized the potential for conflict between different racialized groups but acknowledged that both of them shared similar disadvantages:

> on the inequalities agenda this is a forgotten community and its concerns are being forgotten and one of the lessons he [Blunkett] took from the disturbances was that you had alienated and frustrated communities both Pakistani and white, both of whom looked at each other and thought they were getting all the goodies from government. And that jealousy and envy had created part of that response, part of that condition and therefore we needed a response that understood that, and that any response that just demonized white communities wasn't going to be very helpful, so I think he understood it from that point of view.

These comments suggest that the urban unrest of 2001 served to focus on issues of alienation for some British Muslim communities concentrated in deprived urban areas which seemed ignored or forgotten. They also acknowledge the potential for conflicts, which may easily be racialized, over the allocation of government resources and the need to address this perception and be seen to act fairly (Keith 2008). These are themes which were raised by the Commission on Integration and Cohesion, in particular in their definition of community cohesion.

‹ While interviewees saw the origins of community cohesion policy in response to the urban disturbances of 2001, by the time policy initiatives were being drafted new issues had emerged. In particular, the attacks of 11 September 2001 shifted representations of Muslims in public discourse. This shift was to become more central to government debates about community cohesion with the London bombings in July 2005. As we reflect in more detail below, this meant that right from the outset, and perhaps in contradistinction to the sentiments expressed by David Blunkett and others above, conflicts that were perhaps initially understood in relation to socio-economic causes became overlaid with more ideological and cultural explanations. Second, right from the beginning definitions of community cohesion were shaped by public concerns about migration. ‹

Nick Pearce, adviser to the then Home Secretary, David Blunkett, sums it up:

> I think the summer of 2001 was an incredibly toxic summer, there were the different events that were taking place with, you know, pictures from Sangatte[3] and the riots, and then of course 9/11, I think it was much more about trying to cope with a rising tide of hostility to new migrants coming to Britain, totally different to the [later] post-accession migration that we've had from Poland and the rest of Europe, to deal with the rising hostility to dispersed asylum seekers in northern towns and cities as well as then the riots that followed which then brought up a whole set of issues around settled communities and interaction.

Pearce's statement is interesting because it folds into the emerging public policy debate about community cohesion a whole range of different 'moral panics' about migration and integration. As Mark Carroll concurs:

> I mean on cohesion the biggest challenge is that all the evidence says, polling that the Commission on Integration did as well as other public source polling, says that it's migration and cohesion that's the big thing that people worry about.

What becomes clear is the extent to which, from the outset, community cohesion initiatives are bound up within a complex web of different policy concerns (see Flint and Robinson 2008) within which public fears about Muslim extremism and migration are uppermost.

We asked all our interviewees how they understood the term 'community cohesion', or how they would define it. Ted Cantle described how, in evoking the term in his report, he had drawn on previous research (Kearns and Forrest 2000; Forrest and Kearns 2001; Flint and Robinson 2008):

> Timms, Forest and Kearns has used that term, we thought, well, this is something we can adapt. I think that they had used it particularly in Canada and used the term community cohesion synonymously with social cohesion ... we thought it was obviously still about basic inequalities and disadvantage but we also thought that it was more a fundamental issue about attitudes and values as well.

Reflecting further on why community cohesion is important, Cantle explains:

The obvious one is just to try and avoid complex disorder and disagreements, disaffection of different communities, breakdown ... but I think there is a business case behind it too ... obviously a community that is working together is going to get the best out of all the sections of the community ... there is also a moral case ... an issue of social justice, because I don't believe you can have social justice without community cohesion. I believe that a lot of inequalities are locked into a process of difference and separation.

These definitions suggest that while ameliorating social inequalities is part of the task, community cohesion is also about a more complex process of breaking down differences or developing shared values. While admitting that a 'pragmatic way' to describe societies that were less divided had become an 'edifice' of policy, John Denham also stressed that community cohesion went beyond socio-economic issues: 'there's a lot about disadvantages of different groups, but it was saying that we need that plus, and the plus is the level of interaction between different communities and the question of shared values'.

There is also evidence of the broad scope of the policy. Cantle reflected that the ideas first expressed in his report have been taken up in different ways, so that 'it is just accepted that cohesion now covers a much broader spectrum, it's not just a white versus black or Asian dimension'. Indeed, he sees community cohesion as 'a broader perspective' that is 'locally determined ... if I go and talk to Boston in Lincolnshire they say Muslims, we've never heard of Muslims, this is about Portuguese, Polish, Estonians and Latvians'. This notion of a broad-brush approach was also echoed by Ciarra Wells, director of the Faith and Cohesion Unit, who told us that 'ultimately anyone can be un-cohesive with someone else, you know you're trying, you're trying to have a blanket approach'.

Fiona Mactaggart, former community cohesion minister, acknowledged that community cohesion 'is a terrible weasel word'. She goes on to explain, 'It's one of those phrases – government uses phrases, words, in a way which adapts, changes, develops their meanings.' She continues:

We did do some work on producing a definition of it ... and I think that the thing about 'people around here' having some shared aspirations is actually quite important for community cohesion. Doesn't mean you have to agree about everything, but it means that you have some kind of shared sense of what you want from round here ... it's about a community of place.

Mactaggart was critical of simple definitions of community, drawing instead on the specificity of shared local experience. She drew on her constituency experiences in the ethnically diverse town of Slough to reflect carefully on how community cohesion should not be conflated with integration, a term she rejected as being too close to assimilation:

> I'm actually in favour of a differentiated society, not an integrated society. A differentiated society, but a cohesive differentiated society, which says that we can all have our differences, we need to respect our differences from each other, but we also need to respect some rules and social norms.

Our interviews revealed the slipperiness of the term 'community cohesion'; it was difficult to contain and define and shifted in meaning over time. Cantle himself pointed out that 'community cohesion isn't just a government creature, it's got a life of its own now'.

Some respondents, notably those less constrained by government responsibilities, were more critical. Herman Ouseley expressed a view that other critics have raised (see McGhee 2008):

> Community cohesion is terminology that is much more comfortable to handle than talking about racism, Islamophobia, and communities that actually have no contact with each other even though they lived alongside each other. Therefore community cohesion was another term for, how do we bring better race relations? But community cohesion has a better feel to it because I think by then race was becoming a bit too uncomfortable for people to handle.

For Ouseley this is a new discourse which replaces the more critical discourses of either anti-racism or multiculturalism (Joppke 2004; Hewitt 2005; Alexander 2007). He goes on to point out: 'All community cohesion did was it brought a new set of opportunities for people to get some more crumbs out of central government; you do this and you get a bit more money, which is the old beauty contest that community groups have always been in.'

Certainly in practice community cohesion policies have presented new opportunities for some groups to gain government funding for their activities, at the same time making it more difficult for other groups, particularly those aimed at the needs of a specific ethnic or faith community, to gain money. As John Denham acknowledged:

> when the money became available, I think a lot of people who were doing very good community work said, well, we're trying to make

sure the tenants have got a good voice in the local planning policy, or we're trying to make sure that grungers don't keep beating up the punks, and so they manage to get their hands on some of the money.

Other interviewees were more scathing about the concept of community cohesion. Tony Blair's former adviser Phil Collins admits:

> nobody knows what community cohesion policy is, do they, nobody knows what it is. I mean, it might be the sort of thing that you shouldn't have a policy about … What policy could one imagine that would create cohesion between people? … My own view is that community cohesion breaks down into normal policy. I don't think community cohesion is a credible policy area.

Even Wells, a civil servant charged with implementing the policies, admitted the difficulties of measuring the effectiveness of community cohesion funding initiatives. She describes an evolution of the implementation of community cohesion policy from a short-term approach, which really belonged with policing 'Public Order Community Cohesion', to a longer-term approach of 'how do we embed cohesion into what we're doing?' She suggests that this can only be measured by people's perceptions of their neighbourhood:

> we don't want our measure of cohesion to be whether people are rioting or not … we accept that whether people are rioting or not is not your only indicator of how cohesive an area is. Actually it's people's attitudes to levels [of interaction] they live with and it's the nature of the area they live within.

None the less, she admitted that they were still searching for '*robust*' indicators which might measure such interactions.

This discussion illustrates how a diffuse and contested conception of community cohesion emerged as a basis for public policy. In the next section we turn to consider how this concept is inflected with particular understandings of Muslims

COMMUNITY COHESION AND MUSLIMS

Despite the origins of community cohesion policy, interviewees emphasized that the policy should not be directed only at particular communities. Fiona Mactaggart said: '[policy] initially focused on the experience of places where there had been riots. But that didn't mean it was just for them because it recognized that there wasn't anything unique about those places, actually.'

Expanding on the emphasis noted above on concerns about new flows of migration after the enlargement of the EU in 2004, Wells argued that in practice community cohesion money was often targeted at two specific localities:

> I think how that policy [of community cohesion] plays out in practice, it means we do focus disproportionately, or proportionately depending on how you look at it, on sort of indigenous white working-class and settled Pakistani communities ... we tend to work in areas where the issues are (a) around settled white community versus settled Pakistani community, and (b) around settled white community with no experience of diversity.

How Muslims as a group were positioned by policy-makers was complex. It was clear that, as Ouseley suggests above, a language of religious identity had begun to replace other markers of difference. As Denham says:

> With the benefit of hindsight, you can see that the report came out at a time when outside the Muslim community, and often inside the Muslim community, the Muslim identity was being strongly asserted; had you been five years before, I wonder if it wouldn't have talked about Pakistani and Bengali communities ... what was happening was that within the community ... there was a very clear assertion of the Muslim identity, not just the Pakistani identity, and outside there was a greater perception of this as a faith community rather than as an ... ethnic community.

Wells also explained that a focus on Muslims was perhaps inevitable when thinking about community cohesion:

> Perceptions of difference between people that might generate issues around cohesion are sometimes an odd melange of issues around people's racial identity and their faith identity, or how they are perceived by others ... I think there is a particular issue around Muslim identity and how that affects people's perceptions of each other.

So Muslims become identified as a collective group, their identity shaped by religious identifications rather than ethnic affiliations, and there is also a recognition that Muslim identifications are subject to particular, assumed negative, perceptions.

Ministers we interviewed were conscious that from the outset policies were perceived as targeting Muslims, as Denham explains: 'there were some very loud voices in the Muslim community that rejected Ted

Cantle's report entirely, and said that by the very fact of naming the Muslim community you're blaming the Muslim community'.

For Fiona Mactaggart there was a need to express more carefully the nuances within the policy focus. Echoing the parallel need to focus on both marginalized Asian and white communities, which Blunkett and others had emphasized, she explained:

> The sharpest focus was created because of violent tensions between young people in the northern cities ... the driver was the violence be-tween young people ... you need to conduct policies which reduce the fault lines ... There was a real perception that Asian wards got more money than white wards. So even saying that, stopping and thinking how your policies fall out, stopping and thinking about whether it does reinforce already fragile lines should be a necessary feature of policy-making.

As she continues:

> The initial lesson was when you're tackling the worst housing, if the worst housing coincides with a racial group, the other people might see that the racial group is getting more money spent on housing ... so they feel resentful and the tension between them grows. That can easily happen when you have a discourse, you know, in public, where a certain ethnic or faith group is seen as a problem, and it is true that that is true currently of Islam.

For Mactaggart, then, community cohesion policies had to reduce 'fault lines' between different groups and sometimes this required under-standing when perceptions about inequalities were being produced through social policies. She stressed that the policy also had to do more to address 'the real sense that young Muslims felt very alienated'. If a focus on Muslims was inevitable given the initial impetus of the policy in the Cantle Report, Mactaggart suggests the need to address how negative perceptions of different communities and processes of alienation emerge. She also argued that government needed to engage a range of different stakeholders in policy-making, including Muslim organizations. Events quickly changed the context for public policy concerns, however. As John Denham reflects: 'What actually happened was before we had really rooted an understanding of community cohesion ... of course everything got distorted by 9/11.' This distortion of the original emphasis of community cohesion was felt most strongly, perhaps unsurprisingly, by its original architect, Ted Cantle. In response to a question about the current focus of community cohesion policies, he argued that:

I'm thinking about the entire community, I'm not thinking about any particular group, and I think that part of the problem is the way that focus can move around, for instance at the moment if you talk about community cohesion, the government will probably be focusing immediately on the Muslim community and has attempted to do that, I think wrongly and not very cleverly.

Ted Cantle explained that after the bombs in London in July 2005 there was a shift in focus which was accentuated by the launching of a new government funding stream, 'Preventing Violent Extremism' (PVE), in April 2007.

Well, 7/7 did change a lot. In some senses it didn't change the formal definition of community cohesion or what is was all about, that carried on. But inevitably a lot of the focus of programmes and activity in local authority areas and the government switched to a Muslim community and right through to this April with the Preventing Violent Extremism Fund. So in a way you've got two programmes running.

Cantle was strongly opposed to the emphasis of the PVE funding and pointed out that many local authorities ran programmes, funded by the two different funding streams, in parallel and were anxious not to single out Muslim concerns. He argued that the PVE fund, which came not through local authority funding but directly from the Home Office, was problematic both from a moral standpoint but also in terms of how the same issues were being tackled on the ground by the same agencies. On the moral issue he argued:

I would much prefer the emphasis to be on the whole community in all areas and for them to address the particular issues as they see them. In some cases there are issues that are more focused on Muslim communities but I think it's got to be located within a broader brush [approach]. Otherwise you are, I think, pointing the finger at the Muslim community all the time. You are making the association between extremism and terrorism and the Muslim community all the way through which stigmatizes them. And in the wider public point of view you are just reinforcing a stereotype which I think is unhelpful.

Interestingly, Ciarra Wells, although not involved in the allocation and monitoring of PVE funding, also emphasized that 'local authorities don't want to be stigmatized with money coming in from prevention pathfinders'.

In the aftermath of 7/7 it was clear that ministers and policy-makers were treading a tightrope with regard to how they positioned British Muslim communities in wider public policy discourses. Fiona Mactaggart, describing a letter to her from a young Muslim constituent who felt fearful about travelling into London, argues: 'government had a really important job to do, to say to those people, we don't think that because you're a Muslim you're a bomber. It was really really important that government said that.'

At the same time public anxieties demanded a government response that reassured them that the causes of terrorism were being addressed. Some of the Labour policy advisers we interviewed described the heated debates about how Tony Blair's speeches delivered after 7/7 should talk about the relationship between the young men who planted the bombs and their Islamic identifications.[4] As one adviser said:

> You always get accused, you know, 'you're only talking about Muslims'. In fact, because you're bending over backwards not to only talk about Muslims, the Hindus, and the Sikhs, and the Presbyterians all say hang on, why are you dragging us into this, we haven't done anything. You can't win.

In the wake of 7/7 community cohesion discourses did become entwined with government responses to wider public anxieties about political Islamism and terrorism. Our interviews revealed, however, that these connections were difficult to develop. As Mark Carroll reflects:

> As the Haymarket [attempted] bombing or the Glasgow bombing showed, there isn't necessarily an issue about ... inequalities, we're not necessarily talking about people who are poor or uneducated. Equally we're not necessarily talking about people who aren't very integrated, so these aren't traditional inequality or black and integration issues.

Yet he suggests that none the less involvement in such political activities must reflect disengagement:

> If people are susceptible to political ideology that must mean that they feel less connected to the overriding kind of British narrative, of integration and cohesion, and therefore we need to do more on integration and cohesion.

Following the 7/7 bombings, if government policy on community cohesion had not changed, the ways in which it was being articulated in government speeches appeared to increasingly emphasize the more ideological or cultural elements of the discourse, particularly a focus on the meaning of Britishness.

In our interviews some of the government ministers commented on the focus on Britishness in the speeches of both Tony Blair and then his successor, Gordon Brown. As Mike O'Brien reflected:

> I would like people to feel British, but I don't need them to feel British, that's an individual choice and indeed part of the liberty British people have ... And it shouldn't be for me to tell them that they shouldn't be feeling this way. But it can be for me to say, you know, we expect British people to broadly support a democratic way of doing things rather than terrorism.

For Fiona Mactaggart assertions read as being anti-British were sometimes exaggerated:

> If the rule-makers, if the British government has done something you think is wrong, like going to Iraq, then you can say, 'I'm no longer British', as it were. That's a way of rejecting their values ... but I'm not sure how profound it is, I think it's more a tactic.

These comments can be read as a distancing by a former minister involved with community cohesion policy from the ways in which the policy was implicitly, if not explicitly, expressed in some ministerial speeches in which narratives of Britishness were emphasized. Interviewees pointed out that political speeches were often required to 'respond to short-term angst that people have about particular incidents rather than an overall approach' (Angela Eagle). Indeed, Mark Carroll admitted: 'There is media debate, which is "Muslims, what are we going to do?" I think politicians will inevitably feel that they need to speak to big public debate.'

These responses reveal another tension which clearly runs through the discussion of community cohesion policies at government level. While ministers and civil servants recognize the issues of representation with regard to how negative discourses about Muslims in general are perpetuated, there is also a debate about the extent to which government ministers must be seen to be responding to public fears and media debates. Thus there was pressure to be seen, in particular, to be expressing 'strong' views about crime and immigration (Uberoi and Saggar 2009).

As we suggested in our discussion of the evolution of community cohesion policy, many of those we interviewed traced a shift from articulating concerns about community cohesion using an older multicultural lexicon that emphasized ethnicity or racism to languages of faith or religious identity. They gave a range of reasons for this in relation to the reassertion of a religious identity among Muslims in Britain (Modood 2005), as well as the rise of Islamophobia in the context of wider political conflicts. What emerges from the interviews, however, is also some ambivalence about focusing on religious communities as broad categories. Instead interviewees wanted to emphasize the diversity that they recognized within the broad British Muslim population.

Discussing the difficulties of getting together a 'representative' group of people for a meeting, Phil Collins points out:

> We've only got room for twenty people at the meeting, who are they? Are they 'the community' or not? Clearly they are not. No matter how well meaning they are and how good they are, they're not. The Muslim community, but many other communities, are stratified within themselves, are full of differences. The Muslim community? Well, no such thing in some obvious ways, it's because it's stratified by nation of origin, by those who were born abroad, those who were born here, by generation, by gender, like people are.

For some respondents, recognition of this diversity meant that linking inequalities to religious identity was problematic. As Mark Carroll asserts:

> I don't buy the argument incidentally that religion is a major factor in inequalities. The evidence seems to suggest that there's as much variation within Muslim groups as there is between Muslim groups … Wherever there is data you can clearly see white Muslims doing much better than anybody else, but you also see Indian Muslims doing better than Pakistani or Bangladeshi Muslims. You see Middle East Muslims doing better still; where we've got data (quite limited still) of African Muslims some are doing really well, some doing really badly, depending on who they are.

Carroll goes on to suggest that: 'some Islamophobia remains in employment practices or in education but the prime drivers of people's experiences continue, it seems to me, to be about race not about faith, in terms of inequalities'.

For Trevor Hall the danger was that in prioritizing religious identities broader social concerns were ignored and religion was reified: 'What I felt then, and still feel now, [is] that when we talk about Muslim people we tend to primarily think of them in terms of religion, and not as a holistic person.'

He went on to argue that this reification meant that attention was not focused on people's everyday ordinary concerns:

/ The weakness I want to emphasize, in doing that, we were looking from the centre at Muslim people in terms of religion, neglecting possibly the most important part of their social concerns ... lack of fair treatment, [which] many British born Muslims felt then and still feel now.

Hall was convinced that public policy had been seen to prioritize Muslims both as an object of concern for government, but also as a group that had been able to gain the ear of government with regard to their needs. He argued that this had negative consequences for broader inter-ethnic relations:

What we have done, and I think there is a bit of backlash, we have given the impression that we are only concerned with and we're only responding to concerns about Muslims. We have alienated other minority groups from thinking that government is concerned about them.

This reflection is revealing. While Muslim communities may have felt that they had received undue attention from government policy-makers, the backlash is that other groups were once again concerned that government money was being distributed unfairly and that Muslim concerns were being given too much prominence.

CONCLUSION

In this chapter we have drawn on interviews with some of those most closely involved with the evolution and execution of community cohesion policy to critically examine the policy, particularly in relation to how Muslims are positioned. Our findings provide evidence to concur with some of the critical analysis of community cohesion policy, particularly by illustrating the ways in which the policy evolved and the difficulties in articulating what exactly community cohesion means, or how it might be measured. There is evidence also, however, of some ambition in tackling racism and its causes at local community levels and the need to establish a better framework for communicating and measuring fair resource allocation (Keith 2008). Our analysis also reveals the deeply ambivalent positioning of Muslims in public policy discourse. There is evidence of the difficulties politicians had in articulating their concerns about either the encapsulation of some Muslim communities or the activities of radical political Islamist groups because they did not want to risk either offending Muslim groups or essentializing Islam. At the same time there is political pressure to respond to particular mediated panics about migration and integration which are often susceptible to highly racialized framings. The policies themselves have multiple outcomes. Despite our disquiet about the ways in which Muslims as a group have been pathologized in both public debate and political rhetoric on community cohesion, particularly through the Preventing Violent Extremism fund, policies have delivered new resources to marginalized Muslim communities, including women's groups and young people (Ellery 2009).

It is perhaps too early to see how significant is the shift to discourses of 'community cohesion', despite a plethora of articles signalling the 'end of multiculturalism' (Jopkke 2004; Meer and Modood forthcoming). Certainly it is a policy shift that has provided greater opportunities for civic participation for faith communities in Britain, including Muslims (Furbey 2008; Dinham and Lowndes 2009).[5] This may be important both in enabling Muslims to gain parity with other faith communities in terms of civic participation and for inter-faith initiatives on social issues to be mobilized. At the same time evidence for the enduring significance of socio-economic factors in producing community divisions (Jayaweera and Choudhury 2008; Wetherell et al. 2007) suggests that the emphasis on the cultural or ideological rather than the socio-economic in community cohesion discourses may fail to address the realities of social exclusion for many British Muslims..

NOTES

1 This is research undertaken by Tariq Modood, Centre for Ethnicity and Citizenship, University of Bristol, and Claire Dwyer, Migration Research Unit, University College London, with Varun Uberoi and Nasar Meer, funded by the Leverhulme Trust. For further details see www.bristol.ac.uk/sociology/leverhulme/.

2 Most interviews were conducted by Varun Uberoi and included those listed below. Interviewees agreed to be taped, they all received transcripts and in some cases quotes were cleared before use. Like all interviews, then, these are partial and positioned accounts. List of interviewees:

Lord Herman Ouseley (author of *Community Pride Not Prejudice*), 18 September 2007; Dominic Grieve, MP (Shadow Justice Secretary and spokesman on community cohesion), 18 September 2007; Ted Cantle (head of the independent review team that published *Community Cohesion: A Report of the Independent Review Team*), 4 September 2007; Mike O'Brien, MP (former minister for race equality), 30 October 2007; Angela Eagle, MP (former minister for community cohesion), 15 October 2007; Fiona McTaggart, MP (former community cohesion minister), 5 October 2007; Dame Pauline Neville Jones (shadow security spokeswoman and author of the Conservative Party's *Interim Report on National Cohesion*), 17 October 2007; Trevor Phillips (head of the Equalities Commission), 30 October 2007; John Denham, MP (former chair of the Ministerial Team on Public Order and Community Cohesion), 11 July 2007; Nick Pearce (former adviser to David Blunkett), 31 October 2007; Ciarra Wells (director of the Faith and Cohesion Unit), 22 October 2007; Trevor Hall (former permanent secretary to the Home Office's Race Equality Adviser), 23 October 2007; Mark Carroll (former Director General for Communities, DCLG), 11 December 2007; Charles Clarke, MP (former Home Secretary), 11 December 2007; Phil Collins (former speech writer and adviser to Tony Blair), 14 December 2007; Paul Goodman, MP (shadow spokesman for community cohesion), 4 March 2008; Damian Green, MP (shadow immigration spokesman), 18 April 2008.

3 This is a reference to a controversial refugee camp in Sangatte, France, near the Channel Tunnel, from which attempts to enter the UK were made by asylum seekers. An agreement to close the camp, and house refugees in both the UK and France, was made in 2002.

4 See in particular the context for Tony Blair's speech on 8 December 2007, 'One nation's future, multiculturalism and integration', discussed in Uberoi and Modood (2008).

5 At the same time, however, measures of community cohesion can be used to allay secularist fears, in particular in relation to faith schools. From 2009 OFSTED will have to include measures of fostering community cohesion when reporting on state schools. This can be interpreted as a government response to rising concerns about the role of faith schools in contributing to segregation and exclusion in which Muslim schools have sometimes been singled out (Dwyer 1993, 2007).

REFERENCES

Abbas, T. (2007) 'Muslim minorities in Britain: integration, multiculturalism and radicalism in the post 7/7 period', *Journal of Intercultural Studies*, 28(3).

Alexander, C. (2007) 'Cohesive identities: the distance between meaning and understanding', in M. Wetherell et al. (eds), *Identity, Ethnic Diversity and Community Cohesion*, London: Sage.

Amin, A. (2004) 'Regions unbound: towards a new politics of place', *Geografiska Annaler*, 86B.

Bagguley, P. and Y. Hussain (2008) *Riotous Citizens: Ethnic Conflict in Multicultural Britain*, Aldershot: Ashgate.

Brighton, S. (2007) 'British Muslims, multiculturalism and UK foreign policy: "integration" and "cohesion" in and beyond the state', *International Affairs*, 83: 1.

Burnett, J. (2004) 'Community cohesion and the state', *Race and Class*, 45(3).

Cantle, T. (2001) *Community Cohesion Review*, London: Home Office.

CMEB (Commission on the Future of Multi-Ethnic Britain) (2000) *The Future of Multi-Ethnic Britain*, London: Profile Books.

Crowley, H. and M. Hickman (2008) 'Migration, postindustrialism and the globalised nation state: social capital and social cohesion re-examined', *Ethnic and Racial Studies*, 31(7).

Denham, J. (2002) *Building Cohesive Communities*, London: Home Office.

Dinham, A. and V. Lowndes (2009) 'Faith and the public realm', in A. Dinham, R. Furbey and V. Lowndes (eds), *Faith in the Public Realm*, Bristol: Policy Press, pp. 1–19.

Dorling, C. (2005) 'Why Trevor is wrong about race ghettos', *Observer*, 25 September.

Dwyer, C. (1993) 'Constructions of Muslim identity and the contesting of power: the debate over Muslim schools in the United Kingdom', in P. Jackson and J. Penrose (eds), *Constructions of Race, Place and Nation*, London: UCL Press.

— (1999) 'Contradictions of community: questions of identity for British Muslim women', *Environment and Planning A*, 31.

— (2007) 'Muslim state-funded schools: contested spaces of faith and citizenship', Paper presented at the Annual Conference of the Association of American Geographers, Chicago, IL.

— (2008) 'Geographies of veiling', *Geography*, 93(3).

Ellery, S. (2009) 'Extreme measures', *Guardian*, 28 January.

Etzoni, A. (1995) *The Spirit of Community. Rights, Responsibilities and the Communitarian Agenda*, London: Fontana.

Fekete, L. (2004) 'Anti-Muslim racism and the European security state', *Race and Class*, 46(1).

Flint, J. and D. Robinson (eds) (2008) *Community Cohesion in Crisis? New Dimensions of Diversity and Difference*, Bristol: Polity Press.

Forrest, R. and A. Kearns (2001) 'Social cohesion, social capital and the neighbourhood', *Urban Studies*, 38(12).

Furbey, R. (2008) 'Beyond "social glue"? "Faith" and community cohesion', in J. Flint and D. Robinson (eds), *Community Cohesion in Crisis? New Dimensions of Diversity and Difference*, Bristol: Policy Press.

Hewitt, R. (2005) *White Backlash and the Politics of Multiculturalism*, Cambridge: Cambridge University Press.

Hewstone, M. (2005) 'Intergroup contact in a divided society: challenging segregation in Northern Ireland', in D. Abrams, J. M. Marques and M. A. Hogg (eds), *The Social Psychology of Inclusion and Exclusion*, Philadelphia, PA: Psychology Press.

Jayaweera, H. and T. Choudhury (2008) *Immigration, Faith and Cohesion: Evidence from Local Areas with Significant Muslim Populations*, York: Joseph Rowntree Foundation.

Joppke, C. (2004) 'The retreat of multiculturalism in the liberal state: theory and policy', *British Journal of Sociology*, 55(2).

Kalra, R. (2002) 'Extended view: riots, race and reports: Denham, Cantle, Oldham and Burnley Inquiries', *Race Relations Abstracts*, 27.

Kearns, A. and R. Forrest (2000) 'Social cohesion and multilevel urban governance', *Urban Studies*, 37(5/6).

Keith, M. (2008) 'After the cosmopolitan? New geographies of race and racism', in C. Dwyer and C. Bressey (eds), *New Geographies of Race and Racism*, Aldershot: Ashgate.

Khan, O. (2007) 'Policy, identity and community cohesion: how race equality fits', in M. Wetherell et al. (eds), *Identity, Ethnic Diversity and Community Cohesion*, London: Sage.

Lewis, P. (2007) *Young, British and Muslim*, London: Continuum.

LGA (Local Government Association) (2002) *Guidance on Community Cohesion*, London: LGA.

McGhee, D. (2008) 'A past built on difference, a future which is shared – a critical examination of the recommendations made by the Commission on Integration and Community Cohesion', *People, Place and Policy Online*, 2(2).

McLaren, V. (2005) 'Civil renewal – a matter of trust?', *Proceedings of the Runnymede Conference on Social Capital, Civil Renewal and Ethnic Diversity*, London: Runnymede Trust.

Meer, N. and T. Modood (forthcoming) 'The multicultural state we're in: Muslims, "multiculture" and the "civic re-balancing" of British multiculturalism', *Political Studies*.

Meer, N., C. Dwyer and T. Modood (2008) 'Conceptions of British national identity, citizenship, and gender in the "Veil Affair"', Paper presented at the Post-Immigration Minorities, Religion and National Identities Conference, Bristol, November.

Modood, T. (1992) *Not Easy being British: Colour, Culture and Citizenship*, Stoke-on-Trent: Runnymede Trust.

— (2005) *Multicultural Politics: Racism, Ethnicity and Muslims in Britain*, Edinburgh: Edinburgh University Press.

— (2007) *Multiculturalism*, Cambridge: Polity Press.

Phillips, D. (2006) 'Parallel lives? Challenging discourses of British Muslim self-segregation', *Environment and Planning D: Society and Space*, 24(1).

— (2008) 'The problem of segregation: exploring the racialisation of space in northern Pennine towns', in C. Dwyer and C. Bressey (eds), *New Geographies of Race and Racism*, Aldershot: Ashgate.

Putnam, R. (2000) *Bowling Alone: The Collapse and Revival of American Community*, New York: Simon and Schuster.

Simpson, L. (2004) 'Statistics of racial segregation: measures, evidence and policy', *Urban Studies*, 41(3).

Uberoi, V. and T. Modood (2008) 'Community cohesion, Muslims and multiculturalism', Paper presented at the Political Studies Association Conference, Swansea, April.

Uberoi, V. and S. Saggar (2009) 'Diversity and extremism', in V. Uberoi et al., *Options for a New Britain*, Basingstoke: Palgrave Macmillan.

Uberoi, V., T. Modood and C. Dwyer (2008) 'Re-imagining what it means to be British', Paper presented at the Post-Immigration Minorities, Religion and National Identities Conference, Bristol, November.

Valentine, G. (2008) 'Living with difference: reflections on geographies of encounter', *Progress in Human Geography*, 32(3).

Wetherell, M., M. Laflèche and R. Berkeley (2007) (eds) *Identity, Ethnic Diversity and Community Cohesion*, London: Sage.

12 | Residential integration: evidence from the UK census

M. A. KEVIN BRICE

In the wake of bombings in New York, Madrid and London, and in the context of the so-called war on terror, debates about the integration of Muslims into European and other Western societies have intensified. Many of the contributors to this book provide evidence that Muslims are integrating into Western societies: culturally (see the chapters by Sarah Mills and Reina Lewis), economically (see the chapter by Jane Pollard) and politically (Richard Phillips, Sarah Glynn and Claire Dwyer). Many commentators, however, continue to question the degree of integration of Muslim minorities, and some have gone so far as to suggest that Muslims are simply no longer making any effort to integrate. In the UK, for instance, a documentary on the publicly funded television station Channel 4 entitled *Dispatches: What Muslims Want* asserted that Muslim integration into British society has effectively come to a halt (Snow 2006).

Integration is a complex and contested term, difficult to measure, but several indicators of integration have been adopted across a number of western European countries, and these pay particular attention to residential geographies. As Rudiger and Spencer (2003: 31) argue, 'Where, how and with whom people live influences not only their quality of life, their educational and employment opportunities, but also the relationships they have with each other and their interactions with other members of society.' Two British government reports, commissioned in the aftermath of urban disturbances in the northern cities of Bradford, Oldham and Burnley in the summer of 2001, both highlighted concerns about residential segregation and the effect this may have on a broader process of social integration. The Cantle Report, discussed in the previous chapter by Claire Dwyer and Varun Uberoi, concluded that 'many communities operate on the basis of a series of parallel lives' that 'do not seem to touch at any point, let alone overlap and promote any meaningful interchanges' (Community Cohesion Review Team 2001: 9). Similarly, the Ouseley Report identified a 'very worrying drift towards self-segregation' (Bradford Race Review Team 2001: foreword). According to these reports, then, 'self-segregation' on the part of particular racial, ethnic *and religious* groups was largely to blame for the disturbances. The British media echoed this claim through stories about British Muslims, under headlines such as 'Muslims and whites still worlds apart' (Johnston 2001) and '"Parallel lives" are blamed for the race riots' (Williams 2001). And this idea was restated in September 2005 when Trevor Phillips, then chair of the Commission for Racial Equality, delivered a speech entitled 'After 7/7: sleepwalking to segregation'. In this speech he argued that British society was 'becoming more divided by race and religion' (Phillips 2005), and painted an emotionally charged picture of minority groups isolated from mainstream society, living in ghettoes:

> Residentially, some districts are on their way to becoming fully fledged ghettoes – black holes into which no-one goes without fear and trepidation, and from which no-one ever escapes undamaged. And here is where I think we are: we are sleepwalking to segregation. We are becoming strangers to each other, and we are leaving communities to be marooned outside the mainstream. (ibid.)

The word 'segregation' has very negative connotations; social segregation is 'generally dismissed as a totally negative and abhorrent phenomenon' (Peach 1996: 379). It is suggested that individuals 'experience extra social problems simply because they are living in a segregated world' (Musterd 2003: 624). Moreover, 'a strong spatial concentration of specific population categories is supposed to have a negative impact on integration and upward social mobility' (ibid.: 624). These are powerful, problematic claims.

This chapter interrogates commonplace claims about integration and segregation, disentangling these terms and subjecting each to empirical scrutiny. First, it argues that integration and segregation are not simply opposites. As Sardar and Datta have shown in their different ways, it is possible for segregated – or, to use less pejorative language, Muslim-identified – spaces to coexist with broader processes of social integration, where the latter encompasses equality, participation and interaction (Phillips 2005). On the other hand, it is also helpful to interrogate claims about segregation. Whereas many of the other chapters in this book contest stereotypes about segregation and integration through largely qualitative arguments and social, cultural and political commentaries, this chapter develops its case through quantitative – statistical and demographic – data and analysis.

STATISTICAL ANALYSIS OF INTEGRATION AND SEGREGATION

Segregation is a '*statistical concept*, concerned with the uneven distribution of a variable' (Carling 2008: 554). Muslims can be said to be residentially segregated if they are found in disproportionately high numbers in a particular residential area. Among western European countries, only the United Kingdom gathers census data on populations categorized by both ethnicity and religious affiliation. So, in this chapter, the residential distribution patterns of Muslims in the United Kingdom will be analysed. As there are significant differences in the way ethnicity and religious affiliation are classified in both Scotland and Northern Ireland, the analysis will actually be limited to data from England and Wales.

According to the 2001 Census there are some 1.5 million Muslims in England and Wales, representing just under 3 per cent of the total population. If the population were evenly distributed, Muslims would make up just under 3 per cent of the population in each local authority. In the majority of local authorities, however – 282 of the 376 in England and Wales – Muslims are under-represented (forming less than 1.5 per cent of the population, or half the number we would expect if they were evenly distributed). In 149 of these 'under-represented' local authorities, Muslims form less than 0.3 per cent of the population – less than one-tenth of the expected level. Conversely, Muslims are concentrated in a small number of local authorities: more than 75 per cent of Muslims live in fifty local authorities and almost one-third of Muslims live in just ten local authorities, where the level of Muslim presence is more than four times greater than would be expected .

At first sight, it would appear that this is clear evidence of the segregation of Muslims in England and Wales. Muslims are clearly found in disproportionately high numbers in particular local authorities. We must, however, first clarify what is exactly meant by the term 'Muslims'. Muslims should not be seen as a single homogeneous group; the 2001 Census shows that 'Muslims' are comprised of diverse ethnic groups (Table 12.1). To gain a better understanding of the residential distribution of 'Muslims', the distribution patterns for different Muslim ethnic groups should also be considered. The four key ethnic groups for Muslims are: Pakistani (45.5 per cent of Muslims), Bangladeshi (16.8 per cent of Muslims), Indian (8.5 per cent of Muslims) and Black African (6.2 per cent of Muslims). While the ethnic group Other White is numerically larger than the group Black African, it does not comprise a single ethnic group but instead covers all white persons of non-British

TABLE 12.1 Breakdown of Muslim ethnic groups (England and Wales) (%)

White	11.62	White British	4.08
		White Irish	0.06
		Other White	7.49
Mixed	4.16	Mixed: White & Black Carib/Black African/Black Other	0.77
		Mixed: White and Asian/Other Mixed/Other	3.38
Asian	73.65	Indian (Asian/Asian British)	8.51
		Pakistani (Asian/Asian British)	42.52
		Bangladeshi (Asian/Asian British)	16.79
		Other Asian (Asian/Asian British)	5.82
Black	6.88	Caribbean (Black/Black British)	0.29
		African (Black/Black British)	6.22
		Other (Black/Black British)	0.37
Other	3.70	Chinese	0.05
		Other	3.65

Source: based on data from the 2001 Census, Table S104

descent and so is not of particular use in the current context. The relative breakdown of these four key Muslim ethnic groups was considered for the ten local authorities previously identified as having the highest representation of Muslims.

Table 12.2 indicates that one ethnic group forms the majority of Muslims in six out of the ten local authorities (Bangladeshis form the

TABLE 12.2 Distribution of Muslim ethnic groups (by local authority) (%)

	Muslim	Indian	Pakistani	Bangla-deshi	Black African
Average	2.97	8.51	42.52	16.79	6.22
Tower Hamlets	36.4	0.82	1.84	86.93	3.47
Newham	24.31	11.79	32.33	33.49	10.32
Blackburn with Darwen UA	19.40	49.72	40.32	1.69	0.31
Bradford	16.08	3.84	81.98	5.91	0.19
Waltham Forest	15.07	9.96	48.54	6.12	7.49
Luton UA	14.62	2.47	59.26	26.99	1.38
Birmingham	14.33	3.55	69.63	13.79	1.31
Hackney	13.76	13.42	7.02	17.99	11.06
Pendle	13.43	0.70	93.08	0.21	0.16
Slough UA	13.35	1.70	81.76	0.94	3.15

Source: based on data from the 2001 Census, Table S104

majority in Tower Hamlets; Pakistanis form the majority in Bradford, Luton, Birmingham, Pendle and Slough), despite the fact that no single ethnic group forms a majority of the total Muslim population. Furthermore, one ethnic group forms more than two-thirds of the Muslim population in five out of the ten local authorities (Bangladeshis in Tower Hamlets; Pakistanis in Bradford, Birmingham, Pendle and Slough), with the figure going as high as 93 per cent in Pendle. In four of the local authorities – Tower Hamlets, Bradford, Pendle and Slough – there is a clear pattern of one ethnic group dominating the Muslim population to the exclusion of the other ethnic groups – one group is over-represented and the other three groups are under-represented.

The residential distribution patterns of the four key Muslim ethnic groups in these 'Muslim local authorities' suggest that each ethnic group has its own distinctive distribution pattern and individual Muslim ethnic groups can dominate areas at the expense of other Muslim ethnic groups. The evidence from these local authorities indicates that it is not in fact 'Muslims' who exhibit residential distribution patterns associated with segregation, but rather individual Muslim ethnic groups which are concentrated in specific areas and, according to the definition of segregation given earlier, can be seen as segregated. This is in line with the conclusions drawn by Peach (2006) when he looked at the residential distribution patterns of different Muslim ethnic groups in London. Peach (ibid.: 367) found that 'that there is considerable residential separation between Muslims of different ethnic origins'.

Before drawing firm conclusions from this evidence, however, it may be useful to consider the factors that influence the residential distribution patterns exhibited by the Muslim ethnic groups. Patterns of residential distribution may be explained, to some degree, by considering the reasons behind residential choices made by individuals. An individual's choice of where they live may be determined by many different factors: reputation of the area, local amenities, schools, family circumstances, work, culture or ethnicity, and financial resources. If Muslims are self-segregating, as many commentators suggest, then Muslim residential choice should be strongly influenced by proximity to family and those of the same ethnicity and religion.

A report commissioned by the UK Commission on Integration and Cohesion entitled *Public Attitudes towards Cohesion and Integration* explored reasons for residential choices. The report surveyed a representative sample of adults aged over sixteen in England ('main group') and four 'booster' groups, including a general ethnic minority group (black and minority ethnic groups, or BMEs). While there was not a specific

Muslim 'booster' group, the BMEs group would include Muslims, and so the findings for the BMEs group may be taken as indicative (though not representative) of Muslims. The report looked at motivations for moving and reasons for choosing the current area of residence (Commission on Integration and Cohesion 2007: 18). The most cited motivation for moving was the same for both the main group and BMEs, namely 'expanding family/needed more room' (25 per cent of general group and 21 per cent of BMEs). Twenty-one per cent of the BME group, however, compared with 8 per cent for the population as a whole, said that none of the suggested motivations for moving applied to them. Looking more closely at this group, we see that many did not actively choose where they live; it was the only option available to them. Indeed, turning to the reasons for choosing the current area of residence (Table 12.3), the most frequently cited reason for the BME group is 'did not choose' (23 per cent of the BME group cite this as a reason). The BME group is more than twice as likely to say that they did not choose the current area than the main group (only 9 per cent of the main group cite 'did not choose'). Clearly lack of choice is a major factor for the BME group, and this factor needs to be taken into account when charges of self-segregation are laid against members of this group.

The most frequently cited reason for choosing an area for the main group is to be 'near family' (23 per cent cite this reason). Given that such a reason may be taken as an indicator of self-segregation, it is interesting to note that the general group is 50 per cent more likely than the BME group to cite this as a reason (15 per cent of the BME group cite this as a reason). The main group is also almost twice as likely to cite 'reputation of area' as a reason for choosing an area than the BME group (18 per cent for the main group and 10 per cent for the BME group), again suggesting that the main group is able to be more selective in choosing an area. Two other reasons closely associated with the idea of self-segregation, being near to 'people from the same ethnic group' and being near to 'people of the same religious group', are cited more frequently as reasons for choosing an area by the BME group than by the general group. Both these reasons, however, are relatively minor reasons for the BME group (being cited by only 5 and 2 per cent of the BME group respectively).

What emerges from the survey is that for a significant proportion of the BME group there is not a choice involved in selecting an area of residence. Where a choice was made, 'cost' and a desire to be 'near work' were just as important as being 'near to family' (all cited by 15 per cent of the BME group). Being 'near friends' and 'near shops or other

TABLE 12.3 Reasons for choosing current area of residence (multiple reasons permitted) (%)

Reasons for choosing current area	Main group	BMEs
Did not choose	9	23
Cost	11	15
Near work	16	15
Near schools	13	11
Near family	23	15
Near friends	10	12
Near shops or other facilities	10	12
Reputation of area	18	10
People from the same ethnic group	1	5
People from the same religious group	★	2
Nice area	3	1
Council offered it to me	1	2
Liked the house	3	1
Cheap/affordable housing	1	1
Close to transport	2	1
Born here/always lived here	3	1
Lived here before	2	1
Rural/open environment/quiet/peaceful	4	4
Good access to London	1	★
Parents' house/decision	1	1
Marriage/living with partner	1	1
Other	4	2
None of these	4	4
Don't know	1	3

Note: ★ Represents a value of less than half of 1 per cent, but not zero
Source: Commission on Integration and Cohesion (2007: 69)

facilities' are also both important for the BME group (both cited by 12 per cent of the BME group); these two reasons are also important for the main group, however (both reasons are cited by 10 per cent of the main group). These reasons, which may be considered as indicators of self-segregation, are just as important (if not more so) to the main group as they are to the BME group. The desire to be close to those who are similar to oneself, which results in the residential clustering of particular groups, is not unique to members of Muslim or other BME communities; it is a desire held in common by members of other ethnic and religious minorities, and by the majority society too, as Ziauddin Sardar has argued in this book.

RESIDENTIAL CLUSTERING

Clustering is not only observed based on ethnicity or religion; it can also be based on educational needs (clustering of students in university towns), professional needs (clustering of fishermen in fishing ports), financial situation (clustering of wealthy individuals in gated communities) as well as other needs and traits. Clustering based on these other needs and traits does not appear to cause the same level of concern in the media and with politicians that clustering based on ethnicity or religion does. As Sardar points out, a double standard is at work here, in which some forms of segregation are regarded as acceptable, others dangerous, with Muslim segregation arousing the greatest anxiety.

There is also an understandable tendency to move 'upwards and outwards' from the current area of residence, in other words to disperse, as evidenced by the common motivation to move owing to improvement in circumstances. The pull of the familiar, however, and the requirement to satisfy cultural needs, means that there is a process of 'regrouping' observed in groups that undergo initial dispersal. This pattern of dispersal followed by regrouping is evident in the changing distribution of the Anglo-Jewish community. Newman (1985: 362) notes that the Jewish community requires 'a range of community services, all of which necessitate a minimum threshold population to justify their existence'. He identifies 'the demand for synagogues, Jewish day schools, food outlets and communal cemeteries as constituting the major community services' (ibid.: 362) and argues that the changing spatial distribution of this community represents:

> a classic example of an ethnic group which starts out as an immigrant group concentrated within a well defined residential ghetto, who move out of the inner city to the suburbs ... accompanied by a tendency to regroup within the new locations and recreate group values. (ibid.: 374)

Muslims share many characteristics with the Jewish community in terms of the range of community services that necessitate a minimum threshold population – for Muslims the community services are: mosques, madrasas (Islamic schools), halal shops and Muslim cemeteries. The ability of Muslims to move into new areas is, however, constrained by opposition on the part of the majority group to the establishment of the most fundamental of the community services – the mosque. The London *Sunday Times* reported opposition to the proposed building of a mosque as part of a development led by the Duchy of Cornwall in an article entitled 'Charles's mosque meets a rebellion' (Leppard 2005).

According to the article, some local residents opposed the mosque, claiming it 'would be out of place and unpopular with existing residents' and that 'there are virtually no Muslims in the area'.

Even in areas with large Muslim communities there are difficulties in establishing mosques – in his examination of planning applications for places of worship and education in Birmingham, Gale (2005: 1176) found that 'the planning process continues to present Muslims in Birmingham with a series of constraints that unduly restrict the manifestation of their religious practices'. Thus, Muslim movement out of current areas of concentration will be limited owing to uncertainty about the ability to establish the necessary community services in new areas and the desire to remain close to the established services in current areas.

The motivation behind clustering based on ethnicity, religion or other traits has been seen as evidence that, despite the negative connotations, 'segregation is not all bad' (Peach 1996: 379). Peach identifies two types of segregation – good segregation and bad segregation – and notes that failure to differentiate between the two types 'has led to severe misunderstandings of the social processes underlying spatial patterns in cities' (ibid.: 380). According to Peach, the positive side of segregation is that concentration of particular ethnic groups 'allows the group to maintain its social cohesion. It maintains cultural values, it strengthens social networks, it allows the passing of critical thresholds for the support of institutions and shops' (ibid.: 386). On the other hand, segregation can also represent a form of social exclusion, which keeps 'underprivileged ethnic populations out of the residential areas of the dominant group' (ibid.: 387).

The segregation apparent in the residential distribution patterns of individual Muslim ethnic groups can be seen as having elements of both 'good segregation' and 'bad segregation'. The residential clustering of these groups based on the desire to be close to the familiar and the shared religious and cultural needs allows the formation of cohesive communities that would define this type of segregation as positive. The lack of choice that Muslims have in selecting an area of residence and the limitations imposed on the setting up of necessary facilities (such as mosques) result in negative segregation with Muslims kept out of the residential areas of the majority white ethnic group.

RETHINKING THE RELATIONSHIP BETWEEN SEGREGATION AND INTEGRATION

The relationship between residential segregation and broader forms of social integration is not as straightforward as has been previously supposed. If the relationship between segregation and integration were a simple one, then we would expect to find that all groups with similar levels of segregation would perform similarly in terms of integration. A study of this relationship conducted in the Netherlands, however, found that minority groups with similar levels of segregation had different levels of integration and concluded that 'the thesis that a clear and negative relationship exists between levels of segregation ... could not be supported' (Musterd 2003: 638). A study drawing on the UK Fourth National Survey of Ethnic Minorities (Bisin et al. 2007) examined the veracity of the claim that the process of cultural integration is different for Muslims than for other minority groups in the UK. The study measured cultural integration in terms of 'importance of religion, attitude towards intermarriage, and importance of racial composition in schools' (ibid.: 9). A strong religious identity among Muslims was taken to indicate a lack of cultural integration. As the authors put it:

> living in a more integrated neighbourhood (with a lower percentage of own ethnic/religious minority group) and speaking English at work, which signals a mixed working environment, are both associated with a higher sense of identity. This integration pattern is common to both Muslims and non-Muslims, but it appears to be more marked for Muslims. (ibid.: 6)

In other words, living in less segregated areas actually tended to strengthen religious identity and by definition weaken cultural integration. Such a situation may be explained by the fact that 'intense forms of identities appear to be formed in social contexts in which the minority ethnic/religious trait is more exposed to the interaction with the majority norm of behaviour' (ibid.: 7). This study concluded that while 'Muslims integrate less and more slowly than non-Muslims', there was 'no evidence that segregated neighbourhoods breed intense religious and cultural identities' and there was no 'positive relationship between geographic segregation and identity' (ibid.: 10). So segregation by itself should not be seen as cause of a lack of social integration.

The report from the UK Commission on Integration and Cohesion referred to earlier in this chapter also considered where and how frequently different ethnic groups mix with each other (see Table 12.4). The survey shows that members of the BME group mix more with other ethnic groups than the main group in all circumstances apart from at pubs or clubs. The BME group, however, is much more likely to classify a pub or club as a location that is not applicable for social mixing (and this would be particularly relevant to Muslims considering the prohibition on alcohol for practising Muslims). What is evident from the survey is that when social interaction with members of other ethnic groups takes place, it is most likely to occur at the shops or at work, school or college. What the survey does not show is the level and nature of this interaction.

Some insight into the real nature of interaction in one of the locations where social mixing is seen to be most frequent is provided by research carried out on patterns of seating in a multi-ethnic cafeteria in a university situated in the north-west of England (Clack et al. 2005). The university cafeteria 'represents a space where ethnic and racial mixing was expected to occur' (ibid.: 5) and yet the research revealed that: 'The majority of individuals sat in units comprised exclusively of members of their own ethnic group. In addition, White and Asian customers were often distributed "disproportionately" across different sections of the cafeteria' (ibid.: 13).

It appears that segregation occurs even in locations where different ethnic groups are in proximity with each other. The reasons underlying the segregation witnessed in locations of social mixing may be just as varied and complex as those identified earlier in this chapter for residential segregation. Despite this apparent segregation, it may be claimed that even the limited contact that occurs in these locations can promote integration by reducing prejudice and producing a sense of familiarity with minority groups. There is, however, a growing body of research (for example, Valentine 2008) which suggests that this sort of everyday contact does not in any way impact on the basic prejudices of the majority which are seen to inhibit the integration of minority groups, and that 'proximity does not equate with meaningful contact' (ibid.: 334). The suggestion that proximity does not lead to meaningful contact, and so does not necessarily aid integration, somewhat undermines the argument that segregation must be seen as opposed to integration.

CONCLUSION

Data from the 2001 UK Census show that Muslims are found in disproportionately high numbers in particular residential areas, and so, under more simplistic definitions of this term, they might be said to be residentially segregated. Residential segregation is more complex than is normally supposed, however; it is not simply a Muslim-to-non-Muslim but also an intra-Muslim relationship. Furthermore, measures of segregation are always scale dependent. When considering the national level, overall averages for each group are obtained in absolute terms – 2.97 per cent of the population is Muslim, 42.52 per cent of Muslims

TABLE 12.4 Frequency of social mixing with people from different ethnic groups, % (figures for BME group in brackets)

Location	Daily or at least once a week	Less than weekly, but at least once a month	Less than monthly, but at least once a year	Less than once a year	Don't know/ Not applicable
At your home, or their home	16 (37)	14 (18)	15 (15)	42 (19)	13 (11)
At work, school or college	44 (58)	7 (9)	5 (3)	22 (9)	23 (22)
At a pub or club	16 (16)	12 (12	12 (9)	36 (17)	25 (47)
At a café or restaurant	15 (27)	19 (18)	15 (10)	33 (15)	18 (30)
Socially outside work/school	20 (35)	16 (18)	13 (9)	33 (13)	19 (25)
At child's crèche/nursery/school	13 (29)	3 (5)	3 (3)	25 (10)	55 (52)
At the shops	47 (73)	13 (13)	7 (2)	22 (6)	11 (6)

Source: Commission on Integration and Cohesion (2007: 65)

are Pakistani. When focus moves 'down' to lower geographical levels – government office region; local authority; ward – a divergence from the national average is seen, and thus evidence of residential segregation may begin to emerge. If this were pushed farther – to the level of individual streets – a picture of greater segregation may become more apparent, and at the extreme, at individual household level, total segregation and full isolation would in most cases become evident. Thus supposed evidence for segregation based purely on geographical distribution patterns should be approached with some caution and care should be taken to place the evidence in a more complete context.

It has been argued that the residential distribution patterns of Muslims can be explained (to a degree) by an understandable desire to 'cluster', and this clustering can be classified as 'good segregation'. Also, recent research has suggested that the link between segregation and integration may not be as simple and clear cut as has previously been thought (Musterd 2003), and even that the relationship may at times run contrary to normal thinking with increased residential integration resulting in a weakening of cultural integration (Bisin et al. 2007). Finally, there is evidence that even in areas and places where different ethnic groups mix socially, segregation on the lines of ethnicity (and probably religion) still occurs (Clack et al. 2005) and that casual contact between different groups cannot be taken to be an indication of social integration (Valentine 2008).

Clearly more work needs to be done looking at specific outcomes for Muslims, as much of the evidence presented in the second part of this chapter relates to ethnic minorities generally, and it would be unwise to assume a conformity of experience across all ethnic and religious minorities. What is clear, however, is that many of the commonly held opinions about the segregation and integration of Muslims are unfounded. Simplistic calls for Muslims to integrate that blame residential segregation for a lack of broader social integration fail to take account of the very complex factors at play in residential choices of Muslims and their engagement with society.

REFERENCES

Bisin, A., E. Patacchini, T. Verdier and Y. Zenou (2007) 'Are Muslim immigrants different in terms of cultural integration?', Centre for Economic Policy Research, Discussion Paper 6453.

Bradford Race Review Team (2001)

Community Pride Not Prejudice: Making Diversity Work in Bradford, Bradford Metropolitan District Council.

Carling, A. (2008) 'The curious case of the mis-claimed myth claims: ethnic segregation, polarisation and the future of Bradford', *Urban Studies*, 45(3).

Clack, B., J. Dixon and C. Tredoux (2005) 'Eating together apart: patterns of segregation in a multi-ethnic cafeteria', *Journal of Community & Applied Social Psychology*, 15.

Commission on Integration and Cohesion (2007) *Public Attitudes towards Cohesion and Integration*, London: Home Office.

Community Cohesion Review Team (2001) *Community Cohesion: A Report of the Independent Review Team*, London: Home Office.

Congressional Research Service (2005) *Muslims in Europe: Integration Policies in Selected Countries*, CRS Report for Congress, 18 November.

Gale, R. (2005) 'Representing the city: mosques and the planning process in Birmingham', *Journal of Ethnic and Migration Studies*, 31(6).

Hampshire, J. and S. Saggar (2006) 'Migration, integration and security in the UK since July 7', www.migrationinformation.org/feature/display.cfm?id=383.

Johnston, P. (2001) 'Muslims and whites still worlds apart', *Telegraph*, 11 December.

Kelly, R. (2006) Text of speech launching Commission on Integration and Cohesion, 24 August, www.communities.gov.uk/speeches/corporate.

Leppard, D. (2005) 'Charles's mosque meets a rebellion', *Sunday Times*, 26 June.

Modood, T. (2005) 'Remaking multiculturalism after 7/7', *Open Democracy*, www.opendemocracy.net/conflict-terrorism/multiculturalism_2879.jsp.

Musterd, S. (2003) 'Segregation and integration: a contested relationship', *Journal of Ethnic and Migration Studies*, 29(4).

Newman, D. (1985) 'Integration and ethnic spatial concentration: the changing distribution of the Anglo-Jewish community', *Transactions of the Institute of British Geographers*, NS 10.

Office for National Statistics (2001) *2001 Census*, London: HMSO.

Peach, C. (1996) 'Good segregation, bad segregation', *Planning Perspectives*, 11.

— (2006) 'Islam, ethnicity and South Asian religions in the London 2001 census', *Transactions of the Institute of British Geographers*, 31(3).

Pfaff, W. (2005) 'A monster of our own making', *Observer*, 21 August.

Phillips, T. (2005) 'After 7/7: sleepwalking to segregation', 83.137.212.42/sitearchive/cre/Default.aspx.LocID-ohgnew07s.RefLocID-ohg00900c002.Lang-EN.htm.

Rudiger, A. and S. Spencer (2003) *Social Integration of Migrants and Ethnic Minorities – Policies to Combat Discrimination*, OECD/European Commission.

Snow, J. (2006) 'Muslim integration has come to a halt', *Sunday Times*, 6 August.

Valentine, G. (2008) 'Living with difference: reflections on geographies of encounter', *Progress in Human Geography*, 32(3).

Williams, G. (2001) '"Parallel lives" are blamed for the race riots', *Daily Mail*, 11 December.

13 | Muslim-American hyphenated identity: negotiating a positive path

SELCUK R. SIRIN AND SELEN IMAMOĞLU

Terrorist attacks and the wars in Iraq and Afganistan have led to increasing Islamophobia in Western countries, which has in turn forced Muslims in the West to identify themselves primarily through their religious background. The accelerated emergence of the 'Muslim-' label as a new cultural identity, however, conceals many differences within this group. In this chapter, we will present the case of Muslim immigrants in the United States as a distinct and positive example of identity negotiation. Despite the claims of a 'clash of civilizations' that they hear from both Western intellectuals and politicians (e.g. Huntington 1993, 2004) and from some Muslim scholars, many Muslim-Americans have found a way to create a hybrid, positive identity that successfully claims their religious heritage as Muslims and at the same time their civic and national pride as Americans. Therefore, in this chapter we will examine unique aspects of the *immigrant* Muslim experience in the USA that may point towards ways of generating hope and creating a more positive coexistence. Towards that goal, in addition to relying on others' work, we will also share some of the findings from our own work with young Muslim immigrants in the USA. We believe there is much to learn from the experiences of these young men and women about how we can start a new dialogue regarding nationality and religion across the hyphens. We must note that although more than a third of Muslims in the USA are of African origin, we will not delve into their experiences in this chapter owing to their unique history in the USA (see Turner 2003 for a historical account and Curtis 2002 for a discussion on identity).

Identity is a multifaceted construct. One's gender, nationality, race, religion and various other characteristics all contribute to the development of a sense of identity. In today's world, many consider identity a label that indicates certain boundaries – whom to approach and whom to avoid. Conflicts between various domains of one's identity, however, such as one's race, religion or country of origin, may put one in an ambivalent state, as has been the case for some Muslims who live in

Western countries in the post-9/11 context. One of the most disturbing findings from our studies with Muslim youth over the past five years was the degree to which discriminatory acts have been woven intimately into their lives (see Sirin and Fine 2007, 2008; Sirin et al. 2008; Sirin and Balsano 2007). Through surveys, focus groups and identity maps, Muslim young men and women told us, in no uncertain terms, about the joys, but also the burdens, of being Muslim, young and American at this very point in history. In addition to worrying about how to cope with and protect themselves in a state of heightened surveillance and suspicion, they also worry about the social scrutiny to which they are subjected, and the discrimination they endure.

At the same time, the experiences of Muslims in the United States during the post-9/11 period cannot simply be described in terms of discrimination and stress. Their stories may provide us with an insight into what lies in between, on the hyphen of seemingly polar identifications. Despite many negative experiences, and a pull to identify either with their religious identity (i.e. Muslim) or their national identity (i.e. American), these young people have not 'given up' their American identity for the sake of their Muslim identity. Neither did the opposite occur. This is important, especially at a time when there is a heated debate about the compatibility of Islam and democracy. Our studies show in greater detail that many Muslim youths maintain that they are finding harmonious ways to claim both their American and their Muslim heritages. These American Muslims feel they are thriving, albeit in an unusually difficult environment.

MUSLIM-AMERICANS: A DEMOGRAPHIC PORTRAIT

Not surprisingly there is no single route to being Muslim in the United States. As for most other Americans, the history of Muslim-Americans is also a history of immigration that can be traced back to the very early days of European expedition and the African slave trade, which included some Muslim tribes from sub-Saharan Africa. Their identity as Muslim slaves is not recorded in their papers, but there are accounts of slaves who spoke a language similar to Arabic and who believed in a god called 'Allah'. While there were individual migrants and some converts, the large-scale migration of Muslims did not begin until the late nineteenth century and took place in two waves, one that spread from the late nineteenth century to the early twentieth century and one that began around the mid-1960s and continued through the 1990s. These waves brought about two-thirds of today's Muslims to the United States. We must also add to these waves those, mostly African-American, along with some Caucasian, and most recently Latin American Muslims, who have converted to Islam. For the purposes of this chapter, we limit our focus to immigrant Muslims, those who migrated here themselves (i.e. first-generation) and those who come from households with immigrant parents (i.e. second-generation).

The first major wave of Muslim immigration began between 1870 and 1890 and lasted until the 1925 Johnson-Reed Immigration Act, which restricted all Asians from coming to the United States, including those from most of the Muslim and Arab countries which were also classified as Asian. The majority of Muslim immigrants during this first wave came from the Middle East, Albania and South Asia. They were mostly illiterate peasants and, as a result, had more difficulties in adapting to life in the USA, even when compared to Christian Arabs who migrated around the same time from the Middle East in large numbers from Jordan, Syria and Palestine. Muslims of this era moved to places like North Dakota, Indiana, Iowa and Michigan in the Midwest. Around 1915, the first mosques in the USA began to appear in places like Cedar Rapids, Iowa, and Biddeford, Maine. Around the same time, Muslim Arabs joined Christian Arabs in search of work at the Ford Company around Detroit and in Dearborn, Michigan, which became the home of a large Muslim and Arab community.

The second wave began with the immigration reforms of 1965, which, among several other changes, made it possible for Muslims from the Middle East and South Asia to immigrate to the USA. The Muslim immigrants of this era arrived with much stronger religious and national identities than previous generations of Muslim immigrants, owing to popular movements that had shifted the Muslim and Arab world on to a more Islamic and nationalistic path. As in the previous era, these immigrants also came from Palestine, Egypt, Syria and Iraq, but unlike the previous wave, they also came from the South Asian countries of India, Pakistan and Bangladesh in much larger numbers. Another shift was the composition of Arab immigrants; unlike the first wave of im-migrants in which an overwhelming majority of Arabs were Christians, the second wave was composed of mostly Muslim Arabs. Perhaps the most striking difference between the two waves of immigrants was that, compared to the earlier immigrants, most of the migrants of this era either had a college degree or came here to pursue one. This change likely reflects shifts in US immigration policy. These differences, both immigration status and generations spent in the USA, are two critical factors to consider when it comes to understanding Muslim-American identity formation.

Like many issues that involve Muslims in the USA, their numbers are also a matter of political debate (see Smith 2002 for a methodological discussion). There is really no 'hard' number partly because the US Census Bureau, by law, does not gather any information about religious affiliation, and unlike churches, mosques do not have membership rolls that can be used as a proxy, and even if there were such data, many Muslims do not attend mosques. What makes the count of Muslims even more challenging is the fact that even large-scale surveys fail to fully count the number of new immigrant populations, which represent a large number of Muslims in the USA. Hence, because of these difficulties, the number of Muslims in the USA has been estimated to be anywhere between 2 and 8 million.

As a group, Muslim-Americans are one of the fastest-growing segments of the US population. According to the American Religious Identification Survey (ARIS) conducted twice in 1990 and 2001, the number of Muslims in the USA grew over 108 per cent in a single decade (Kosmin et al. 2001). Although not exactly reflecting the trends for all Muslims, an evaluation of census ancestry data for those with birthplaces in Islamic countries also confirms the same trend as it shows that the number of US citizens from predominantly Muslim countries has grown dramatically since the 1970s. A third source of evidence for this huge gain is the findings from the 2000 FACT survey, which shows that the number of mosques in the USA is growing faster than for any other type of religious centre in the USA. At the time of the FACT survey, there were more than 1,200 mosques in the USA, a 25 per cent increase from an earlier survey conducted in 1994. Not only is the number of mosques growing rapidly, but the average attendance in each mosque has more than tripled during the same period, from an average of 485 in 1994 to an average of 1,625 in 2000. Although one would expect the number of immigrants from Muslim countries to drop from its historical peak, the high birthrates and growing number of converts are likely to keep the numbers growing over the next few decades. It is projected that Islam will likely become the second-largest religion in the USA, second only to Christianity.

In terms of racial/ethnic background we have more reliable data. Overall the three major groups of Muslim communities in the USA are of South Asian, African-American and Arab origin (Zogby 2004). South Asians represent about 30 per cent of the Muslim-American population, and they come from Pakistan, Bangladesh and India. This group is quite well educated and they are a relatively new immigrant group compared to other groups of Muslims in the USA. African-American

Muslims are mostly converts to the religion and they represent the largest indigenous Muslim group in the USA, constituting around 25 per cent of the Muslim-American population. One-third of the new converts to Islam in the USA are African-American. The third major group is Arab Americans, who represent an additional 25 per cent of the US Muslim population. The rest of the Muslim-American population represents much more diverse ethnic backgrounds, including a very large Iranian population and much smaller immigrant groups from Malaysia, Indonesia, Turkey, Afghanistan, sub-Saharan Africa, and central and eastern Europe, as well as Caucasian and Latin American converts.

Muslim-Americans today are, therefore, diverse in terms of race, ethnicity, sectarian differences (e.g. Shia, Sunni), immigration status and historical roots in the USA, as well as many different cultural practices of Islam, ranging from highly conservative to more liberal interpretations. Given this diversity, it is reasonable to question the very existence or accuracy of the label 'Muslim-American'. Just imagine the differences in the practice of Islam between a Palestinian immigrant who fled his/her country because of a civil war that ended with a Muslim fundamentalist government on one side and a secular government on another and a Bosnian immigrant who fled his/her country because of another civil war and a genocide against Muslims in 1990s. Similarly, think of Turkish women, who left their secular but 99 per cent Muslim country because of the ban on headscarves in schools, and Muslim Arab gays who fled their country for fear of imprisonment. The former came so they could practise a stricter version of Islam and the latter so they could practise a more flexible version, possible only in the West, which makes it feasible to be gay and Muslim at the same time. Also, think of the many young Muslim professionals who chose to live and work in the USA to enjoy better academic opportunities or to achieve a higher quality of life, just like many other immigrants in the USA. While all these individuals are at times grouped under the umbrella of 'Muslim-American', their degree of identification with Islamic and American values, and hence how they negotiate the hyphen, will be quite different. And yet, albeit reluctantly, we continue to rely on this label as it captures the general experiences of a group of people in the post-9/11 world, where they are increasingly viewed as a single group by others, whether they agree with such a label or not. At the same time it is important to note that the popular media, government agencies and, more importantly, Americans of Muslim origin have increasingly adopted the label 'Muslim-American' to refer to Americans of specific religious or Middle Eastern geographical origins (Grewal 2003). Particularly since the 9/11 attacks, a growing number of Americans have joined organizations under the label of 'Muslim-American', at both the national and local levels (Leonard 2003). The Council on American-Islamic Relations, a small organization with eight chapters in 2001, is now the largest Muslim organization in the country with more than thirty-two chapters. There are Muslim student organizations on most college campuses instead of ethnic (e.g. Arab student clubs) or home-country-based organizations (e.g. a Pakistani Student Organization). Thus, while we use the term 'Muslim-American' in this chapter to illustrate a unique phenomenon of collective identity that emerged amid recent historical events in the USA and the Islamic world, it is important to remember that there is no singular, monolithic category of people called 'Muslim-Americans'. Rather there are many 'groups of people' who can be labelled as Muslim-American (ibid.).

HOW YOUNG PEOPLE IN THE UNITED STATES CONSTRUCT A POSITIVE IDENTITY AS MUSLIM-AMERICANS

What makes me myself rather than anyone else is the very fact that I am poised between two countries, two or three languages and several cultural traditions. It is precisely this that defines my identity. Would I exist more authentically if I cut off a part of myself? (Amin Maalouf)

For immigrants, identity formation involves becoming a member of a collective group based on racial, ethnic or religious backgrounds and negotiating between different cultural frameworks (Berry 1990; La Fromboise et al. 1993; Suárez-Orozco 2004). Berry (1990) formulated the most widely researched acculturation framework, which suggests an orthogonal model with two independent domains: a) the degree to which one is willing to identify with and is allowed to participate in one's home (e.g. Muslim) culture and b) the degree to which one is willing to identify with and is allowed to participate in the host (e.g. US) culture. Several studies investigate the relationship of ethnic (country of origin) and national (host country) identities (Berry et al. 2006; Phinney and Devich-Navarro 1997). According to Berry's model, a positive correlation between measures of ethnic and national identifications indicates an integrated identity or biculturalism. In contrast, ethnic and national identities are irreconcilable if they are negatively correlated (that is, revealing either a strong home-country or a strong host-country orientation). Alternatively, the two identities may vary independently, which would suggest that they are not incompatible but not related either (see Berry et al. 2006 for an updated review of this model).

Much research also examined the links between discrimination

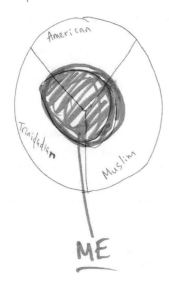

ME

Figure 13.1 'Identity map' drawn by young Muslim-Americans, illustrating the integration of civic/national, religious and ethnic identities (*source*: the authors)

and the identity negotiation process. Tajfel and Turner's (1986) Social Identity Theory can be useful in situating the emergence of Muslim-American identity during the past decade. According to this model, one's identity can be represented on a continuum from personal identity to social identity. In that vein, an individual's behaviour may be governed by personal concerns or by the implications of group membership, depending on whether the former or the latter identity is salient in a particular situation. That is, when one's social identity as a Muslim-American is salient, then the individual's behaviour may be more likely to be determined by concerns of perceived inequalities or discriminatory acts between groups. On the other hand, when one's personal identity is salient, then his/her individual characteristics may be more likely to have an impact on behaviour than inter-group relations (Kelly and Breinlinger 1996). The rejection-identification model (Branscombe et al. 1999; Major and O'Brien 2005) also made a similar point: those who perceive more personal discrimination are strongly identified with their own targeted groups. Identification with a targeted group, therefore, correlates highly with perceptions of and experiences with stress related to discrimination.

In our own work we tested several of these conceptual models, including the influence of discrimination-related stress on Muslim-American young adults' identification with Muslim communities and the mainstream US society. More specifically, we used a multitude of research methods including psychometrically validated paper-pencil surveys, open-ended questions, focus groups, individual interviews and a novel technique called identity maps (for more detail, please see Sirin et al. 2008; Sirin and Fine 2008, 2007). A total of 134 people (ages 18–25), 77 women and 60 men, participated in this mixed-methods study. Despite the fact that participants saw their Muslim identity as more important, and evaluated it more positively than their American identity, it appeared that the more they saw themselves as members of the Muslim community, the more likely they were to identify with mainstream American society. Furthermore, 61 per cent of the participants constructed identity maps that indicated a positive, integrated Muslim-American identity, and 29 per cent indicated separated (but compatible) Muslim and American identities. In this chapter, we present two maps that illustrate different ways of integrating multiple sources of one's identity. In both figures we can clearly see the integration of civic (i.e. USA), religious (the word 'Muslim' in Figure 13.1 and the crescent in Figure 13.2) and ethnic identities (Trinidad in Figure 13.1 and the continent of Africa in Figure 13.2). Only 11 per cent of the participants constructed maps that reflected a conflicted identity.

Also, when asked about their preference for certain social and cultural activities, the majority of the participants showed a preference for engaging in activities that integrated both mainstream US and their home-country orientations. For example, for items such as 'I am most comfortable being with people from ...', 'My best friends are from ...', 'The way I do things and the way I think about things are from ...', the majority of Muslim-American adolescents gave answers

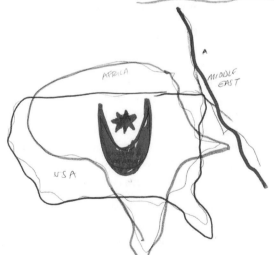

Figure 13.2 'Identity map' drawn by young Muslim-Americans (*source*: the authors)

that encompassed both cultures, indicating an integrated pattern. These findings fail to confirm the clash-of-civilizations hypothesis that is so commonly observed in public discourse. It appears that young Muslim-Americans do not seem to have too much of a problem adapting to the mainstream US culture, or creating a hybrid social and cultural world where they integrate various characteristics of both cultures.

In addition to the identity maps and survey data, the participants in our focus groups shared with us how they view themselves as Muslims in the USA, which again reflected a more integrated identity. Most of our participants presented their integrated identities, creatively engaging both their Muslim and their American heritages. One of the participants explained this process as follows: 'It's like those new restaurants that mix ... you're like a *fusion* ... a new fusion. And it's just interesting to be you, you know, because you're fusing two cultures in one.' Another person spoke of his multiple identities in a more descriptive way:

> ... A big part of my identity is American. My mentality has been
> shaped by the way things are run here but I also see myself as a
> Muslim. I have to adapt to the religion and that's more like a way
> of life. You know it could also affect my mentality. I see myself as
> not just being American but having other identities as well. I lived
> in Switzerland for two years, I feel I actually acquired a lot there ...
> Swiss taste. Also I was in the Italian part of Switzerland so, you know,
> you get their style a little bit. And I come from Albania so the culture
> there also has an influence on the way you think.

Finally, another participant highlighted similar points:

> ... To me, America is like a melting pot of all these cultures. I'm
> one piece of that. ... There's so many more parts to our culture, the
> American culture ... And you know I had those values of like Pakistan
> or Islam but I also have the American customs and culture too 'cause
> I grew up here, I can't, I don't totally alienate myself from it 'cause if
> I didn't like it, I wouldn't live here any more. But I do like it, as much
> as we say we don't agree with it. Yes, there are some things that totally
> don't agree with Islam either, but I'm living here and I choose to live
> here, 'cause I do like some of the stuff, whether it is un-Islamic or not
> ... I don't see why I can't call myself American and Muslim.

Following Berry's model, in order to fully understand how Muslims in the USA managed to positively negotiate their identities at a time when most expected the worst after the 9/11 attacks, one must first examine their demographic portrait. As we will illustrate below, unlike many other immigrant groups in the USA and the West in general, Muslims in the USA were well into accumulating their social capital to be a part of mainstream US society. In terms of educational attainment, Muslim-Americans are one of the most educated groups in the USA, owing partly to the immigration of professionals and the influx of international students who came from Muslim countries to the United States during the past four decades (Pew Research Centre 2007; Zogby 2004). In fact, the percentage of Muslims with professional degrees is much larger than the US average (Pew Research Centre 2007). According to the Zogby survey, close to two-thirds of Muslim-Americans have at least a college degree, compared to the United States average of 28 per cent. Despite the high numbers of professional degrees and the low numbers of college dropouts among Muslims, they are on par with the national average when it comes to having no high-school degree, both around 5 per cent, indicating the possibility of a segment of immigrants who came here with no formal education.

Muslim-Americans are also wealthier than most other identifiable social groups in the USA. According to the Zogby survey (2004) a third of respondents earn an average of $75,000 or more and an additional 20 per cent reported incomes of $50,000–75,000. While half of Muslim-Americans make more than $50,000 a year, the median income for the same year was $44,389 compared to the US average of $42,158. The Pew survey (Pew Research Centre 2007), however, also shows that family income among Muslim-Americans is comparable with that of the US population, with a slight advantage for foreign-born Muslims. The occupational statuses of Muslim-Americans also reflect the middle-class status of the majority of Muslims. About 23 per cent of adults work in professional/technical jobs, with an additional 10 per cent working in managerial positions and 9 per cent in medical fields. Furthermore, a majority of Muslim-Americans own stock, either personally or through pension plans, and own their own home.

Unlike other immigrant groups, Muslims in the USA have also built social capital in terms of citizenship status, political participation and language proficiency. According to the American Muslim survey conducted by Zogby International, close to 90 per cent of adults are US citizens (Zogby 2004). This is a surprisingly high citizenship ratio considering the finding from the same survey that two-thirds of Muslim adults in the USA were not born in the country. Muslim-Americans are also more willing to assert their civic identities as Americans, as indicated by the finding that about 82 per cent of them are registered to vote (ibid.). Another indicator of social capital is the use of the English language at home. According to the 2000 census data that documented language use at home among the fourteen largest immigrant groups in the USA, families from Pakistan, Bangladesh, Iraq and Afghanistan were the most likely to be bilingual, around 80 per cent, which is well above the US average for other immigrant groups.

Thus, given the higher levels of educational attainment, income and citizenship rates, it is not surprising that many Muslims in the USA were able to claim their Islamic and American identities while those in other parts of the world, especially in Europe, struggled during the post-9/11 context. So the question, then, becomes what predictions can we make regarding the future of Muslim immigrants in the West in general and in the USA in particular? We believe that since the Muslim-Americans constitute quite a heterogeneous group, more than one identity negotiation path may need to be considered. First, as noted above, it should be pointed out that the majority of Muslim-Americans have high status in terms of education and income, and so, as predicted by social identity theory (Tajfel and Turner 1986), are expected to continue having a positive sense of social identity and self-esteem, and regard themselves as much 'Americans' as their fellow citizens. As our studies show (Sirin et al. 2008; Sirin and Fine 2008), a large segment of US Muslim immigrants fall into this category.

On the other hand, those Muslims who perceive themselves as members of a low-status group may be likely to have a negative social identity. This may be the case for a small minority of Muslim-Americans but also perhaps a large segment of European Muslims, as indicated with polling data provided by the Pew study. According to social identity theory, this group of Muslims is more likely to be motivated to improve their status through individual upward mobility *if* they perceive the host society as an *equal opportunities* society and the existing group boundaries as *permeable*. Hence, those individuals are more likely to make internal attributions for their existing status and believe that improving it is *feasible* if they work hard enough. If they perceive their status as *illegitimate*, however, because, for example, of the discriminatory actions of the dominant group, and the group boundaries as *impermeable*, then they might be more likely to identify with other members of their own groups and seek collective solutions to their issues.

When trying to understand Muslim-Americans' likely future responses in terms of their individual characteristics, the Balanced Integration Differentiation (BID) model of self-systems (Imamoğlu, E. O. 2003) may provide a useful framework. According to the model, all people are assumed to have natural propensities for both *intrapersonal differentiation* (i.e. a self-developmental tendency towards *individuation* in order to actualize their unique potentials) and *interpersonal integration* (i.e. an interrelational tendency towards *relatedness*), but differ in the degree to which they are able satisfy those needs. Four self types are achieved by combining the low and high ends of those dimensions. Accordingly, people who are able to satisfy their needs for both (or neither) individuation and relatedness are referred to as having a *balanced* (or *unbalanced*) self-type, whereas those who are able to satisfy their needs for only individuation *or* relatedness are referred to as having *differentiated* or *integrated* self-types, respectively. For our present purposes, it is important to note that the psychological functioning of those four self-types was found to show similar trends among American and Turkish samples (Imamoğlu and Karakitapoğlu-Aygün 2004, 2006, 2007). Those findings suggest that people everywhere may seem different (as, for example, in terms of learned cultural or subcultural expectations) but yet similar trends may be observed in terms of the basic psychological functioning of those with similar self-types across or within cultures. Findings from different studies support the assertion of the BID model that the balanced self-type is associated with optimal psychological functioning, whereas the unbalanced type tends to be associated with the least favourable psychological outcomes in different contexts (Imamoğlu, E. O. 2003; Imamoğlu and Güler-Edwards 2007; Imamoğlu and Imamoğlu 2007). Thus, on the basis of those findings, we can suggest that these American Muslims are enjoying 'balanced' psychological health, even in politically turbulent and socially divisive times.

COMPARISON AND CONCLUSION

The encouraging results of the research described above must be set in context. On the one hand, this chapter has been concerned with a particular, relatively privileged section of American Muslim society; comparable research among African-American Muslims would likely yield very different findings. On the other hand, the social advancement and integration of these American Muslims is instructive. It presents a particularly striking comparison with similar – first- and second-generation immigrant – Muslims in Europe. A brief comparison between these American and European Muslims puts the findings of this chapter into context, and helps establish the basis for a conclusion.

The international survey conducted by Pew in twenty-two countries between 2002 and 2007 found American Muslims integrated in many areas of national life (Pew Research Centre 2007). This survey concluded that 'the views of Muslim Americans resemble those of the general public in the United States' and depart from Muslims in Europe and elsewhere (ibid.: 4). These conclusions reflect a range of social, economic and attitudinal variables. For example, whereas 49 per cent of the general public were employed full time in 2007, this was true of 41 per cent of American Muslims. While 71 per cent of Muslim-Americans believe that one can get ahead with hard work, 82 per cent of the general public believe so. Most Muslims said that they were happy with their lives (24 per cent 'very happy', 54 per cent 'pretty happy'), which was quite similar to the general public expressing this view (36 per cent 'very happy', 51 per cent 'pretty happy').

Furthermore, the Pew survey drew some striking comparisons between American and European Muslims. It found the former more integrated in national life. For example, although 81 per cent of Muslims in Britain chose to identify themselves as 'Muslim first', only 47 per cent of US Muslims felt the same way, the rest identifying as 'American first' (ibid. 2007). Compared to their counterparts in Europe, American Muslims are well educated and wealthy, an ambitious and successful minority (Rath and Buijs 2002). For example, unlike the somewhat underclass status of South Asian immigrants in the United Kingdom whose unemployment rate is several times higher than the UK average, South Asian immigrants to the USA have one of the lowest unemployment rates in the country (Sirin and Fahy 2006).

To begin to explain the higher levels of integration apparent among American Muslims, it is possible to point to different legal frameworks. Whereas Muslim immigrants in the United States have one of the highest rates of citizenship, most Muslims in Europe are still struggling to gain full citizenship, even when they have been legal employees for several decades. But different experiences of immigration are not simply a function of migration and citizenship law, but also of contrasting immigrant cultures and national identities. A young person in one of our studies suggested that:

> America is unique because we have such a diverse group of people and the only other place I have seen this is in Mecca. All of us went last year, and there were people from Africa, Asia, and Europe. The only place elsewhere where you see it is here [the USA]. The US is indeed a melting pot that unites people from different cultures under the umbrella of 'American'.

We would like to end with the words of Amin Maalouf, the famous writer who was born in Lebanon, and who has been living in the West for more than thirty years:

So am I half French and half Lebanese? Of course not. Identity can't be compartmentalized. You can't divide it up into halves or thirds or any other separate segments. I haven't got several identities: I've got just one, made up of many components combined together in a mixture that is unique to every individual. (Maalouf 1996: 3)

For Maalouf, as for the young Muslim-Americans described in this chapter, identity is not a matter of either/or, and faith does not necessarily set Muslims apart.

REFERENCES

Berry, J. W. (1990) 'Psychology of acculturation: understanding individuals moving between cultures', in R. W. Brislin (ed.), *Applied Cross-cultural Psychology*, Newbury Park, CA: Sage.

Berry, J. W., J. S. Phinney, D. L. Sam and P. Vedder (eds) (2006) *Immigrant Youth in Cultural Transition: Acculturation, Identity, and Adaptation across National Contexts*, Mahwah, NJ: Lawrence Erlbaum.

Beydoğan, B. (2008) 'Self-construal differences in perceived work situation and well-being', Unpublished doctoral dissertation, Middle East Technical University, Ankara.

Branscombe, N. R., M. T. Schmitt and R. D. Harvey (1999) 'Perceiving pervasive discrimination among African-Americans: implications for group identification and well-being', *Journal of Personality and Social Psychology*, 77.

Curtis, E. E. (2002) *Islam in Black America: Identity, Liberation, and Difference in African-American Islamic Thought*, Albany, NY: SUNY Press.

Fine, M. and S. R. Sirin (2007) 'Theorizing hyphenated lives: researching marginalized youth in times of historical and political conflict', *Social and Personality Psychology Compass*, 1(1).

Grewal, I. (2003) 'Transnational America: race, gender and citizenship after 9/11', *Social Identities: Journal for the Study of Race, Nation & Culture*, 9(4): 535–61.

Güler-Edwards, A. (2008) 'Relationship between future time orientation, adaptive self-regulation, and well-being: self-type and age-related differences', Unpublished doctoral dissertation, Middle East Technical University, Ankara.

Gündoğdu, A. (2007) 'Relationship between self-construals and marital quality', Unpublished master's thesis, Middle East Technical University, Ankara.

Huntington, S. P. (1993) 'The clash of civilizations?', *Foreign Affairs*, 72(3).

— (2004) *Who are We: The Challenges to America's National Identity*, New York: Simon & Schuster.

Imamoğlu, E. O. (2003) 'Individuation and relatedness: not opposing but distinct and complementary', *Genetic, Social, and General Psychology Monographs*, 129(4).

Imamoğlu, E. O. and A. Güler-Edwards (2007) 'Geleceğe ilişkin yönelimlerde benlik tipine bağli farklılıklar' [Self-related differences in future time orientations], *Turkish Journal of Psychology*, 22.

Imamoğlu, E. O. and S. Imamoğlu

(2007) 'Relationships between attachment security and self-construal orientations', *Journal of Psychology*, 141(5).

Imamoğlu, E. O. and Z. Karakitapoğlu-Aygün (2004) 'Self-construals and values across different cultural and socioeconomic contexts', *Genetic, Social, and General Psychology Monographs*, 130.

— (2006) 'Actual, ideal, and expected relatedness with parents across and within cultures', *European Journal of Social Psychology*, 36.

— (2007) 'Relatedness of identities and emotional closeness with parents across and within cultures', *Asian Journal of Social Psychology*, 10.

Imamoğlu, S. (2005) 'Secure exploration: conceptualization, types, and relationships with secure attachment, self-construals, and other self-related variables', Unpublished doctoral dissertation, Middle East Technical University, Ankara.

Kelly, C. and S. Breinlinger (1996) *The Social Psychology of Collective Action: Identity, Injustice and Gender*, London: Taylor & Francis.

Kosmin, B. A., E. Mayer and A. Keysar (2001) *American Religious Identification Survey*, New York: City University of New York.

La Fromboise, T., H. L. K. Coleman and J. Gerton (1993) 'Psychological impact of biculturalism: evidence and theory', *Psychological Bulletin*, 114(3).

Leonard, K. I. (2003) *Muslims in the United States: The State of the Research*, New York: Russell Sage.

Maalouf, A. (1996) *On Identity*, London: Harvill.

Major, B. and L. T. O'Brien (2005) 'The social psychology of stigma', *Annual Review of Psychology*, 56.

Pew Research Centre (2007) *Muslim Americans: Middle Class and Mostly Mainstream*, www.pewresearch.org/pubs/483/muslim-americans.

Phinney, J. S. and M. Devich-Navarro (1997) 'Variations in bicultural identification among African American and Mexican American adolescents', *Journal of Research on Adolescence*, 7(1).

Portes, A. and R. G. Rumbaut (2001) *Legacies: The Story of the Second Generation*, Berkeley: University of California Press.

Rath, J. and F. Buijs (2002) 'Muslims in Europe: the state of research', Essay prepared for the Russell Sage Foundation, New York.

Sirin, S. R. and A. Balsano (2007) 'Pathways to identity and positive development among Muslim youth in the West', *Applied Developmental Science*, 11(3).

Sirin, S. R. and S. Fahy (2006) 'What do Muslims want? A voice from Britain', *Analyses of Social Issues and Public Policy*, 6(1).

Sirin, S. R. and M. Fine (2007) 'Hyphenated selves: Muslim American youth negotiating their identities across the fault lines of global conflict', *Applied Developmental Science*, 11(3).

— (2008) *Muslim American Youth: Understanding Hyphenated Identities through Multiple Methods*, New York: New York University Press.

Sirin, S. R., N. Bikmen, M. Mir, M. Zaal, M. Fine and D. Katciaficas (2008) 'Exploring dual identification among Muslim-American emerging adults: a mixed methods study', *Journal of Adolescence*, 31(2).

Smith, T. W. (2002) 'The Muslim

population of the United States: the methodology of estimates', *Public Opinion Quarterly*, 66: 404–17.

Suárez-Orozco, C. (2004) 'Formulating identity in a globalized world', in M. M. Suárez-Orozco and D. B. Qin-Hilliard (eds), *Globalization: Culture and Education in the New Millennium*, Berkeley: University of California Press.

Tajfel, H. and J. C. Turner (1986) 'The social identity theory of intergroup behaviour', in S. Worchel and W. G. Austin (eds), *Psychology of Intergroup Relations*, Chicago, IL: Nelson Hall.

Turan, G. (2007) 'Relationship between materialism and self-construals', Unpublished master's thesis, Middle East Technical University, Ankara.

Turner, R. B. (2003) *Islam in African American Experience*, Bloomington: Indiana University Press.

Waters, M. (1990) *Ethnic Options: Choosing Identities in America*, Berkeley: University of California Press.

— (1999) *Black Identities: West Indian Immigrant Dreams and American Realities*, Cambridge, MA: Harvard University Press.

Zogby, J. (2004) 'Muslims in the American public square: shifting political winds and fallout from 9/11, Afghanistan, and Iraq', Online press release and report, www.projectmaps.com/AMP2004report.pdf.

14 | 'After 7/7': challenging the dominant hegemony

TAHIR ABBAS

In the wake of 7/7 – the London bombings of 7 July 2005 – the focus on British Muslim communities has been greater than ever. Issues of identity, gender, political representation, cultural relativism and the alleged growth and spread of Islamism have all been brought to the fore, particularly through a series of government initiatives, designed to establish and improve relations with British Muslim minorities (Abbas 2009). This chapter, complementing others in this book by Sarah Glynn and Claire Dwyer, examines the threats and opportunities presented by these developments and initiatives, considering their implications for future community relations between Muslims and non-Muslims. Drawing together many of the threads that run through this book, it reviews the economic, social, political and cultural challenges facing Muslims in Britain as these groups begin to come to terms with increasing problems of exclusion, vilification, alienation and isolation.

Then, considering possible 'spaces of hope' for British Muslims, the chapter looks at the development of particular identity politics, which seek to modify notions of Islam and modernity in a Western liberal secular democratic context, potentially overriding many elements of the existing Islamic and Muslim British hierarchy (Lewis 2007). There is an inevitable problem as sweeping changes are introduced as part of the amalgamation of certain community mobilizations and government-orchestrated modes of action, where attention concentrates on 'the Muslims' but largely ignores the socio-historical factors that have led to the wider presence of Islam in British society (Ansari 2004). As certain Muslims in Britain are increasingly recognizing the importance of engagement and the potential to impact on political decisions in relation to social policy, most remain dislocated and voiceless (Modood et al. 1997; OSI 2004). Indeed, through the 'war on terror' and since 7/7, a great deal of stress has been placed upon the roles and responsibilities of Muslims in positions of power and influence. The traditional *ulema* (religious hierarchy) are said to be culturally, socially and theologically

disconnected from younger people, who dominate the Muslim population profile in Britain (see Peach 2005).

The following sections discuss the notion of Islamophobia and its
effects on how Muslims and Islam are regarded and treated in public
space. Next, there is a discussion of the ways in which political mobilization and in particular New Labour party politics have made an impact
upon Muslim activity within the government. Finally, there is discussion
of the role of the 'war on terror' and how this period in history has
had a significant impact on developments in political and community
relations in Britain in relation to Muslims (Phillips, R. 2008). In conclusion, it is argued that the current period is a testing time for Muslims
as they engage with the politics *and* the reality of participation *and*
representation. Ironically, writing at the beginning of 2009, I suspect that
the local and national challenges of a global economic downturn may
well have more of a bearing on community relations between Muslims
and non-Muslims than the international 'war on terror'. This is simply
because so many of the challenges facing British Muslims relate to the
socio-economic realm.

ISLAMOPHOBIA AND ITS SHIFTING CONTOURS

While a concentration on historical, economic, social and political
issues that affect Muslims in Britain is important, it is also necessary
to raise a range of cultural concerns. Islamophobia has become part of
established academic, practitioner and societal parlance over the last
two decades, developing an especially malevolent form after the end
of the cold war and the beginning of the 'clash of civilizations' thesis
(Runnymede Trust 1997). In Britain, the term took on a well-accepted
meaning and application after the events of 'The Rushdie Affair' of
the late 1980s (Modood 1990). There was also the development of
a government-orchestrated analysis of social and cultural exclusion
facing ethnic minorities in the mid- to late 1990s, based on groups
differentiated by virtue of 'race', ethnicity, class, gender or religion. In
the post-9/11 and post-7/7 climate, Islamophobia has gathered pace
as a lived experience, but also in the way it is utilized as an analytical
concept in various research and policy development arenas.

It is important to explore the ways in which the government relates
to its citizens and defines its roles and responsibilities in relation to
them. That is, how is the problem of Islamophobia stated and what are
its precise characteristics? What can be done to alleviate it? To this end,
the 1997 Runnymede Trust commission into Islamophobia is used as
a starting point. Case studies based on the publication of *The Satanic*

Verses by Salman Rushdie in 1988, the more recent examples relating to
the Danish cartoons controversy of 2006, and the comments made and
the debate in relation to the veil by former Home Secretary Jack Straw,
also in 2006, are highlighted to explore the ways in which the discourse
has shifted over time. It is argued that there are changing notions in
relation to the ways in which ethnicized and racialized minorities are now
regarded with religio-cultural characteristics at the fore and how they
are 'othered' by wider society. In this regard, Islam and Muslims have
the greatest exposure. This experience has implications for human social
relations in the context of a failing global 'war on terror', developments
in international information communication technologies and the ways
in which the state (i.e. through 'elite racism' – after Dijk 1993) regards
its minority citizens in the context of devolution, Europeanization and
'the problem' of Muslim minority youth and their radical identity politics
(Abbas 2007). This new – but age-old – racism takes the form of an
assault on groups through the lens of culture and language, rather than
direct forms of colour discrimination (Blackledge 2006).

    Although it is apparent that Islamophobia is a useful term, it does
have its share of problems. For some it is an inflexible concept and it
does not always inform about degree, scope or magnitude. It can hide
internal practices inside Muslim communities, where accusations of
Islamophobia can mask gender inequalities, regressive cultural practices
and significant power imbalances within the domestic sphere or community context. Further, it conflates Islam and Muslim into single
entities, hiding tremendous variations in ideology and practice. It covers
huge ground to include those who have limited or no knowledge of Islam
and fear it as a whole with those who are seemingly fighting against
radical Islamism, which would also include many Muslims within this
sphere. There are also confusions in how some would focus on aspects
of discrimination with a deliberate concentration on anti-Islamic rhetoric
or doublespeak but also somehow see that as contradiction in relation to
internal struggles within the Muslim communities. Nevertheless, the idea
of Islamophobia has significant purchase among intellectuals, scholars,
influential think tanks and government departments. It does capture a
certain social momentum and it is therefore important to discuss it as
a social concept with implications for reality.

    There are indeed significant challenges facing Muslims in Britain
and in western Europe but they are compounded by the ways in which
the state and the Western world at large regards Muslims as somehow
the central feature of 'the problems' experienced. This is particularly
noticeable with reference to the experiences of Muslim young men, for

example in relation to the 'Northern Disturbances' in 2001 and since (Dwyer et al. 2008) – Britain's worst 'race riots' for more than two decades. These largely focused on second- and third-generation South Asian Muslims from the former mill towns in the north of England whose frustrations in relation to alienation, lack of an effective political voice, discrimination, racism and far-right hostility led to five months of violence and destruction, principally in Bradford, Oldham and Burnley, but less significantly in Stoke and in Leeds. The particular characteristics to note here in relation to these groups is that the experience is of the poorest white English indigenous groups pitted against the poorest of second- and third-generation South Asian Muslims competing for the essential aspects of social life: education, jobs, housing, local and national identity. As much as these events were born out of economic, social and political disaffection, the cultural phenomenon of Islamophobia was also present in those towns at the time (and remains to this day).

As Sarah Glynn, Claire Dwyer and M. A. Kevin Brice have all observed in this book, the British government responded to the 'Northern Disturbances' by attempting to promote 'community cohesion', in the face of 'self-styled segregation' and 'parallel lives'. This led to discourses on the 'death of multiculturalism', disseminated by liberal commentators such as Trevor Phillips, David Goodhart and Keenan Malick, and its counter-arguments by Professors Tariq Modood and Bhikhu Parekh. Meanwhile, aspects of the liberal bourgeoisie and political establishment have begun to recognize the potential of Muslim political mobilization based upon changing social, cultural and demographic trends in relation to inter-generational change and adaptation to questions of modernity, particularly in a western European context where the space for debate and the potential to carve out a European Muslim identity relevant to Muslims across the globe is arguably greatest. The challenges of discrimination, racism and Islamophobia are often significant, but the opportunities for focused debate and rational argument are perhaps superior than in the Muslim world per se (Ramadan 2009; Kepel 2008).

LOBBYING GOVERNMENT AND ESTABLISHING POLITICAL SPACE

Despite their long-standing presence in the country, no British government seriously or systematically reached out to Muslims in Britain until 1997, when New Labour swept to power after eighteen years of Conservative rule (Cathcart 1997; Rawnsley 2001). During its first term in office, New Labour introduced genuinely progressive equality policies and practices, including the Race Relations (Amendment) Act

(2000), the Human Rights Act (1998) and the Social Exclusion Unit. This encouraging momentum was lost after 9/11, however. The 'war on terror' undermined and reversed initiatives and policies that were aimed at remedying social exclusion in society, which, until then, had been focused upon groups seen through the lens of ethnicity, religion and identity, as well as social class and social cohesion (Birt 2005).

The formation of the Muslim Council of Britain (MCB) in 1997 and its relations with New Labour are of particular interest in this context. The MCB aims to promote a united forum on Muslim matters in Britain by: working with existing individuals, groups and organizations; encouraging an enlightened awareness of Islam and Muslims in Britain; determining fair and equitable outcomes for Muslims in society; helping to remove patterns of disadvantage and discrimination; and improving cultural and intellectual relations between Muslims and non-Muslims for the betterment of society as a whole. The MCB was created to supplant the National Interim Committee for Muslim Unity (NICMU). Over the years, the MCB has been publicly criticized by commentators who argue that it is not reflective of the Muslim community in Britain, nor is it wholly able to shed certain ideological, sectarian and factional influences within its senior ranks. It attempts to function as an umbrella body, currently with around five hundred members, consisting largely of mosques and Islamic centres, but also including a host of voluntary, community, charitable, civic, student and professional organizations and associations. The MCB aims to reflect the diversity of ethnicity, culture and religiosity of Muslim communities in Britain today, although there continues to be criticism of its effectiveness (Klausen 2005; McLoughlin 2005). Although it has strong working links with the British government, the MCB's relationship with it has been tenuous at times, specifically in the aftermath of the 'war on terror'.

After the 9/11 attacks the MCB was originally encouraged by the British government to show support for the efforts in Afghanistan, and it did. Soon afterwards, however, the MCB publicly dissociated itself from the government's position. This led to a public distancing between the MCB and the government more generally. Similarly, after the terror attacks in Madrid and Amsterdam in 2004, the government called on the MCB to help in its efforts to deradicalize young British Muslim men increasingly regarded as a threat to British society. The leafleting of all the known mosques and Islamic centres in Britain was met with scepticism among many British Muslims, who regarded the actions of the MCB as 'selling out'. That is, support for political-ideological groups, which sprang up in the wake of colonialism in the Middle East and India, organized itself around various national and international concerns in the post-colonial period. After 7/7, the government again sought to dissociate itself from the MCB, and promote a 'new' Muslim leadership in Britain, namely the British Muslim Forum and Sufi Council of Britain. Today, the MCB remains an organization that consists of volunteer officers. Although still under test, the umbrella model of the MCB has now been replicated in other countries, notably France, Indonesia and Australia to name but a few.

By 2001, as I have said, the MCB was out of favour, but by then it had managed to place key personnel in various government departments. It was a heady period for the MCB, which was given unprecedented access to documentation, and the ears of ministers and important advisers to government. At the same time as the MCB was enjoying its honeymoon, and certainly after the 'war on terror', a new brand of Muslim political activist emerged, someone who was comfortable with their British and Muslim credentials but prepared to challenge the workings of the state from within, and, more specifically, without the patience of the generations before them and with the foresight to think many generations ahead. Muslim pressure groups and Muslim civil servants in the heart of Whitehall have variously briefed and counter-briefed, lobbied and counter-lobbied, and have thereby impacted – if not with a single or coherent voice – on a range of policy developments.

So Muslims have entered the political establishment in various ways, though they have done so unevenly, and this is reflected in their limited presence in electoral politics. For example, with only four Muslim members of the House of Commons (at the time of writing: early 2009), all Kashmiri or Pakistani in ethnic origin, two who are now in the cabinet, the representation of Muslims in Parliament has been skewed. Things are better in the House of Lords, where the twenty or so peers are of both genders and various ethnicities, cultures and indeed sects of Islam (and parties). In May 2010, it does appear that there are four Muslim women who have a chance to be elected into parliament: Rushnara Ali, as she attempts to win back the seat of Bethnal Green and Bow from George Galloway of RESPECT (Respect, Equality, Socialism, Peace, Environmentalism, Community, and Trade Unionism); Yasmin Quereshi, for the 'safe' New Labour seat of Bolton South East; Shabana Mahmood, for the New Labour seat previously held by Clare Short in Ladywood, Birmingham; and Salma Yaqoob, a headscarf-wearing Muslim woman, a civil and political activist of some note, standing as prospective parliamentary candidate for RESPECT in the constituency of Hall Green, Birmingham. In 2010, it could well be the case that the number of Muslim MPs will double, with half of them women, although the South Asian ethnic profile will still continue to dominate (a function of history and demographics). In the future it will be important to recognize the needs and aspirations of Muslims who are of very different origins, particularly from eastern Europe, the Middle East and North and East Africa.

Some improvements to the breadth of Muslim representation have taken place in the difficult circumstances of the war on terror, and in the context of government attempts to combat violent extremism. The events of 7/7 helped to mobilize a generation of British Muslims in response to New Labour's efforts to engage with 'liberally minded', 'progressive' and 'moderate' individuals to help tackle the problems of extremism from within. This departed from and advanced upon an earlier generation of attempted engagement between government and Muslims – a malign form of communitarianism – that propped up existing Muslim community elites in an effort to maintain control and resist dissenting voices, while creating a semblance of representation. In 2007, the government introduced the policy of PVE (Preventing Violent Extremism), whereby funding would be handed to Muslims to improve dialogue and engagement, build resilience and to deliver counter-ideological programmes of education and capacity-building. In essence, the debates and policies on preventing 'Muslim extremism' have focused on 'it' being challenged by Muslims themselves, with such initiatives as the 'Radical Middle Way', as well as funding for other Muslim organizations and institutions driving this policy agenda forward. In particular, new Muslim organizations have emerged: those which could act as counter to the MCB, which is seen to have underperformed. Here, the formation of the British Muslim Forum (BMF), Sufi Council of Britain, British Muslims for Secular Democracy and, more recently, the Quilliam Foundation are important examples. The Muslim Association of Britain (MAB), also formed in 1997, is of interest, as it set itself up as an alternative to the MCB at the time. More recently, the development of MINAB (Mosques and Imams National Advisory Board), made up of four prominent organizations (MAB, MCB, BMF and Al Khoei), to help advance imam and mosque development is also significant. While many of these organizations have forged close relations with New Labour, others have established links with the Conservatives, these including the Quilliam Foundation and right-wing think thanks such as Policy Exchange and the Centre for Social Cohesion (Kundnani 2008). The British government, under this political direction, has opted for a populist stance by looking to 'the Muslim' for solutions to the problems faced by and associated with

Muslim communities, while wider social, economic and geopolitical issues remain underemphasized.

In my research I have emphasized that radicalization or violent extremism among British-born Muslims has nothing at all to do with Islam per se and everything to do with history, politics, economics and sociology (Abbas and Siddique 2009). The identity vacuum that is created within second- and third-generation British Muslims is exacerbated by class and ideological struggles that continue to plague the Muslim world (which finds itself still recovering from hundreds of years of imperialism, colonialism, post-colonialism and neocolonialism). The events of 7/7 have as much to do with Islam as the Irish conflict had to with Protestantism versus Catholicism or the 1947 partition of India with Muslim–Hindu antipathy. All are indeed political projects with the enduring history of British imperialism. The uncomfortable place of Muslims in contemporary Britain is not unique, but is comparable in many ways with that of the Irish or West Indians in the 1950s and 1960s, the 'Invading Asians' in the 1970s and 1980s, or African and Arab 'asylum seekers and refugees' in the 1990s.

Rather than looking to the Muslim for the sources of both problems and solutions, it is therefore important to maintain a broad frame of reference, and always to acknowledge the contexts that have shaped current experiences and predicaments. Looking forward, as I have tried to do in this chapter, it is important always to remember broader histories and geographies. It is well documented that Islam has been in Britain for over a thousand years, chiefly in the last four hundred (Matar 1998), and that the social, cultural and political positions of British Muslims have developed differentially in the post-war era. In the post-war era, Britain was short of domestic labour and its response was to encourage former colonial subjects to come to the 'mother country' and take employment that few others wanted (Castles and Koscak 1973; Fryer 1984). In this post-war period, a range of ethnic, cultural and religious groups arrived and settled in Britain, permanently making their home in a nation that was once their colonial overlord. 'New Commonwealth' citizens including Afro-Caribbeans and South Asians arrived in increasing numbers from the 1940s in attempts to improve their lot and that of their children. By the 1970s the descendants of these first-generation immigrants were finding a dominant society hostile towards 'dark strangers' (Patterson 1965). Zealous policing, racism on the television screens, low educational attainment, high unemployment and poor housing were the hallmarks of this era as Britain's black communities tried in vain to find a foothold in society (IRR 1985).

The Brixton disorders of 1981 marked a particular nadir in community relations (Scarman 1982). Those disorders, and their representation in the media, focused upon Afro-Caribbean communities. But, in the 2000s, it is 'Muslims', whose cultural difference conveniently intersects with skin colour, who are seen to represent that which is regarded as being most outside perceived boundaries of Englishness or Britishness, however defined (see Hussain and Miller 2006). Thus, initiatives that focus entirely upon Muslims – their faith and their communities – can never fully explain or ameliorate the unrest among Muslims, or the tensions between these and other groups in the West or between the West and the countries in which Muslims form a majority.

THE WAY AHEAD

Though relations between the British government and the Muslim community and political establishment deteriorated in the aftermath of 7/7, efforts have since been made to build trust and generate confidence. Some of the intended and unintended consequences of these initiatives may be encouraging. In this chapter I have been critical of many of the British government's approaches to Muslims, but having said this, I remain convinced from my ongoing research that many Muslims operating in policy and community contexts are savvy enough to know what is going on, and to turn recent developments to their communities' advantage. The government is wielding its stick, but the carrot is that mosques, imams and women's networks, which have for years lacked not only physical resources but also emotional and intellectual confidence, are being offered resources and support with which to develop and invest. It is now an important time to work on these concerns, when there is high-level ownership linked with dedicated funding. It is not going to remain in place for too long, and if this recent 'Preventing Violent Extremism' push can help to build resilient communities, the more strongly they will be able to fight racism, discrimination, fascism and vilification, and the better they will be as effective citizens who can look more confidently to the future. Similarly, the adverse circumstances faced by Muslims since 7/7 are being turned to advantage in other ways, including through the incorporation of Muslims into the political and lobby systems of Whitehall. A new Muslim political leadership is now coming forward, which does not simply attempt to rally support behind archaic community 'representatives', but increasingly sees younger Muslims establishing themselves in their own right as individuals with distinctively shaped political projects of their own. Here, in the initiatives of Muslims themselves, there may be some space for hope.

NOTE

I would like to thank Malcolm Dick of the University of Birmingham and the anonymous referees for their valuable comments on an earlier version of this paper.

REFERENCES

Abbas, T. (2007) 'British Muslim minorities today: challenges and opportunities to Europeanism, multiculturalism and Islamism', *Sociology Compass*, 1(2).

— (2009) *British Islam: The Road to Radicalism*, Cambridge: Cambridge University Press.

Abbas, T. and A. Siddique (2009) '"Preventing Violent Extremism": perceptions of radicalisation and de-radicalisation among British South Asian Muslims', *Ethnic and Racial Studies*, May.

Ansari, H. (2004) *The Infidel Within: The History of Muslims in Britain, 1800 to the Present*, London: Hurst.

Back, L. and J. Solomos (1992) 'Black politics and social change in Birmingham, UK: an analysis of recent trends', *Ethnic and Racial Studies*, 15(2).

Birt, Y. (2005) 'Lobbying and marching: British Muslims and the state', in T. Abbas (ed.), *Muslim Britain: Communities under Pressure*, London and New York: Zed Books.

Blackledge, A. (2006) 'The racialization of language in British political discourse', *Critical Discourse Studies*, 3(1).

Castles, S. and G. Koscak (1973) *Immigrant Workers and Class Structure in Western Europe*, Oxford: Oxford University Press for the Institute of Race Relations.

Cathcart, B. (1997) *Were You Still Up for Portillo?*, London: Penguin.

Dijk, T. A. van (1993) *Elite Discourse and Racism*, Newbury Park, CA: Sage.

Dwyer, C., B. Shah and G. Sanghera (2008) '"From cricket lover to terror suspect" – challenging representations of young British Muslim men', *Gender, Place & Culture*, 15(2).

Fryer, P. (1984) *Staying Power: The History of Black People in Britain: Black People in Britain since 1504*, London: Pluto.

Giddens, A. (2007) *Over to You, Mr Brown: How Labour Can Win Again*, Cambridge: Polity.

Hussain, A. M. and W. L. Miller (2006) *Multicultural Nationalism: Islamophobia, Anglophobia, and Devolution*, Oxford: Oxford University Press.

IRR (Institute of Race Relations) (1985) *How Racism Came to Britain*, London: Institute of Race Relations.

Kepel, G. (2008) *Beyond Terror and Martyrdom: The Future of the Middle East*, Cambridge, MA: Harvard University Press.

Klausen, J. (2005) *The Islamic Challenge: Politics and Religion in Western Europe*, Oxford and New York: Oxford University Press.

Kundnani, A. (2007) *The End of Tolerance: Racism in 21st Century Britain*, London: Pluto.

— (2008) 'Islamism and the roots of liberal rage', *Race & Class*, 50(2).

Lewis, P. (2007) *Young, British and Muslim*, London: Continuum.

Matar, N. (1998) *Islam in Britain: 1558–1685*, Cambridge: Cambridge University Press.

McLoughlin, S. (2005) 'The state,

new Muslim leaderships and Islam and a resource for public engagement in Britain', in J. Cesari and S. McLoughlin (eds), *European Muslims and the Secular State*, Aldershot: Ashgate.

Modood, T. (1990) 'British Asian Muslims and the Rushdie Affair', *Political Quarterly*, 61(2).

Modood, T., R. Berthoud, J. Lakey, J. Nazroo, P. Smith, S. Virdee and S. Beishon (eds) (1997) *Ethnic Minorities in Britain: Diversity and Disadvantage*, London: Policy Studies Institute.

OSI (Open Society Institute) (2004) *Muslims in the UK: Policies for Engaged Citizens*, New York and Budapest: Open Society Institute.

Patterson, S. (1965) *Dark Strangers: A Study of West Indians in London*, London: Penguin.

Peach, C. (2005) 'Britain's Muslim population: an overview', in T. Abbas (ed.), *Muslim Britain: Communities under Pressure*, London and New York: Zed Books.

Phillips, D. (2006) 'Parallel lives? Challenging discourses of British Muslim self-segregation', *Environment and Planning D: Society and Space*, 24(1): 25–40.

Phillips, R. (2008) 'Standing together: the Muslim Association of Britain and the anti-war movement', *Race & Class*, 50(2).

Ramadan, T. (2009) *Radical Reform: Islamic Ethics and Liberation*, New York: Oxford University Press.

Rawnsley, A. (2001) *Servants of the People: The Inside Story of New Labour*, London: Penguin.

Runnymede Trust (1997) *Islamophobia: A Challenge for Us All*, York: Runnymede Trust.

Scarman, Lord (1982) *The Scarman Report: The Brixton Disorders, 10–12 April, 1981*, London: Penguin.

Van Dijk, T. A. (1993) *Elite Discourse and Racism*, London and New York: Sage.

NOTES ON CONTRIBUTORS

Tahir Abbas, FRSA, is Reader in Sociology and founding director of the University of Birmingham Centre for the Study of Ethnicity and Culture. He is author of *British Islam* (2009) and *The Education of British South Asians* (2004), and editor of *Muslim Britain* (2005) and *Islamic Political Radicalism* (2007).

M. A. Kevin Brice is a research associate with the Centre for Migration Policy Research (CMPR) based at Swansea University, and he is the general secretary of the Muslims in Britain Research Network. Brice is the author of a number of papers about the demographic and socio-economic profiles and identities of white British Muslims.

Raj Brown is Professor of International Business at the School of Management, Royal Holloway College. She works on Asian and Arab entrepreneurship in South-East Asia.

Ayona Datta is lecturer in the Cities Programme of London School of Economics and co-convenor of the MSc Culture and Society degree. She has an interdisciplinary background in architecture, environmental design and planning. She is currently working on books about the slums of Delhi and trans-local geographies.

Kevin M. Dunn is Professor of Human Geography at the University of Western Sydney. His areas of research include: immigration and settlement; Islam in Australia; geographies of racism and multiculturalism. His books include *Landscapes: Ways of Imagining the World* (2003) and *Globalisation, Difference and Inequality* (2000).

Claire Dwyer is a senior lecturer in geography at University College London. Her research focuses on migration, transnationalism and multiculturalism, with a particular interest in religious identities. She is the co-editor of *New Geographies of Race and Racism* (2008) and *Transnational Spaces* (2004).

Fodil Fadli is an architect and researcher at the University of

Liverpool. His research interests focus on sustainable architecture and tourism, and the restoration of heritage buildings. He has published in journals including the *International Journal of Architectural Research* and the *Global Built Environment Review*.

Sarah Glynn has recently returned to architectural practice after lecturing in geography at the University of Edinburgh, and is an honorary research fellow at the University of Strathclyde. She has published on immigrant political mobilization, Islamism, social housing and the impacts of regeneration.

Peter Hopkins is Lecturer in Geography at Newcastle University. His publications include *Masculine Identities for British Muslims* (2008), the co-edited *Muslims in Britain* (2009) and *Geographies of Muslim Identities* (2007), and articles in *Transactions of the Institute of British Geographers* and *Children's Geographies*.

Selen Imamoğlu (Tezcan) is an assistant professor of psychology at Bahcesehir University in Istanbul, Turkey. She completed her PhD in social psychology at the Middle East Technical University (METU). Her main research interests include attachment theory, close relationships, self and gender.

Jamil Iqbal is currently researching his PhD on Transnational Religious Movements at Leeds Metropolitan University. He is an outreach consultant for the International Organization for Migration (IOM). He is the co-editor of *Tales of Three Generations of Bengalis in Britain*, an oral history project funded by the Heritage Lottery Fund.

Alanna Kamp is a researcher at the University of Western Sydney who has worked on indigenous peoples' attitudes to multiculturalism, the exclusion of non-whites through Australia's Immigration Restriction Act (1901), and the place of female Chinese-Australians in understandings of national belonging and identity.

Reina Lewis is Artscom Centenary Professor of Fashion Studies at the London College of Fashion. She is author of *Rethinking Orientalism* (2004) and *Gendering Orientalism* (1996), and the co-editor of *Gender, Modernity and Liberty: Middle Eastern and Western Women's Writings* (2006), and *Feminist Postcolonial Theory: A Reader* (2003).

Hilary Lim teaches at the University of East London. Her research interests are in the fields of trusts, land and Islamic law. Her recent publications include *Land, Law and Islam* (2006) and *Perspectives on Land Law* (2007), which were written and edited with Siraj Sait and Anne Bottomley respectively.

Sarah Mills is a research student in human geography at Aberystwyth University in Wales. Her doctoral work focuses on the cultural politics of British youth movements, specifically the Scout movement.

Jane Pollard is a senior lecturer in the Centre for Urban and Regional Development Studies at Newcastle University. Her interests include geographies of money and finance, the role of financial intermediaries in regional economic development and the changing nature and practices of economic geography. Her current research focuses on the social, cultural and religious elements of financial networks.

Ziauddin Sardar is professor in the School of Arts at City University, London, and is one of Britain's foremost public intellectuals. A prolific writer, broadcaster and cultural critic, he is the author of over forty books, including *Why Do People Hate America?* (2002), *Islam, Postmodernism and Other Futures: A Ziauddin Sardar Reader* (2003) and *How Do You Know?: Reading Ziauddin Sardar on Islam, Science and Cultural Relations* (2006). He is the editor of *Futures*, the monthly journal of policy, planning and futures studies, co-editor of *Third Text*, the critical journal of visual art and culture, and a columnist for the *New Statesman*.

Magda Sibley is an architect and senior lecturer in architecture at the University of Liverpool. She is a specialist in vernacular architecture and urban settlements in North Africa and the Middle East and the lessons of sustainability associated with them. Her current research is concerned with documenting and preserving public bathhouses in Islamic cities.

Selcuk R. Sirin is an assistant professor in applied psychology in New York University's Steinhardt School. His research focuses on the lives of immigrant and minority children. With Michelle Fine, he is co-author of *Muslim American Youth: Understanding Hyphenated Identities Through Multiple Methods* (2008).

Varun Uberoi is a post-doctoral fellow in the Department of Politics and International Relations at the University of Oxford. His research focuses on how unity can be fostered among the citizens of culturally diverse societies.

INDEX